Measurement and Interpretation in Accounting

Recent Titles from Quorum Books

The Employment Contract: Rights and Duties of Employers and Employees
Warren Freedman

Lobbying and Government Relations: A Guide for Executives
Charles S. Mack

U.S. Protectionism and the World Debt Crisis
Edward John Ray

The Social and Economic Consequences of Deregulation: The Transportation Industry in Transition
Paul Stephen Dempsey

The Accountant's Guide to Corporation, Partnership, and Agency Law
Sidney M. Wolf

Human Information Processing in Accounting
Ahmed Belkaoui

Alternative Transportation Fuels
Daniel Sperling

The Design and Implementation of Administrative Controls: A Guide for Financial Executives
John P. Fertakis

Financial Futures and Options: A Guide to Markets, Applications, and Strategies
Todd E. Petzel

Problem Employees and Their Personalities: A Guide to Behaviors, Dynamics, and Intervention Strategies for Personnel Specialists
William T. Martin

The Banking System in Troubled Times: New Issues of Stability and Continuity
Jeremy F. Taylor

Real Interest Rates and Investment Borrowing Strategy
Peter S. Spiro

The Political Limits of Environmental Regulation: Tracking the Unicorn
Bruce Yandle

Summary Judgment and Other Preclusive Devices
Warren Freedman

Measurement and Interpretation in Accounting

A *Living Systems Theory* Approach

G.A. SWANSON
and
JAMES GRIER MILLER

Q

QUORUM BOOKS
New York • Westport, Connecticut • London

Library of Congress Cataloging-in-Publication Data

Swanson, G. A.
  Measurement and interpretation in accounting:
  a living systems theory approach /
  G.A. Swanson and James Grier Miller.
      p.   cm.
   Bibliography: p
   Includes index.
   ISBN 0–89930–422–2 (lib. bdg. : alk. paper)
   1. Finance, Public—Accounting. 2. Information measurement.
  3. System analysis. I. Miller, James Grier. II. Title.
  HJ9745.S92   1989
  657'.835—dc19   89–3857

British Library Cataloguing in Publication Data is available.

Library of Congress Catalog Card Number: 89–3857
ISBN: 0–89930–422–2

First published in 1989 by Quorum Books

Greenwood Press, Inc.
88 Post Road West, Westport, Connecticut 06881

Printed in the United States of America

The paper used in this book complies with the
Permanent Paper Standard issued by the National
Information Standards Organization (Z39.48–1984).

10 9 8 7 6 5 4 3 2 1

Copyright Acknowledgment

We are grateful to McGraw-Hill for granting us permission to use material from *Living Systems*
(1978) by James Grier Miller.

CONTENTS

LIST OF FIGURES AND TABLES

FIGURES

TABLES

ABBREVIATIONS

AI	Artificial Intelligence
AIA	American Institute of Accountants
AICPA	American Institute of Certified Public Accountants
ALEXSYS	Adaptive LST Expert System
ALIGH	Analyses on Interactions of Components within an Organization
APB	Accounting Principles Board
CAPM	Capital Asset Pricing Model
COMFLOW	Communications Flow
CPA	Concrete Process Analysis
CPC	Concrete Process Classification
DPLM	Dynamically Programmable Logic Module
EMH	Efficient Market Hypothesis
FAS	Financial Accounting Standards Board Statement
FASB	Financial Accounting Standards Board
FRB	Federal Reserve Board
GAAP	Generally Accepted Accounting Principles
GI	Gross Inflows

Terms of equations that stand for accounting concepts or entities (found especially on pp. 163ff.) were not considered abbreviations for purposes of this list, even when in letter form.

GSG	Gross Matter-Energy System Generant
GST	General Systems Theory
IMPACT	Analyses on Interactions between an Organization and the Market in which It Competes
LSPA	Living Systems Process Analysis
LST	Living Systems Theory
MATFLOW	Materials Flow
MIM	Money-Information Marker
MONFLOW	Money and Money Equivalents Flow
NASA	National Aeronautics and Space Administration
NME	Net Matter Energy Flows
PERSFLOW	Personnel Flow
SEC	Securities and Exchange Commission
SPDS	Space Personnel Deployment System

PREFACE

Robert N. Anthony, in his conceptual framework for financial accounting entitled *Tell It Like It Was,* recognizes that premises in applied disciplines should be based on evidence gathered by underlying sciences. He states that economic entities are systems and thus general systems theory provides insights into the nature and behavior of systems that concern accounting. He cites James Grier Miller's living systems theory as the primary source of his information about general systems theory.

For many years the accounting profession has attempted to construct a conceptual framework that logically ties together its many ideas and procedures. Although many frameworks have been constructed, no consensus on which one should guide the profession has developed yet. We agree with Anthony's statements and, consequently, have developed in this book a coherent theory of accounting measurement based on living systems theory (LST). Although this theory does not encompass all possible insights that may be drawn from LST, it does provide a fundamental framework for classifying the various accounting ideas and procedures into those that concern measurements of concrete economic processes and interpretations of those measurements.

If accounting is viewed in the context of a general theoretic framework about concrete systems, eventually a book like this must be written. The main dynamic that resulted in this book is a continuing collaboration of its authors, combining general scientific theory and applied accounting theory. Over the last decade, however, several other people have encouraged our research extending LST to accounting theory.

The late Norman X. Dressel, Professor of Accounting at Georgia State University, first raised the hope that a dissertation year could be devoted to this study. Dean Emeritus of the College of Business Administration of the University of Alabama Paul Garner took interest in the project from the beginning, providing academic criticism and inspiration through his personal discussions and letters throughout the period. Al Hartgraves, Associate Dean of the School of Business Administration at Emory University, read many manuscripts and provided valuable assessments of ideas and arguments. John Cook, dissertation committee chair at Georgia State University, wrestling with these ideas in the context of modern accounting theory, raised our awareness of the painstaking efforts that would be required to communicate such ideas to accountants and inspired determination to do so. The extensive works of archaeologist Denise Schmandt-Besserat of the University of Texas–Austin, along with her personal assistance, contributed extensively to our recognizing just how fundamental accounting is to social process. Tim Allen, ecologist at the University of Wisconsin–Madison, provided valuable insights to hierarchy theory. Nuclear physicist and communications expert at the University of Paris Peter Winniwarter provided a practical awareness of both the power and the inaccuracy of measurements used in statistical analyses. Ken Burkhardt of Ryerson Polytechnical Institute, Ontario, Canada, provided insights into the meanings and uses of rigorously stated classical theory in physics.

Referees for the journals *Advances in Accounting, Systems Research*, and *Behavioral Science* (whose names are unknown to us) also encouraged this research, suggesting on more than one occasion that a monograph should be written concerning it. Tennessee Technological University has provided numerous research grants through its University Faculty Grant Program and the College of Business Administration Foundation.

Three professors provided advice directly on the book manuscript itself. Richard V. Mattessich, Arthur Andersen & Company Alumni Professor of Accounting emeritus, read portions of Chapter 8, making important suggestions. Edwin Waters, Professor of Accounting, and Deryl Martin, Professor of Finance, both of Tennessee Tech, made valuable recommendations on portions of Chapters 5, 6, and 7.

LST has been applied in many areas, for example, medicine, biology, psychology, psychiatry, organization theory, sociology, and international relations. We hope that this conceptual framework can make a contribution to accounting theory as well.

Measurement and Interpretation in Accounting

1
THE BIG PICTURE

The Problem and a Solution at a Glance

An eclectic approach to accounting theory has resulted in obscuring information about concrete processes (movements of goods and services) in public accounting reports. Living systems theory (LST) (Miller, 1978) may be used to arrange the many specific and disconnected theories of the eclectic approach in a coherent mosaic that forms a basis for providing information about concrete processes to the public.

Generally accepted accounting principles (GAAP), the eclectic body of accepted theory, obscure information about concrete processes by not distinguishing between the measurements taken on such processes and various interpretations of those measurements based on different special theories. Modern measurement theory may be used in conjunction with LST to distinguish between those measurements and various interpretations.

Consequently, accounting quantities may be sorted into measurements of concrete processes and interpretations of those measurements. Because measurements of concrete processes constitute the most fundamental accounting information, such measurements should be disclosed in public accounting reports. This basic information may then be used in different specific decision models. When model builders know the meaning of information being manipulated by a model and understand the manipulations permitted by the model, they can derive the meaning of the manipulated information. When obscure information is entered into a model, the information output is ambiguous.

The Problem—GAAP Does Not Report Concrete Processes Clearly

Modern accountancy is a paradox. On the one hand, business actors, when surveyed, consistently rate its profession high on trustworthiness and professional ethics. On the other hand, as Kenneth Boulding (1962, p. 55) observed, a common perception of accounting reports is that they are untrue. "A known untruth is better than a lie, and provided that the accounting rituals are well known and understood, accounting may be untrue but it is not lies; it does not deceive because we know that it does not tell the truth, and we are able to make our own adjustment in each individual case, using the results of the accountant as evidence rather than as definitive information."

This paradox may be the result of modern theoretic developments in the accounting discipline. Over the last few decades, accountants have made extensive efforts to develop comprehensive conceptual frameworks, both official and academic, to guide them in developing accounting principles or, as termed in recent years, "standards" for example, Anthony (1983); Chambers (1966); FASB, the Financial Accounting Standards Board, (1978, 1980a, 1980b, 1980c, 1984); Ijiri (1981); Mattessich (1964); Sherman (1984); and Sterling (1979). These efforts generally have not been considered successful, however. As a consequence, the profession has accepted a discipline guided by an eclectic approach to accounting theory. Such an approach has been rationalized on the basis that decision usefulness should be the most prominent quality of accounting information. Because different types of decisions require different concepts of costs, numerous limited-scope theories influence accounting procedures.

The eclectic approach to accounting theory increasingly has led the accounting profession to adopt procedures that report GAAP-defined variables that correspond less and less to measurements taken on concrete system processes. Despite the concrete characteristics of the dual-entry measurement method underlying accounting quantities, more and more the processes of concrete (physical) economic systems, themselves the ultimate objects of accounting measurement, are being ignored.

Information about concrete processes has become so vague that statement users are now asking for reports that somehow connect to actual transactions of goods and services. The Financial Accounting Standards Board, or FASB (1987), has responded by issuing FAS (Financial Accounting Standards Board Statement) 95. This standard mandates that cash flow statements be provided along with balance sheets and income statements. This response may be reactionary, in some sense a return to cash-basis accounting. Such atavisms may impede the evolution of accounting thought rather than advance it.

Current accounting theory only vaguely recognizes that accrual basis accounting basically identifies the flows of concrete elements, that is, matter, energy, and information. As a consequence, individual accounting reports freely mingle estimates based on certain limited-scope interpretations with actual measurements of the concrete elements—goods, services, and money. Nevertheless, the determined adherence of many accountants to the "historical cost" concept and double-entry bookkeeping techniques has generally maintained the fidelity of the actual measurements in the basic accounting systems, limited as they may be. However, given the terminology of the accounting theorists involved in the FASB's Conceptual Framework Project, for example, "assets are probable future economic benefits" (FASB, 1980b), the accounting profession may be on the verge of obscuring measurements with interpretive estimates in the accounts themselves.

We believe that economic actors are not rejecting accrual-based accounting. This basis for accounting likely emerged within organizations in response to management needs for information that made it possible to plan and control organization activities (Swanson and Gardner, 1988; Winjum, 1972). Those needs continue to exist. If cash-basis accounting was insufficient in a period when business was less complex than it is today, it is likely insufficient today. Economic actors are asking for information about the movement of concrete elements among organizations. Those elements are still being monitored by accounting information systems. Consequently, they may be reported unambiguously.

GAAP Obscures Information about Concrete Processes by Not Distinguishing between Measurements and Interpretations

When compared with other modern professions such as medicine, law, and science, the accounting profession is young and, perhaps, yet emerging. The year 1987 marked the centennial of one of its most influential professional organizations—the American Institute of Certified Public Accountants (AICPA, 1987).

Although the history of the accounting function itself may be traced back to at least as far as 8500 B.C. (Swanson, 1984), the profession began to emerge in modern times as the ownership and management functions in organizations were separated. As a result, the corporate legal form of organization evolved to create a need for an independent attest function. However, a major impetus for its direction and acceleration did not occur until the securities acts of 1933 and 1934 were passed by the United States Congress. Additional impetus came even later in the area of federal income tax practice (Gardner and Swanson, 1987).

Parallels often can be drawn among similar societal components. It may be instructive to draw such parallels between the accounting profession and the medical, legal, and scientific professions (Swanson, 1987a). The particular parallel that concerns us is a means for distinguishing between information that is collected on concrete systems, commonly called "facts," and various interpretations of those facts. Such facts are discovered by using well-defined methods to sort out attributes of interest to investigators from a generally large set of attributes that do not concern directly an issue at hand. Interpretations, on the other hand, are based on theories arrived at by consensus within a particular profession. Medicine, law, and science clearly distinguish between these two actions. The distinction is less clear in accounting.

In science, information on concrete systems is gathered under the guidance of accepted research design and measurement theory. Measurement theory requires that numbers be assigned to concrete system phenomena so that they are isomorphic to an understood numeric system. As a result, the interpretation of the numbers representing the concrete phenomena may be enhanced by performing certain mathematical operations allowed by the understood numeric system. The medical profession makes similar measurements that are distinguished clearly from their interpretations.

The legal profession also distinguishes facts from interpretations. Legal facts are established within rigid rules by the lower courts. The prosecutor and defense counsel present the facts, the judge monitors the categorical boundaries (the law that governs admission of evidence), and the jury interprets the facts under the guidance of the law (a form of consensus).

In accounting, public statements report a set of numbers governed by GAAP. These principles are interpretation-driven; that is, decision usefulness, not concrete system measurement, is the primary consideration. This methodology mingles the information gathered on concrete systems with various interpretive manipulations, inclusions, and omissions. Because the whole accounting system is report-oriented, measurements and interpretations are often mingled in the accounts themselves.

While there is no question that interpretation is as vital as raw measurement, the older professions have found it useful to distinguish clearly between the two actions. Why? The answer is quite straightforward. Measurement and interpretation are validated on different bases—measurement on the basis of empirical demonstration, and interpretation on the basis of consensus within a profession. We believe that the accounting profession can make a useful step forward by distinguishing clearly between these actions. The social actors served by the profession would be better able to evaluate accounting reports, and accounting numbers would be more useful for various scientific investigations.

Consequently, we have proposed to reassert the usefulness of accounting measurements of the concrete processes of organizations. However, a simple reassertion of their usefulness is not likely to produce much more than a "so what?" response, because many economic actors believe that summarized measurements of concrete processes are what accounting reports now provide. Therefore, we must precisely identify measurements of concrete processes and sort such measurements from quantities that represent interpretations of those measurements.

Living Systems Theory May Be Used to Distinguish Clearly between Measurements and Interpretations

Living systems theory (Miller, 1965, 1978) is a set of related definitions, assumptions, and propositions that views reality, from the vantage point of living systems, as an integrated hierarchy of matter, energy, and information. It defines living systems in a scheme of all systems as concrete open systems, ranging in a hierarchy from cells to supranational systems. This hierarchy includes organizations and societies that unquestionably concern accounting. LST is a particular mosaic of concepts identified with what is commonly termed *systems thinking*.

For four decades, systems thinking has increasingly penetrated virtually all disciplines of thought. The systems approach is based on the idea that the key to asking useful questions about existence and answering those questions is to be found in the relationships existing among the parts making up the whole, not in isolating parts of a particular whole. This revival of the holistic Aristotelian view that the whole is greater than the sum of its parts reinstates the question of cosmic order. For a time, the Scientific Revolution of the sixteenth and seventeenth centuries obscured this question by emphasizing analytical methodologies based on causal mathematical laws. With the revival of the holistic view, synthesis is emerging as a method of scientific investigation that parallels and enhances analysis.

While systems thinking may be generally characterized as a transdiscipline way of thinking because of its rapid diffusion among the recognized disciplines, a new discipline, systems science, is emerging that concerns knowledge about general, as opposed to specific, systems themselves. This emerging discipline is at the heart of the holistic view revival.

During the first half of this century, important contributions to the revival occurred in at least three separate disciplines—physics, biology, and psychology. Those contributions provided theoretical justification for extending rigorous investigation procedures among disciplines. In physics, Einstein, Lorentz, and Minkowski (Einstein, 1961) formulated relativity theory, identifying the relationships among the elements of energy and matter existing in three dimensions of physical space and a fourth dimension, time. Somewhat parallel developments in biology and psychology converged on the formulation of another important theory, open systems theory. This theory asserts that, while relatively closed physical systems—being subject to the law of thermodynamic degradation—can endure over only limited periods, relatively open systems can endure indefinitely by taking on resources. Kohler (1921, 1927, 1938) formulated a theory of open systems out of Gestalt psychology, and von Bertalanffy (1950, 1956, 1968) arrived at essentially the same theory from the biological perspective. Both Kohler and von Bertalanffy used Hill's (1931) concept of a dynamic steady state maintained by a continual expenditure of energy as a vital aspect of the theory. This theory makes it possible to extend research methodology from physical sciences to the biological sciences in a rigorous fashion instead of trying to draw insights from loose analogies.

Methodology for formalizing exact mathematical relationships may be extended from physics to biology by generalizing Gibb's (1902) second law of thermodynamics from relatively closed systems to relatively open systems. And indeed, since the open system is the generalization of which the closed system is a subset, the extension may be made to engineering, social science, management, and so forth. Moreover, this very generalization of a doctrine considered by classical physics as consummate in its specialized form implies the "formal correspondence of general principles, irrespective of the kind of relations or forces between the components" (von Bertalanffy, 1950, p. 29). In other words, the patterns themselves may be significant, totally divorced from the elements and criteria of relationships that constitute a particular system. This "formal correspondence" leads to the idea of a scientific doctrine that concerns the principles that apply to such pure systems (arrangements in which kinds of relationships or forces and kinds of components may be varied without changing the arrangement). Von Bertalanffy called this scientific doctrine General Systems Theory (GST), and it became a centerpiece of systems science.

GST is applied by attempting to discover "isomorphisms" (formal similarities) between pure systems and concrete (physical) and abstracted systems. Where isomorphisms of pure systems are discovered, the principles of relationship applicable to the pure system can be applied to the isomorphous systems. A particular pure system may be isomorphous to various concrete and abstracted systems in numerous disciplines. Consequently, the application of GST synthesizes, to some extent, the research of various disciplines.

This application of GST appears to be very much like the application of modern measurement theory. It is important to realize that GST does not advocate the synthesis of various disciplines by loose analogy that may obscure rather than illuminate useful relationships. It rather advocates the rigorous construction of formal identities that may be confirmed or denied by empirical evidence.

What the emerging discipline will become remains to be seen. It may become an applied science concerned with the correspondence between quantitative representations of elements in systems, concrete and abstracted, that are being investigated—a science of measurement. On the other hand, this emerging discipline may be concerned with a second level of correspondence—constructing mathematical models with more narrowly defined understood limits and other characteristics than those of measurement scale models. Such second-level-of-correspondence models would allow full manipulation of quantities according to the rules of a measurement scale but only within the constraints of a pure system. Thus evidence would be presented that the method for assigning numbers to elements of a system under investigation is isomorphic (in the mathematical usage of the term) to an understood measurement scale and, further, evidence that the system under investigation itself is "isomorphous" (in the GST usage of the term) to a particular quantitative model would be required.

GST has had only limited exposure in the accounting literature. Smith (1968, 1971), Talbert (1973), and Mattessich (1978) have discussed GST directly and in some depth. Willingham (1964) used some GST concepts in his attempt to define the accounting entity. Others, such as McNerney (1964), Amey (1979), Ansari (1979), and Ridel (1982), have provided overviews or suggested limited applications of some GST concepts.

All disciplines have many factions. In mature disciplines, the prominent ones can be identified and described, but the factions of emerging disciplines are less easily identified. Consequently, systems science itself may not provide a synthesis of systems thinking that is useful for application to other disciplines. Individual theorists in the movement, however, have provided useful applications to several disciplines.

Miller's LST is well suited for applying systems thinking to accounting information systems. It asserts that all living systems must take in and put out (process) various sorts of matter, energy, and patterns of transmissions that convey information. The accounting information system is based on an input-output mathematical model. Therefore, LST asserts broadly that schemes for assigning numbers to certain aspects of all living systems can be isomorphous to the accounting input-output model; that is, such systems may be described by that model.

As GST may synthesize the research of various disciplines, LST may be used to integrate the research of various related disciplines with that of accounting. Accountants have recognized for some time that the accounting system is influenced by the aspects of reality studied by related disciplines such as mathematics, sociology, economics, management science, systems science, information and communications theories, and computer science. In fact, subdisciplines have emerged in accounting, for example, behavioral accounting (Rhode, 1972), social accounting (Tinker, 1986), and accounting information systems (Cushing, 1978; Robinson and Alderman, 1982), reflecting this emerging cross-disciplinary awareness. Also, accounting journals have carried major articles interfacing accounting with other disciplines, for example, *The Accounting Review*, April 1983.

Many accounting theorists—Sprague (1913), Scott (1931), Littleton (1933), and Sterling (1970) among them—have recognized that a conceptual framework is needed to guide the integration of concepts from other disciplines with those of accounting theory. Bedford views this need as a paramount theoretic consideration. He states "The agonizing fact is that 'a priori' research needs a guiding theory for the *evaluation* of a priori theories and to stimulate the development of relevant a priori theory and research. The proposal is awesome in its implications. The change in direction necessary for a priori research to achieve impact on practice directly is fully as great as the change that occurred when alchemy was changed to chemistry" (Bedford, 1978, pp. 26–27). Because such guidance lies at the heart of distinguishing between measurements and interpretations in accounting reports, the general theory accepted for that purpose should itself clearly distinguish between these two actions. LST makes such a distinction.

Additionally, the general theory should be stated in sufficient detail to establish a connection between a priori research and practice. Bedford further states:

Faced with the practical impossibility of developing a causal relationship between the mass of a priori research and accounting practice because some a priori research precedes practice, some follows it, and some is never used, another approach to the problem of relating a priori research and accounting practice seems to be needed. The problem takes the form of determining the type of a priori research that has or should be immediately accepted in practice. To select this type, some criteria are needed to distinguish the relevant theories. In this sense a theory of accounting theories, one that will identify the "good" theories, is needed. (Bedford, 1978, p. 5).

LST is stated in practical detail. Table 1–1 provides an outline showing the detail in which the theory is stated. The theory provides this level of detail for each of eight hierarchical levels of living systems, that is, (1) cell, (2) organ, (3) organism, (4) group, (5) organization, (6) community, (7) society, and (8) supranational system. Accounting directly and obviously involves the four higher levels beginning with organizations.

Rather than developing such a detailed conceptual framework for judging theories, Bedford states six general criteria and terms them a theory of accounting theory. Those criteria, however, are so general that, while they may eliminate some "bad" theories, they offer no guidance for the practical integration of acceptable ones. LST provides both criteria for judging the usefulness of various sorts of theories and a framework for integrating such theories into a coherent whole. Furthermore, LST itself clearly distinguishes between measurements of concrete processes and interpretations of those measurements.

Some applications of LST to accounting have been made. Anthony (1983) used some LST concepts in developing his conceptual framework. He specifically cites Miller's work as the source of his ideas from GST and states, "Because entities are systems, ideas from general systems theory are also relevant. General systems theory does not have a set of concepts in its own right. Rather, its purpose is to investigate the similarity (technically, the isomorphy) of models and systems in various fields so that concepts from one field can be usefully transferred to another field" (Anthony, 1983, p. 23).

LST has been applied to various aspects of accounting at a general level of abstraction (Swanson, 1987a). A general theory of accounting using syllogistic logic chains to describe the connection between LST and accounting information systems theory has been established. It identifies basic accounting functional advances as a progression of living systems evolving from relative simplicity toward complexity (Swanson, 1982, 1983, 1984).

At a more detailed and applied level, the interface of accounting information systems and specific subsystems of living systems has been described by Swanson

Table 1–1
Outline of LST

1. Structure
    1.1 System size
    1.2 Structural taxonomy of types of systems
2. Process
    2.1 System and subsystem indicators
    2.2 Process taxonomy of types of systems
3. Subsystems
    3.1 Subsystems which process both matter-energy and information
         3.1.1 Reproducer
                3.1.1.1 Structure
                3.1.1.2 Process
         3.1.2 Boundary
                3.1.2.1 Structure
                3.1.2.2 Process
    3.2 Subsystems which process matter-energy
         3.2.1 Ingestor
                3.2.1.1 Structure
                3.2.1.2 Process
         3.2.2 Distributor
                3.2.2.1 Structure
                3.2.2.2 Process
         3.2.3 Converter
                3.2.3.1 Structure
                3.2.3.2 Process
         3.2.4 Producer
                3.2.4.1 Structure
                3.2.4.2 Process
         3.2.5 Matter-energy storage
                3.2.5.1 Structure
                3.2.5.2 Process
         3.2.6 Extruder
                3.2.6.1 Structure
                3.2.6.2 Process
         3.2.7 · Motor
                3.2.7.1 Structure
                3.2.7.2 Process
         3.2.8 Supporter
                3.2.8.1 Structure
                3.2.8.2 Process
    3.3 Subsystems which process information
         3.3.1 Input transducer
                3.3.1.1 Structure
                3.3.1.2 Process
         3.3.2 Internal transducer
                3.3.2.1 Structure
                3.3.2.2 Process
         3.3.3 Channel and net
                3.3.3.1 Structure
                3.3.3.2 Process
         3.3.4 Timer
                3.3.4.1 Structure
                3.3.4.2 Process
         3.3.5 Decoder
                3.3.5.1 Structure
                3.3.5.2 Process
                3.3.6 Associator
                       3.3.6.1 Structure

Table 1–1 (Continued)

Table 1–1 (Continued)

and Miller (1986). That study provides a discussion of how accounting procedures and information flows are involved in each of nineteen critical subsystem processes of organizations. A study reported in *Behavioral Science* asserts that accounting information systems, as viewed in LST, are concerned with statements about measurable attributes, data simplification, prediction, and history in much the same manner as science is concerned about these phenomena (Swanson, 1987b). This study reverses the perspective and suggests that accounting information can be used for scientific investigation.

Weekes (1984) has developed a general systems approach to management accounting in extensive detail, using LST and other related systems principles. He provides accounting methods based on replacing the basic assumptions of "authority" and "accountability" with, respectively, "participation through the seeking of legitimate advice" and "the feedback processes of scientific methodology." He thus effectively connects the principles of feedback, studied extensively by systems scientists, with the principles that underlie accounting systems.

Finally, Swanson and Miller (1988) provide in-depth discussion of how LST may be used to distinguish clearly between measurements and interpretations in public accounting reports, rigorously developing the fundamental relationships among elements of information in accounting reports. This book expands that discussion and ties together various other studies to provide a practical means of improving accounting information gathering and disclosure procedures.

A Preview

To distinguish between accounting measurements and interpretations requires an action somewhat analogous to fine-tuning a television set. All of the elements for a good picture are present on the blurred screen. They are simply not arranged properly. We must rearrange the elements of accounting theory and procedure. A quick twist of a knob, however, will not get the job done. Several small adjustments at different places in the eclectic theoretic framework are needed, and thus the big picture of what we are doing may be lost in the detail. Therefore, a preview of how we approach the task may be helpful.

Chapter 2, "Concrete Processes and Accounting Information Systems," clearly distinguishes concrete systems from abstracted and conceptual ones and identifies accounting information systems as concrete systems. In that chapter we answer questions like these: What is information in concrete systems? Why measure concrete processes? Do accounting information systems measure concrete processes? What is the prediction power of accounting measurements of concrete processes? How did accounting processes evolve?

Chapter 3, "Incipient Money–Information Markers" discusses the concept of money in terms of LST and traces the emergence of money–information markers from bone tallies and pebbles used for counting to coins. This chapter clarifies the characteristics of money–information markers in the context of four ideas: (1) the accounting unit, (2) mobility (negotiability), (3) certification, and (4) value.

Chapter 4, "Living Systems Theory and Accounting," defines important terms and concepts used in LST and then discusses how accounting information systems are connected to each of twenty critical LST-defined subsystems. The twenty subsystems are:

1. Reproducer	11. Input transducer
2. Boundary	12. Internal transducer
3. Ingester	13. Channel and net
4. Distributor	14. Timer
5. Converter	15. Decoder
6. Producer	16. Associator
7. Matter–energy storage	17. Memory
8. Extruder	18. Decider
9. Motor	19. Encoder
10. Supporter	20. Output transducer

Chapter 5, "A Theory of Concrete Process Measurement," describes how the accounting information system uses human observers, electronic sensors, meters, clocks, and so forth to monitor the inputs and outputs of various forms of matter and energy by organizations. The chapter emphasizes the measurement scale used in this process. Consequently, it discusses what measurement is, what distinguishes measurement from surrogation generally, the monetary three-dimensional scale, and the four-dimensional accounting scale that includes three dimensions of physical space and one dimension of time.

Chapter 6, "An Accounting Model of Concrete Processes," discusses the system of accounts for recording accounting data, clarifying its characteristics as a system that maps the circuitous relationship between matter–energy flows and money–information marker flows. The chapter provides a rigorous development of important relationships within this accounting system. It specifically discusses the relationship of measurement and bias, defines unbiased accounting measurement, determines whether the double-entry bookkeeping measurement method converges on an unbiased global measurement, derives the variable net matter–energy flows (NME), and illustrates the utility of NME for referring accounting reports to raw accounting measurements.

Chapter 7, "Accounting Measurement of Concrete Processes Applied to Organizations," discusses how this LST-based theory would change accounting information-gathering and reporting procedures and how it may be applied. Extensive illustrations are provided for applying it under full measurement conditions and under partial measurement conditions. The first illustration uses typical accounting adjustments to restate information about concrete processes into the GAAP-governed quantities reported on balance sheets, income statements, and cash flow statements. The second illustration reverses the procedure and restates typical accounting information into concrete process information. Finally, we suggest how information about concrete processes may be reported to the public.

Chapter 8, "Concrete Process Analysis (CPA) and Living Systems Process Analysis (LSPA)," discusses how LSPA is applied to investigations of various living systems and how LSPA and CPA may be integrated to support holistic research on organization processes. It discusses both multilevel reseach based on an LST hierarchy of levels of life and LSPA at the organization level. One application of LSPA is illustrated with a synopsis of proposed NASA research on human space habitation on a space station and later on the moon.

Chapter 9, "LST General Research Hypotheses and Accounting Information Systems," distinguishes between conceptual frameworks for accounting research and those for accounting practice and provides an LST interpretation of scientific methodology, experimentation, and hypothesis testing. General research hypotheses are developed from the LST conceptual framework. It compares empirical research based on concrete systems with research based on "positive accounting theory" and suggests that accounting information can be used for empirical scientific investigations of organizations, communities, societies, and supranational systems.

Chapter 10, "Accounting Measurement of Concrete Processes Applied to Societies," proposes a society-level application of the theory that is applied mainly to organizations throughout the text. It explains how Leontief's input-output economics may be adapted for use with accounting measurements of concrete processes. The importance of cross-level upward-flow information disconnects between organizations and the society level of living systems is discussed. The Financial Accounting Standards Board and its conceptual framework are discussed in the context of cross-level information disconnects.

Chapter 11, "Summary and Conclusions," briefly summarizes the book.

References

American Institute of Certified Public Accountants (AICPA). *Centennial Issue Journal of Accountancy* (May 1987), entire issue.

Amey, Lloyd R. "Towards a New Perspective on Accounting Control." *Accounting, Organizations, and Society* Vol. 4, No. 4 (1979), pp. 247–58.

Ansari, Shahid L. "Towards an Open Systems Approach to Budgeting." *Accounting, Organizations, and Society* Vol. 4, No. 3 (1979), pp. 179–191.

Anthony, Robert N. *Tell It Like It Was*. Homewood, IL: Richard D. Irwin, 1983.

Bedford, Norton M. "The Impact of a Priori Theory and Research on Accounting Practice." In *The Impact of Accounting Research on Practice and Disclosure*, ed. A. Rashad Abdel-Khalik and Thomas F. Keller (Durham, NC: Duke University Press, 1978).

Boulding, K. "Economics and Accounting: The Uncongenial Twins." *In Studies in Modern Accounting Theory*, ed. W. Baxter and S. Davidson. Homewood, IL: Richard D. Irwin, 1962.

Chambers, R. J. *Accounting, Evaluation and Economic Behavior*. Englewood Cliffs, NJ: Prentice-Hall, 1966.

Cushing, B. E. *Accounting Information Systems and Business Organizations*. Reading, MA: Addison-Wesley, 1978.

Einstein, Albert. *Relativity, the Special and General Theory*, trans. Robert W. Lawson. New York, NY: Crown Publishers, 1961.

Financial Accounting Standards Board (FASB). *Objectives of Financial Reporting by Business Enterprises* (SFAC 1). Stamford, CT: FASB, 1978.

_____. *Qualitative Characteristics of Accounting Information* (SFAC 2). Stamford, CT: FASB, 1980a.

_____. *Elements of Financial Statements of Business Enterprises* (SFAC 3). Stamford, CT: FASB, 1980b.

_____. *Objectives of Financial Reporting by Nonbusiness Organizations* (SFAC 4). Stamford, CT: FASB, 1980c.

_____. *Recognition and Measurement in Financial Statements of Business Enterprises* (SFAC 5). Stamford, CT: FASB, 1984.

_____. *Statement of Cash Flows* (FASB Statement No. 95). Stamford, CT: FASB, 1987.

Gardner, John C., and G. A. Swanson. "From Bercu to Sperry—Significant Legal Landmarks in the Development of Tax Practice." *Journal of Accountancy* (May, 1987), pp. 163, 189–91.

Gibbs, J. W. *Elementary Principles of Statistical Mechanics*. New Haven, CT: Yale University Press, 1902.

Hill, A. F. *Adventures in Biophysics*. University of Pennsylvania Press, 1931.

Ijiri, Y. *Historical Cost Accounting and Its Rationality: Research Monograph No. 1*.

Vancouver, Canada: The Canadian Certified General Accountant's Research Foundation, 1981.

Köhler, W. *Die physischen Gestalten in Ruhe und in stationären Zustard.* Braunschveig: Vieweg, 1921.

————. "Zurn Problem der Regulation," *Roux's Archiv.* 112 (1927).

————. *The Place of Values in the World of Fact.* New York: Liveright, 1938.

Littleton, A. C. *Accounting Evolution to 1900.* New York: American Institute Publishing, 1933.

Mattessich, Richard. *Accounting and Analytical Methods.* Homewood, IL: Richard D. Irwin, 1964.

————. *Instrumental Reasoning and Systems Methodology.* New York: D. Reidel, 1978.

McNerney, John P. "Accounting and Its Relation to the Systems Concept," *The Ohio CPA* (Spring, 1964), pp. 53–58.

Miller, James Grier. "Living Systems: Structure and Process." *Behavioral Science* Vol. 10 (1965), pp. 337–79.

————. *Living Systems.* New York: McGraw-Hill, 1978.

Rhode, J. G. "Behavioral Science Methodologies with Application for Accounting Research: References and Source Materials, Chapter 7 of Report of the Committee on Research Methodology in Accounting." *The Accounting Review* (Supplement 1972), pp. 494–504.

Ridel, Ronald J. "Systems Approach: Applying Big Picture Thinking," *The Internal Auditor* (April, 1982), pp. 24–26.

Robinson, A., J. Davis, and C. Alderman. *Accounting Information Systems.* New York: Harper & Row, 1982.

Scott, D. R. *The Cultural Significance of Accounts.* New York: Henry Holt, 1931.

Sherman, H. D., ed. *Conceptual Frameworks for Financial Accounting.* Boston: The President and Fellows of Harvard College, 1984.

Smith, Charles H. "Systems Theory as an Approach to Accounting Theory." Ph.D. dissertation, Pennsylvania State University, 1968.

————. "The Modern Systems Approach, General Systems Theory, and Accounting Theory Development in the Age of Synthesis." *The International Journal of Accounting Education and Research* 6 (Spring, 1971), pp. 59–73.

Sprague, Charles Ezra. *The Philosophy of Accounts.* New York: Ronald Press, 1913.

Sterling, Robert. *Theory of the Measurement of Enterprise Income.* Lawrence: University Press of Kansas, 1970.

————. *Toward a Science of Accounting.* Houston, TX: Scholars Book Co., 1979.

Swanson, G. A. *A Living Systems General Theory of Accounting.* Ph.D. dissertation, Georgia State University, 1982. University Microfilms Order No. DEO 82–16502.

————. "A Proposed Framework to Aid Historical Investigations of the Development of Accounting and Accounting Thought." *Proceedings of the AAA Midwest Regional Meeting, 1983* Iowa City, IA: University of Iowa, 1983, pp. 133–38.

————. "The 'Roots' of Accounting." *The Accounting Historians Journal* Vol. 11, No. 2 (Fall, 1984), pp. 111–16.

————. "An Inquiry into the Utility of a Parallel System for Providing Insights Into the Development of an Accounting Conceptual System." *Advances in Accounting* Vol. 4 (1987a), pp. 3–12.

_____. "Accounting Information Can Be Used for Scientific Investigation." *Behavioral Science* Vol. 32, No. 2 (1987b), pp. 81–91.

Swanson, G. A. and James Grier Miller. "Accounting Information Systems in the Framework of Living Systems Theory and Research." *Systems Research* Vol. 3 (1986), pp. 253–265.

_____. "Distinguishing Between Measurements and Interpretations in Public Accounting Reports." *Behavioral Science* Vol. 33 (1988), pp. 1–24.

Swanson, G. A. and John C. Gardner. "Not-for-Profit Accounting and Auditing in the Early Eighteenth Century: Some Archival Evidence." *The Accounting Review* Vol. 63, No. 3 (July, 1988), pp. 436–47.

Talbert, William L. "Application of a New Systems Model of Social Organization to the Theory and Practice of Financial Accounting." Ph.D. dissertation, The University of Texas at Austin, 1973.

Tinker, Tony. *Social Accounting for Corporations*. New York: Markus Wiener Publishing, 1986.

von Bertalanffy, L. "The Theory of Open Systems and Biology," *Science* 3 (1950), pp. 23–29.

_____. "General Systems Theory," *General Systems* (1956), pp. 1–3.

_____. *General Systems Theory*. New York: Brazilles, 1968.

Weekes, W. H. *A General Systems Approach to Management Accounting*. Salinas, CA: Intersystems Publications, 1984.

Willingham, John J. "The Accounting Entity: A Conceptual Model." *The Accounting Review* 34 (July, 1964), pp. 543–52.

Winjum, J. O. *The Role of Accounting in the Economic Development of England: 1500–1750*. Chicago: Center for International Education and Research in Accounting, 1972.

2
CONCRETE PROCESSES
AND ACCOUNTING
INFORMATION SYSTEMS

Introduction

This chapter distinguishes precisely among concrete systems, abstracted systems, and conceptual systems. The accounting information system is described as a subsystem of concrete living systems that constructs conceptual systems by abstracting relationships from concrete systems. The following relevant questions are answered: What are concrete systems? What is information in concrete systems? Why measure concrete processes? Do accounting information systems measure concrete processes? What is the prediction power of accounting measurements of concrete processes? How did accounting processes evolve?

What Are Concrete Systems?

The term *system* refers to any set of related and interacting elements. This is an extremely broad definition and, at the same time, sufficiently precise to be useful. The elements of a system can be anything. The important notion is that relationships and interactions among elements can be identified. The relationships and interactions of some fairly simple systems may be identified mathematically, while constructing transformation functions that can identify, relate, and reduce to comprehensible complexity all the relationships and interactions of highly complex living systems is still beyond the ability of the most advanced mathematicians.

The two basic qualities to which a system owes its existence are relationship and interaction of elements. Relationship of elements is a necessary but not sufficient quality. For a system to exist, the elements must also be interdependent;

the actions of one must influence the actions of another. By this definition, random disorder is a nonsystem.

The universe of all systems may be usefully divided into three types of systems, two with subtypes. (1) A *concrete system* is a structured accumulation of matter, energy, and information in a physical region organized into interacting interrelated subsystems or components. (2) An *abstracted system* is a limited set of relationships abstracted or selected by an observer. Such systems are studied by conceptual systems. (3) A *conceptual system* is a set of words, symbols, patterns, or numbers, including those in computer simulations and programs, that has one or more subsets ordered in similar ways.

It is an axiom of systems theory that all systems have certain common attributes. They all consist of units coupled in particular relationships. The units are similar in some of their properties. The units of abstracted systems are relationships abstracted or selected by an observer. They are roles that may be filled by different actors at different times. These relationships are observed to inhere to and interact in selected concrete, usually human, systems. The units of concrete systems, on the other hand, are other concrete systems (components, parts, or members). The relationships of concrete systems are spatial, temporal, causal, or resultant from information transmissions. For us to study such systems with conceptual ones, we must abstract relationships from the concrete systems. Thus, our conceptual systems that describe both concrete and abstracted systems are the result of the process of abstraction or observation. Relationships among the elements of concrete systems, however, may be empirically confirmed or denied by accepted public observation methods.

According to Campbell (1958), an observer distinguishes concrete systems from unorganized elements by applying these four criteria: (1) physical proximity of the units, (2) similarity of the units, (3) common fate of the units, and (4) distinct or recognizable patterning of the units. The boundaries of such systems are discovered by empirical operations available to the general scientific community rather than set conceptually by a single observer.

This distinction is important for separating interpretations from measurements of concrete processes. While we do not claim ontologically that concrete systems thus identified constitute reality, we do strongly assert that during the evolution of modern civilization an information system, commonly termed accounting, emerged which itself may be distinguished in this fashion and which processes information about entities so distinguished.

There are two subtypes of conceptual systems: *numerical* and *verbal*. Numerical systems may represent nominal, ordinal, or cardinal information. Consequently, it is useful to classify numerical systems as truly *quantitative* and *nonquantitative*.

Also, there are two subtypes of abstracted systems: *measured* and *surrogated*. Measured systems are always quantitative and are selected by an observer by comparing elements of a concrete system with some standard or unit contained in the concrete system. What constitutes measured systems is discussed in Chapter 5. Surrogated systems may be quantitative or nonquantitative and are selected by an observer by comparing elements of a conceptual system with elements of a concrete system. This is a process of loose analogy. Because there is no standard or unit within the concrete system to which the observer compares the concrete element, there is no explicit assurance that the surrogated abstraction is, in fact, drawn from a particular concrete system. Surrogated abstracted systems provide no traceable connection between units of the conceptual system and elements of the concrete system that concern an observer. The strength of surrogated abstractions (or analogies) rests with the ingenuity of the argument constructed to relate the conceptual system elements to the concrete system elements.

Using this classification of systems, the accounting information system may be described as a concrete subsystem of a concrete human system, consisting of elements like people, buildings, equipment, energy, and money. The accounting information system, then, selects measured abstracted systems from concrete systems and constructs quantitative conceptual systems in order for managers and other social actors to study the abstractions and thus the concrete systems. The distinction between measured and surrogated abstractions is important. This distinction has been blurred by modern accounting theorists as well as many social scientists. The view of accounting information systems as concrete systems is even more important.

Historically, accountants have held a narrow view of accounting. They considered it to include only the system of accounts. The bookkeepers who manipulated the accounts were considered to be entirely separate from them. Therefore, the accounting system was believed to be free from their personal biases and neutral in its influence on the people within the corporation or other social organization whose economic activities are described, in part, in the accounts. More recently many accountants have come to realize that the accounting system cannot be divorced from the people and the organization of which it is a part.

The primary tool of this concrete accounting information system is a quantitative conceptual system that is commonly called double-entry bookkeeping. The accounts themselves form a quantitative conceptual system that describes a measured abstracted system. This is the case because the amounts in the accounts are determined by comparing flows of materials, energy, communications, personnel, and money with various forms of money information markers (described below) in each exchange at the boundary of the entity. The money exchanged is the standard by which the other flows are quantified. Therefore, the monetary unit in exchange is the measurement unit. Because this unit is used to account for the other flows, it is termed the *accounting unit*. In sum, the amounts flowing through the accounts constitute a conceptual system, quantified by comparison to the monetary units exchanged.

What Is Information in Concrete Systems?

Fundamentally, information in concrete systems is defined as the patterned arrangement of the matter and energy in the system. Information transmitted on channels in space or stored over time is borne on many sorts of markers including stone tablets, papyrus, paper, neural impulses, gestures, sound waves, radio and television waves, and electronic currents. The movement of information markers through physical channels and nets constitutes *communication* or *information flow*. If both the transmitter and the receiver of communications use the same language or code and if the transmission alters the behavior of the receiver in some way, the impact of the transmission is called its *meaning*.

In the accounting information system, we are concerned with information defined in the sense of Shannon's (1948) information theory. We are not so much interested, however, in calculating quantities of information content or complexity within systems as we are in tracking the rearrangements of matter–energy elements occurring between or within systems over time. Consequently, whereas information theory emphasizes cardinal numbering and manipulation, accounting's first priority is ordinal numbering. Cardinal numbering (quantities) emerges secondarily. For example, the accounting process is triggered by exchanges (rearrangements) and its reports are based on "accounting periods" (a time sequence). Then, within this general frame, accountants become concerned with quantification.

Money, money equivalents, and economic data such as costs and prices constitute a special subclass of information flow that first emerged in human societies. While money serves numerous purposes, fundamentally, it tracks the matter–energy and communications flows within and between societies. In modern societies, money–information markers include coins, currency, promissory notes, checks, bills, invoices, electronic transfers, and accounting entries. While most track the matter–energy flows directly, money–information markers such as promissory notes and accounts like accounts payable and accounts receivable are designed to create timing lags and leads between the currency money–information marker flows and the other matter–energy flows.

Money is legal tender that can be exchanged directly among the components of society, that is, organizations, groups, and individual persons, for various forms of matter, energy, and information at established or negotiated prices. Thus the flow of money as a medium of exchange directly reflects the flows of materials, energy, personnel, communications, and even money itself (e.g., costs of minting, exchanging, storing, and transferring money). This process uses prices and costs as a means to reduce all sorts of flows or processes in social systems to a common denominator of monetary units like dollars (Chambers, 1969, pp. 560–61; Churchman, 1961, p. 102). Such monetary units make it possible to create a very useful monetary information system that describes major aspects of the economy of any human system.

Why Measure Concrete Processes?

Some systems scientists describe systems science as the science of complexity; that is, it searches for solutions to multidisciplinary questions. For example, solutions to questions arising from nuclear disasters, epidemics, and the effects of natural calamities all require some combination of fields like economics, psychology, biology, medicine, atmospheric sciences, nuclear physics, engineering, law, and accounting. Effective interaction of different disciplines requires rigorous communication of measured information.

Eventually, it should be possible to write transformation equations to reduce dimensions of any of the disciplines of physical, biological, or social science into common dimensions compatible with the centimeter-gram-second system of measurement so that specialists in different fields can communicate precisely. The use of a common language, such as English, may be a good way to begin; but it is often so ambiguous that it leads to misconceptions. One sign of maturity in a science is the ability to write such transformation equations. At an early stage of conceptual development, it may be necessary to use measurements that are unrelated to others even in the same field. For example, there is no important known relationship between scores on the Stanford-Binet measurement of intelligence and the Rorschach test of personality.

Experimenters in physical and biological sciences almost always measure in dimensions identical to those used by other scientists in those fields, or in dimensions which have known transformations to those used by others. Investigators studying LST attempt to use such concrete system dimensions whenever possible. If some phenomena of living systems cannot be measured along such dimensions, one or more additional ones might have to be employed. If this is done, however, an explicit statement should always be made that those particular dimensions are incommensurable with the established dimensions of natural science.

Since all biological and social living systems exist in the same four-dimensional physical space as nonliving systems and the meters or indicators that measure them all do so in physical space, there is no reason why all dimensions and units employed for living as well as nonliving systems should not be ultimately commensurable. When that time comes, the average probable error of measurements made on living systems is likely to decrease dramatically.

Common dimensions for living and nonliving systems are increasingly useful as matter–energy and information processing technologies become more sophisticated and are more widely employed throughout the world. The design of person-machine interfaces will be much more precise and efficient when comparable dimensions are used to measure both.

Using transformation equations that relate other measurements to concrete ones is advocated rather than trying to go directly to some system of common dimensions, because people in the different disciplines ordinarily feel that the measurements to which they are accustomed are preferable. Transformation equations are a reasonable first step to common dimensions and, thus, to more precise understanding of interdisciplinary problems. Managers of organizations and other societal actors are concerned with many such problems. Consequently, transformation equations should be written to restate accounting information as well as other management information in terms of concrete processes.

It is possible to carry on scientific work in terms of abstracted systems such as roles. In scientific propositions generally, however, it is practical and easy to refer to concrete objects with nouns and to their relationships with verbs or predicates. The reverse is less practical and more difficult. The straightforward language we learned as children states that the ball rolls or the child loves the mother. It is confusing and achieves nothing important to reverse this common mode of speech and say that fatherhood is assumed by another man when a woman with children remarries after a divorce, or that the presidency was occupied first by Lincoln and later by Kennedy.

Typically, such roles are so complex and individual actors simultaneously play so many roles that it is impossible to determine what role is responsible for a particular action. On the other hand, actions of concrete elements can be observed and studied in relationship to other actions. This is how we have learned what we have by scientific method in the physical and biological sciences. We have not yet exhausted the knowledge obtainable by this method in the social sciences. In fact, we have hardly begun to obtain it. Unfortunately, abstracted systems theory about roles has produced no large body of quantitative research to support it because the theoretical statements that characterize it are difficult to test by any form of data collection.

Do Accounting Information Systems Measure Concrete Processes?

Sombart (Most, 1979, p. 251) clearly identifies the basic connection between accounting and physical processes.

If its [double-entry bookkeeping's] significance is to be correctly understood, it must be compared with the "knowledge" which scientists have built up since the 16th century, concerning relationships in the physical world. . . . By the same means it organizes perceptions into a system, and one can characterize it as the first cosmos constructed on the basis of mechanistic thought. . . . Double-entry bookkeeping is based on the methodological principle that all perceptions will be manipulated only as quantities, the basic principle of quantification which has delivered up to us all the wonders of nature.

Accounting provides a comprehensively integrated circuitous system based on the equality of total inputs and outputs over time that makes it possible to measure increases and decreases in differentiated concrete system processes as coherent wholes.

Mattessich believes that this system parallels the thermodynamic law of conservation of energy.

It is much more than a coincidence that *Heisenberg's S-Matrix Theory* and the various *gauge theories of particle physics* are nowadays recognized as "accounting systems of nature.'' Thereby, many interactions between nuclear and subnuclear particles are precisely accounted for, such that in terms of energy equivalents (including such properties as electrical charge, spin, and so on), the total output equals its total input. It may sound far-fetched to bring consideration of physics into management accounting, but it seems much less so if the *second* law of thermodynamics, the *Law of Entropy,* is also taken into consideration. Georgescu-Roegen (1976, p. 277, 283) reminds us that the law of entropy is an *economic* and not a mechanistic law of nature, that ''our whole economic life feeds on low entropy,'' that ''the basic nature of the economic process is entropic and that the Entropy Law rules supreme over this process and over its evolution.'' Through this law, the total (thermal) energy of the universe is separated into two distinct categories: (i) the *free* or *available* energy for activating change, and (ii) the *bounded* or *''wasted''* *energy* which no longer is available to instigate any kind of change or transformation. (1984, p. 408)

Burkhardt (1987) reverses the direction of the logical connection between physics and accounting measurement theories made by Mattessich to that asserted by Sombart and confirms this connection by actually developing a uniform approach to classical physics using the balancing accounting input-output algorithm. Dividing all extensive (substance-like) quantities into ''constituents'' (quantities that cannot be converted into one another) and ''components'' (quantities that form part of a constituent), he describes seven constituents with a set of simultaneous and usually coupled balance equations. The seven constitutents are: volume, ''V''; mass, ''M''; energy, ''E''; momentum, ''P''; angular momentum, ''L''; electrical charge, ''Q''; and entropy, ''S.'' This surprisingly short list of extensive quantities makes it possible to establish a frame for complete coverage of classical physics.

Karl Marx (Eastman, 1932, p. 236) clearly states the fundamental connection between accounting and concrete economic processes.

There is nevertheless a certain difference between the costs arising out of the process of bookkeeping and those arising out of the process of buying and selling. The latter arise solely from the fact that the product is a commodity, and would consequently disappear as soon as the process of production assumes another social form. Bookkeeping, on the contrary, insofar as it controls the process and epitomizes it in an ideal manner, becomes all the more necessary in the measure in which the social scale of production develops, and in which the process of production loses its individualist character. Bookkeeping is, therefore, more necessary in the capitalist system of production than in the split-up systems of handicraft and peasant production—and still more necessary in a system of production by the community itself, than in the capitalist system.

Although they may be used to surrogate many abstractions, such as roles, incorporated in various decision models, raw accounting values are basically measurements of concrete system processes. That is to say, they are numbers assigned to observations of such processes according to prescribed measurement rules.

Consequently, accounting information systems do measure concrete processes. The tenacious persistence of the accounting profession in retaining historical costing procedures, despite the equally persistent urging of various theorists to abandon them, has ensured the measurement of concrete system processes. Actually, the profession has moved, at the same time, both toward and away from a concrete systems view of organizations.

This conceptual development causes some members of the profession to believe that many issues with which accounting is concerned are inherently conflicting; thus an eclectic arrangement of special theories serves the profession better than a general theory. We believe that when information from accounting measurements is distinguished from interpretations of those measurements, a general theory based on concrete systems will emerge that identifies the proper position of the various accepted special theories in a mosaic of accounting practice. A brief overview of the conceptual developments to which we refer is useful.

Influenced by a growing acknowledgment of the dynamic qualities of the economic environment, indeed of physical existence itself, corporate managers increasingly have become concerned with concrete processes. For example, bank managers seek ways to decrease money "float" between spatially separated components of organizations and to increase the rate of information processing, as seen in creating integrated on-line management information systems. Given this state of mind, terms such as *flow* or *stream* are commonly used to describe the movement of resources among entities and over time. Not surprisingly, accountants have become process oriented and commonly call reports that accumulate inputs or ouputs of various classifications of data over time, flow statements.

In 1940, Paton and Littleton popularized the "matching concept" by publishing *An Introduction to Corporate Accounting Standards* and thus providing a theoretical basis for associating the concept of income with each item of goods sold or services performed. This concept justified the already shifting attention of accountants from the balance sheet, a statement of residuals in an organization at an instant, to the income statement, a statement of process over time (FRB, 1918, 1929; AIA, 1936). In the ensuing years, the authoritative pronouncements asserted more and more the importance of measurements of process at the expense of measurements of residuals (AICPA 1940, 1953; Mason, 1961; Grady, 1965; APB, 1963, 1971b), and the trend continues today (FASB, 1987).

Concurrent with the evolution of process reporting, the perception of the accounting entity has developed from a conceptual system bounded by legal considerations of proprietorial rights and fiducial obligations to one based on "economic reality." Official pronouncements first suggesting and later mandating the consolidation of the statements of separate legal entities (e.g., Chevrolet and Buick) into one accounting entity (General Motors) (AIA, 1936; AICPA, 1959), procedures that account for mergers based on economic reality, for example, pooling procedures, must be used when two economic entities are unified and continue to exist as one organization (APB, 1970, 1971a), and the going-concern concept—the idea that the organization continues regardless of changes in its components—is part of this development.

As an important subset of the set of all concrete systems, human (living) systems can be usefully classified on a hierarchy of increasing complexity as cells, organs, organisms, groups, organizations, communities, societies, and supranational systems (Miller, 1978). Fiduciary and proprietary considerations generally set entity boundaries based on the individual, that is, the organism level. As they have become aware that organizations produce their own cultures and that certain accounting-information filters can create organization-level decisions that would not be necessarily the person-level decisions of any particular organization member, accountants have begun to recognize that organizational behavior may have as much to do with its managers, suppliers, employees, creditors, and so forth, as with its owners. Thus a systems view of the accounting entity is emerging.

The confluence of these two developments, process reporting and a systems view, implies that the accounting information system measures the processes of concrete economic systems. Furthermore, the development suggests that research on accounting information systems may be served by general conceptual frameworks that instruct the various disciplines associated with concrete systems, for example, physics, biology, sociology, psychology, management science, decision science, economics, information science, and systems science, among others.

During the same period that conceptual developments toward a concrete systems view of organizations and societies were occurring, the views that accounting should measure a myriad of abstractions, for example, current value, social welfare, national economic good, just or fair information, purchasing power, capital maintenance, economic income, and others, were also emerging (Paton, 1922; Canning, 1923; Sweeny, 1936; Scott, 1941; Sprouse and Moonitz, 1962; Chambers, 1969; Belkaoui, 1975; Zeff, 1978). The conceptual systems constructed to study such abstracted systems have been intermingled with those constructed to study concrete systems. The result is a conglomeration of overlapping and often conflicting theories (some suggest paradigms [Belkaoui, 1981]), the applications of which have often removed much of the original information measured on concrete elements from commonly used accounting measurement derivatives, for example, net income and earnings per share.

LST may be used to sort out the influence on published accounting derivatives of these various theories. It is especially suited for this purpose because a consensus among accountants and other business participants has developed that decision usefulness is the overriding consideration for determining when, what, where, and how accounting information should be processed. In LST terms, the accounting information system is a component of the internal transducer subsystem of organizations and societies. The internal transducer is "the sensory subsystem that receives, from subsystems or components within a system, markers bearing information about significant alterations in those subsystems or components, changing them to other matter–energy forms of a sort which can be transmitted within it'' (Miller, 1978, p. 3). The purpose of this and another seven information-processing subsystems identified by LST is to process information to and from the decider subsystem. The decider subsystem is defined as ''the executive subsystem which receives information inputs from all other subsystems and transmits to them information outputs that control the entire system'' (Miller, 1978, p. 3). Thus the LST view of the centrality of decision usefulness is consistent with the consensus among accountants.

The notion is not new that identifying an internal locus of decision-information-based control is central to identifying the accounting entity. Goldberg's (1965) ''commander'' theory expresses the same idea. What may be new is the assertion that this information-gathering decision-control process may be usefully described in terms of the concrete system elements of matter–energy and money–information marker flows (Swanson and Miller, 1986).

This assertion does not reject using other abstracted systems for many different specific decision models. It rather provides a conceptual system that may be empirically confirmed or disconfirmed as an anchor to which conceptual systems describing other abstracted systems (interpretations), which might not be empirically confirmable, may be connected. Thus it provides a point of reference for evaluating the influence on accounting derivatives of any one theory or combination of theories.

The concrete inputs, throughputs, and outputs of organizations constitute fundamental aspects contributing to the success or failure of any organization. These flows are measured by accountants. Therefore, accountants may provide this information as a point of reference for determining the effects of various interpretive accounting adjustments on accounting derivatives such as total assets, net income, comprehensive income, net worth, earnings per share, debt to equity ratio, and current ratio. Such a disclosure would provide accounting-derived measurements that could be manipulated only by economic action, benchmarks by which bookkeeping manipulations could be independently judged by accounting information users.

What Is the Prediction Power of Accounting Measurements of Concrete Processes?

Accountants talk about economic resources, assets, liabilities, equities, and the like, not matter–energy flows. Many of the differences between accounting terms and LST terms are semantic. Significant conceptual differences, however, also exist. For example, when modern accountants define net assets as economic or financial resources minus obligations, they include not only matter–energy and money–information marker flows, but also certain flows that have not yet occurred but might. Furthermore, they invert the effects of outflows and inflows recorded in such accounts as accounts receivable and accounts payable. Increases in accounts payable obviously give the entity a resource of some form that may be manipulated for its own purposes. Increases in accounts receivable give up such power. Nevertheless, within the logic of modern accounting theory, accountants correctly consider accounts receivable to be a resource and accounts payable a reduction of resources when calculating net assets.

Various explanations of the meaning of accounting reports have been proposed; for example, they report measurements of the value of using a resource or the value a resource would have if exchanged in a market, or they predict future cash flows. Such explanations have little or no prediction power.

Allen and Hoekstra (1985) suggest that different explanations require different criteria by which they may be reduced and thus reduce to different primitives. In this context, the term *primitives* refers to the structural givens in an explanation. The degree to which the primitives persist over time determines the degree of prediction power an explanation may have.

This position relies on the concept of near-decomposability put forward by Simon (1973). Near-decomposable systems have primitives that display relatively tight closure of their own internal processes. Thus the system persists and may be predicted. An explanation is not predictive if a system that it purports to explain shows only decompositions that are competitive with those required by the reduction criterion of the proposed explanation. Such decompositions are unstable with respect to the reduction criterion; thus a match between the two cannot be expected regularly.

Accounting reports generate statements of "what was" in terms that attempt to describe physical reality (concrete systems). The reduction criterion for this explanation can be formalized as matter–energy flows. Reduction based on this criterion achieves near-decomposability in that physical reality is widely understood to consist of arrangements of these fundamental (primitive) elements.

The relatively tight closure of this near-decomposability enhances the prediction power of this explanation. Such closure signals that the criterion, matter–energy flows, isolates primitives that are sufficiently persistent to serve as explanatory principles with some degree of prediction power. In other words, most of the accounting numbers can be explained in terms of matter–energy flows. This is not generally true of other explanations.

The scientific notion of prediction as it relates to concrete systems is tied to the possibility of discovering commonalities in a universe of infinitely diverse elements. If all elements are only different and have no similarities, no element can be used to study and enhance the understanding of another. On the other hand, if commonalities can be discovered among elements, these similarities can be used to extend our understanding of various relationships among the elements of this universe.

Concrete systems are arrangements of various elements of matter and energy in physical space ordered over time. These systems are subject to the laws of thermodynamic degradation; that is, in terms of negative entropy they are moving from order toward random disorder. If no commonalities existed, there would be no arrangement and order and such systems would be nonexistent; that is, their elements would be unrelated and noninteracting and thus indistinguishable from the elements of any other system.

When studying these systems, scientific prediction is not concerned with estimating or guessing the future, although such predictions may imply continuity, within limits of change, into the future. These predictions are relatively specific and generally consist of statements about how new combinations of previously discovered commonalities will relate and interact under controlled conditions.

This distinction is important when examining the prediction power of accounting reports because the meaning of the term *prediction* may be confused with the common meaning of the term *prophecy*, an estimate of future events by an observer who has neither control nor understanding of the elements that produce the events. Scientific prediction hypothesizes an event based on a particular construction of specific elements and what is known about those elements.

Because accounting reports are hierarchically nested data reductions of measurements of a concrete system (termed *accounting entity*), they contain information about the many and complex interrelationships of the internal and environmental elements. As with all scientific predictions, the prediction power of these reports is a function of how complete the data base is and how well it is understood. Data bases generated by basic accounting systems generally are fairly comprehensive. When these data are recognized as certain measurements of exchanges of various bundles of matter and energy, they may be understood in the framework of what science is learning about physical reality.

What is true of the data bases of the basic accounting systems is not necessarily true of the common accounting reports. Clearly, the record of matter–energy flows is contained in the accounting data. Reports produced by the current accrual accounting system, however, commingle information about the rearrangement of bundles of matter–energy with information about the rearrangement of various forms of money–information markers and accounting adjustments. This process obscures the information about matter–energy flows.

Information about matter–energy flows, however, can be separated from other kinds of information contained in the common accounting reports, and the prediction power of such information may parallel that of some other data bases used in scientific investigations. The method of producing the primary measurements (before various reductions and transformations are applied to produce reports) used by the basic accounting system may rival the best scientific methods of data collection. This is so because legal, ethical, and financial considerations constrain the collection process. Consequently, the basic accounting systems may provide a massive data base with prediction power that rivals those used for scientific investigations.

How Did Accounting Processes Evolve?

History is an important part of all disciplines. Because all human systems exist in a four-dimensional space-time continuum, all action, including the ac-

Table 2–1
Hierarchy of Accounting Processes

Accounting Processes	Information Added
1. Concrete system rearrangement	
2. Abstract record keeping	Duplication
3. Classification	Ordinal or categorical synthesis
4. Aggregation	Cardinal synthesis
5. Money	Synthesis of diverse objects and processes into coherent wholes and information flow or mobility
6. Conceptual modeling	Mechanistic (methodical) thought systems that reconcile measurements and interpretations
7. Accrual accounting	Reconciliation of money information flow and matter-energy flow per time

cumulation of knowledge, occurs over time. Thus, any applied discipline must have a history. The requirement that new information be connected to existing knowledge provides a standard to evaluate the new information and estabishes an orderly historical file describing the evolution of the applied discipline.

LST asserts that human systems generally evolve toward increased complexity. A similar evolution occurs in subsystems and components of such systems. By conceptualizing the simplest expression of accounting process and progressing step-by-step in the direction of more complex expressions, one can construct a hierarchy that predicts the chronology of the emergence of accounting processes (Swanson, 1982, 1984), as seen in Table 2–1. Information about the past accumulated by archeologists, anthropologists, and historians provides evidence that accounting processes emerge in this order.

The first step in the development of accounting is the rearrangement of concrete systems to reflect a required information. There is evidence that the concept of ordinal (directly space-time related) numbering may have preceded that of cardinal (quantitative) numbering (Boyer, 1968; Seidenberg, 1962). The ceremonial rites of very ancient peoples enacting creation myths required the specific time ordering of the actors. A similar rudimentary sense of numbering has been shown to exist in certain higher animals as well (Bell, 1945). Ball (1960, p. 123) describes the spatial ordering required by the counting efforts of primitive people as follows: "Up to ten it is comparatively easy to count, but primitive people find great difficulty in counting higher numbers; apparently at first this difficulty was overcome by the method (still in use in South Africa) of getting two men, one to count the units up to ten on his fingers, and the other to count the number of groups of ten so formed.'' Therefore, the proposition that the first step in accounting is rearranging a concrete system seems to be compatible with the development of counting.

Boyer (1968, pp. 1–2) recognizes the primitive characteristic and central position of concrete system rearrangement in this statement:

It is clear that originally mathematics arose as a part of the everyday life of man, and if there is validity in the biological principle of the ''survival of the fittest,'' the persistence of the human race probably is not unrelated to the development in man of mathematical concepts. At first the primitive notions of number, magnitude and form may have related to contrasts rather than likenesses—the difference between one wolf and many.

Scott (1969, p. 1) makes more explicit the elements of early mathematical development. In the context of discussing the Sumerians, he states: ''There is unmistakable evidence that a rudimentary form of mathematics played no small part in their lives. Barter leads at once to the fundamental operations of counting and adding, of weighing and measuring, and an appreciation of simple geometric forms. . . . Moreover, peoples depending upon the fruits of the earth for their existence had need of some form of calendar to indicate the recurrence of the seasons.'' Ball (1960, p. 3) reveals the possible instrument of transition from ordinal to cardinal numbering when he points out that ''the almost universal use of the abacus or swan-pan rendered it easy for the ancients to add and subtract without any knowledge of theoretical arithmetic . . . [T]hey afford a concrete way of representing a number in the decimal scale, and enable the results of addition and subtraction to be obtained by a merely mechanical process.'' Therefore, not only is concrete system rearrangement compatible with early counting developments, but the economic element—the need to account for matter-energy flows—might also have been the impetus for the development of counting (primitive mathematics).

The prehistoric emergence of abstract recordkeeping is documented by the work of Denise Schmandt-Besserat. Tokens, models made of clay of various shapes representing specific commodities begin to appear in the archaeological assemblages of the Middle East about 8500 B.C. (Schmandt-Besserat, 1979a, 1977a, 1977b, 1974). With the emergence of cities, about 3500 B.C., the token system underwent evolutionary changes and clay envelopes containing tokens began to appear (Schmandt-Besserat, 1980, 1979b). Schmandt-Besserat draws parallels between the shapes of these tokens and those of the first signs of writing and describes the relationships and continuity between the token system of recording and the pictographic system of writing.

Except for rare occasions, the tokens found at large were made with great care and fired and enclosed in clay or metal vessels. From this evidence Schmandt-Besserat suggests that ''tokens of specific accounts were kept in special containers'' (1980, pp. 365, 368). On the other hand, the tokens found in envelopes, while identical in shape, were smaller and cursorily manufactured. This difference suggests that the tokens and envelopes might have been manufactured in the presence of involved parties and that the purpose of the invention of the envelopes may have been the need to confer an official character on certain transactions by using a seal.

While the envelopes form the direct impetus for the invention of writing, it is particularly important to observe that the tokens themselves formed a widespread abstract recording system over a period of some five thousand years and over a wide spatial area. "The homogeneity of the group of artifacts strongly suggests that they all served an identical function and that the messages contained in the form of tokens were intelligible from Elam to Palestine" (Schmandlt-Besserat, 1980, p. 371). It should further be observed that all of this happened in prehistory, before the invention of writing.

Schmandt-Besserat concludes:

About 200 spherical clay envelopes (including fragments) have been recovered in an area extending from Palestine to Iran, including Saudi Arabia. The seals impressed upon their surface indicate their formal character, and it seems clear that the tokens they contained stood for goods and stated liabilities. The envelopes would have remained of esoteric interest but for the discovery of their relationship to the invention of writing. Indeed, their evolution illustrates no less than the transition between an archaic abacus and writing according to the following sequence: (1) the invention of envelopes to hold tokens of specific transactions; (2) the impression of markings on the surface of the envelopes to indicate the shape and number of tokens included inside; (3) the collapse of the envelopes into clay balls or tablets bearing impressed signs; and (4) the elaboration of the impressed signs into incised pictographs (1980, p. 385).

Braidwood (1967) and Bell (1945) indicate that the development of writing can be traced step-by-step from the pictographs to cuneiform writing. Modern written language is traceable to the cuneiform.

Not only is the foregoing supportive of the notion that abstract recordkeeping is a primitive development of civilization, but it also attributes to the recording subsystem the invention of the artifact of written language.

The roots of classification, the next step in the development of the accounting subsystem, may be seen in the spatial separation of tokens into specific accounts in special containers and the spatial separation of tokens by transaction in the envelopes. The evolution of the token toward complexity and then toward simplicity may indicate a form of classification (Schmandt-Besserat, 1980, pp. 378–379).

The roots of aggregation likewise may be seen in the finding of specific accounts in special containers and the use of specially shaped tokens to express a collection of goods (1980, pp. 373–376). The early development of the abacus also supports the proposition that aggregation is a relatively early functional advancement of the accounting subsystem.

While it would not serve the purposes of this section to trace extensively the

development of these basic accounting advancements to the present, it is worth-
while to observe that the spatial rearrangement of matter–energy into information
to achieve economic transactions has continued. The emergence and decline of
the counting house, the persistence of the abacus in many parts of the world
even to today, and the electronic addressing of information in the most advanced
computer systems demonstrate that such elementary rearrangement of concrete
elements is not transitory and is quite fundamental to today's complex society.
Werner Sombart has been criticized for claiming that one can see in double entry
the germs of the ideas of the force of gravity, the circulation of the blood, and
the conservation of energy, and for setting A.D. 1202 as the beginning of modern
capitalism because the *Liber Abaci*, a primer of commercial arithmetic, appeared
that year. Perhaps he was more perceptive than his colleagues realized.

Money is such an important functional advancement of accounting that we
devote an entire chapter to its discussion. Conceptual modeling and accrual
accounting are closely tied and are of relatively recent origin. Consequently, we
omit discussions of them at this stage.

Today, there are growing bodies of literature which, by their very existence,
imply that accounting is a concrete process of concrete systems. That literature
dealing with the accounting profession—peer review, independence, management advisory services, proposed internal control system audits, compliance
audits, to name a few issues—is most explicitly concrete-system–oriented. Much
of modern managerial accounting views the system it serves as a social behavioral
system. This has given rise to such specialty areas as social accounting, behavioral accounting, and increased attention to performance measurement. The accounting department is made up of the same elements (matter–energy in space-
time) as the rest of the entity of which it is a part. Many accountants already
recognize this broader character of the accounting subsystem, and some have
begun to address it in a more formal sense. A third important body of literature
is that generated by the accounting historians. Implicit in their methodologies
and writings is the significance of the human element in the development of
accounting and accounting thought. Littleton (1933, p. 368) summarized this
when he wrote, "The evolution of accounting . . . is another cross section of the
unending stream of history wherein ' . . . all events, conditions, institutions,
personalities, come from immediately preceding events, conditions, institutions,
personalities' (Cheyney).''

Recognizing that accounting is a fundamental process of social systems is
important. It is not the invention of a monk who lived in the fifteenth century.
Pacioli's contribution need not be minimized, but it should be recognized in the
context of a process evolution that is much more fundamental to the advancement
of civilization than accountants and other social actors have generally allowed.
If accounting is recognized in this broader fashion, accounting theorists can
consider what differentiates accounting information from other forms of management information. When this happens, accounting will be identified not by

the services an accounting department or public accounting firm offers but rather by a scientific discipline upon which such applications are based.

Summary

In Chapter 2, we distinguish clearly among concrete systems, abstracted systems, and conceptual systems and define concrete systems as matter, energy, and information in physical space-time. Accounting information systems are components of the internal transducer subsystems of higher-level living systems. Living systems comprise a special case of the general case of concrete systems. We discuss this special case extensively in Chapter 4.

Information in concrete systems is the arrangement of their elements in three dimensions of space and order over time. To be communicated or retained over time, information must be borne on information markers. Money–information is an important subset of the set of all information. Money–information is borne on money–information markers.

Accounting information systems process information borne on money–information markers to provide a coherent view of the diverse concrete processes of human systems such as organizations. Such accounting systems have evolved over many centuries and likely contribute significantly to the advancement of civilization.

Because the concept of money–information markers is so important in a theory of the accounting measurement of concrete processes, we devote Chapter 3 to a discussion of their incipient developments. In that chapter, we describe their characteristics in detail. We hope that discussion clarifies what we mean by money–information marker.

References

Accounting Principles Board (APB). *The Statement of Source and Application of Funds.* APB Opinion No. 3, New York: AICPA, 1963.
————. *Business Combinations.* APB Opinion No. 16, New York: AICPA, 1970.
————. *The Equity Method of Accounting for Investments in Common Stock.* APB Opinion No. 18, New York: AICPA, 1971a.
————. *Reporting Changes in Financial Position.* APB Opinion No. 19, New York: AICPA, 1971b.
Allen, T. F. H., and T. W. Hoekstra. "The Instability of Primitives and Unpredictable Complexity." *Systems Inquiring* (Proceedings of SGSR International Conference, 1985). Seaside, CA: Intersystems Publications, 1985, pp. 41–44.
American Institute of Accountants (AIA), *Examination of Financial Statements.* New York: AIA, 1936.
American Institute of Certified Public Accountants (AICPA) "Consolidated Financial Statements." *Accounting Research Bulletin No. 51*, New York: AICPA, 1959.

_____. Accounting Procedures Committee. *Comparative Statements*. ARB No. 6, New York: AICPA, 1940.

_____. Committee on Terminology. *Review and Resume*. Accounting Terminology Bulletin No. 1, New York: AICPA, 1953.

Ball, W. W. Rouse. *A Short Account of the History of Mathematics*. New York: Dover Publications, 1960.

Belkaoui, A. "The Whys and Wherefores of Measuring Externalities." *The Certified General Accountant* (January–February, 1975), pp. 29–32.

_____. *Accounting Theory*. San Diego, CA: Harcourt Brace Jovanovich, 1981.

Bell, E. T. *The Development of Mathematics*. New York: McGraw-Hill, 1945.

Boyer, Carl B. *A History of Mathematics*. New York: John Wiley, 1968.

Braidwood, Robert J. *Prehistoric Man*. 7th ed. Glenview, IL: Scott Foresman, 1967.

Burkhardt, H. "System Physics: A Uniform Approach to Branches of Classical Physics." *American Journal of Physics* Vol. 55, No. 4 (April, 1987), pp. 344–350.

Campbell, D. T. "Common Fate, Similarity, and Other Indices of the Status of Aggregates of Persons as Social Entities." *Behavioral Science* (1958), pp. 3, 14–25.

Canning, J. B. *The Economics of Accountancy*. New York: The Ronald Press, 1923.

Chambers, R. J. *Accounting, Finance, and Management*. New York: Arthur Andersen & Co., 1969.

Churchman, C. West. *Prediction and Optimal Decisions*. Englewood Cliffs, NJ: Prentice Hall, 1961.

Eastman, Max, ed. *Capital, the Communist Manifesto, and Other Writings of Karl Marx*. New York: The Modern Library, 1932.

Federal Reserve Board (FRB). *Applied Methods for Preparation of Balance Sheet Statements*. Washington, DC: Government Printing Office, 1918.

_____. *Verification of Financial Statements*. Washington, DC: Government Printing Office, 1929.

Financial Accounting Standards Board (FASB). *Statement of Cash Flows* (FASB Statement No. 95). Stamford, CT: FASB, 1987.

Georgescu-Roegen, N. *Energy and Economic Myths*. New York: Pergammon Press, 1976.

Goldberg, L. *An Inquiry into the Nature of Accounting Principles for Business Enterprises* (AAA Monograph No. 7). Sarasota, FL: American Accounting Association, 1965.

Grady, P. *Inventory of Generally Accepted Accounting Principles for Business Enterprises* (ARS No. 7). New York: AICPA, 1965.

Littleton, A. C. *Accounting Evolution to 1900*. New York: American Institute Publishing Co., 1933.

Mason, P. *Cash Flow Analysis and the Funds Statement* (ARS No. 2). New York: AICPA, 1961.

Mattessich, R. *Modern Accounting Research: History, Survey, and Guide*. Vancouver, B.C.: CGA Research Foundation, 1984.

Miller, James Grier. *Living Systems*. New York: McGraw-Hill, 1978.

Most, Kenneth. "Sombart on Accounting History," Working Paper No. 35 in *The Academy of Accounting Historians Working Paper Series*, Vol. 2, ed. Edward N. Coffman. Alanta, GA: The Academy of Accounting Historians, 1979, pp. 244–262.

Paton, W. A. *Accounting Theory*. New York: Ronald Press, 1922.

Paton, W. A., and A. C. Littleton. *An Introduction to Corporate Accounting Standards*. Sarasota, FL: American Accounting Association, 1940.

Schmandt-Besserat, Denise. "The Beginnings of the Use of Clay in Zagros." *Expedition* Vol. 16, No. 2. (1974), pp. 11–17.
————. "The Earliest Use of Clay in Anatolia." *Anatolian Studies* Vol. 27 (1977a), pp. 133–150.
————. "The Earliest Use of Clay in Syria." *Expedition* Vol. 19, No. 3 (1977b), pp. 28–42.
————. "An Archaic Recording System in the Urak-Jemdet Nasr Period." *American Journal of Archaeology* Vol. 83, No. 1 (1979a), pp. 23–31.
————. "Reckoning Before Writing." *Archaeology* Vol. 32, No. 3 (1979b), pp. 23–31.
————. "The Envelopes that Bear the First Writing." *Technology and Culture* Vol. 21, No. 3 (July, 1980), pp. 358–385.
Scott, D. R. "The Basis of Accounting Principles." *The Accounting Review* (December, 1941), 341–349.
Scott, J. F. *A History of Mathematics*. New York: Barnes & Noble, 1969.
Seidenberg, A. "The Ritual Origin of Counting." *Archives for History of Exact Sciences* 2 (1962), pp. 1–40.
Shannon, C. E. "A Mathematical Theory of Communication." *Bell System Technical Journal* (1948), pp. 27, 379–423, 623–656.
Simon, H. H. "The Organization of Complex Systems." In H. H. Pattee, ed., *Hierarchy Theory: The Challenge of Complex Systems*. New York: Braziller, 1973.
Sprouse, R. T., and M. A. Moonitz. *A Tentative Set of Broad Accounting Principles for Business Enterprises* (ARS No. 3). New York: AICPA, 1962.
Swanson, G. A. "A Living Systems General Theory of Accounting." Ph.D. dissertation, Georgia State University, 1982. University Microfilms Order No. DEO 82–16502.
————. "A Proposed Framework to Aid Historical Investigations of the Development of Accounting and Accounting Thought." In *Proceedings of the AAA Midwest Regional Meeting, 1983*. Iowa City, IA: University of Iowa, 1984, pp. 111–116.
Swanson, G. A., and J. G. Miller. "Accounting Information Systems in the Framework of Living Systems Theory and Research." *Systems Research* (1986), pp. 4, 253–265.
Sweeny, H. W. *Stabilized Accounting*. New York: Hayer & Brothers, 1936.
Zeff, A. S. "The Rise of Economic Consequences." *The Journal of Accountancy*, (December, 1978).

3
INCIPIENT MONEY–
INFORMATION MARKERS

Introduction

An understanding of money as a form of information, indeed of communication, is central to the proposition that accounting information systems measure the diverse processes of organizations as coherent wholes. In fact, the concept that money is information is so important that accounting information systems might be viewed as extensions of monetary systems, and monetary systems might be viewed as components of accounting systems.

The monetary quantification of information by exchanging money–information markers for various forms of matter and energy is a unique type of quantification. This type of quantification typically emerges at the society level of human systems. At this level of system organization, it provides, as part of the system itself, a means to measure the interrelationships among system elements from the perspective of individual societal actors. That is to say, it is a type of quantification that places the observer of the system within the system being observed. This situation is what Einstein's theory of relativity attempts to provide for measurements taken on objects and processes existing in physical space-time.

While placing the observer in the system being observed must be done conceptually for many systems that concern physics, this situation is a physical reality in concrete social systems; that is, the observer is an integral aspect of these systems. As such, the observers are the actors and every observation is both an action and an observation.

When an economic actor gives up money–information markers bearing a certain quantity of specific monetary exchange value to obtain certain items of goods and services, economic characteristics of the concrete social system such as scarcity and personal preferences cause the actor to be unlikely to consummate a second identical transaction. Consequently, with virtually every action-observation there is a restructuring of the relationships among the societal components, including the relationships among money–information markers and other matter–energy forms. This quality of concrete social systems effectively prevents the construction of *enduring general* transformation equations that describe the connection between specific types of matter and energy forms and the specific monetary exchange value borne on money–information markers. That is to say, in a particular concrete social system no general equation is available that will always convert x number of tons of steel into y number of dollars of specific monetary exchange value, or vice versa.

As a consequence of this condition, specific monetary exchange value emerges as an attribute of the concrete elements that comprise social systems. It is important to realize that this attribute exists only in the context of a higher-order system that has components connected by a money–information marker subsystem. It is a relational attribute and not intrinsic to the elements themselves. It is a true emergent of the higher-order system.

How an attribute such as specific monetary exchange value may have evolved is interesting. In a concrete system, artifacts used to measure and communicate information about the attribute may be expected to reflect this evolution. The artifactual development of money–information markers provides a history that helps us distinguish between the common meaning of the term *money* and the meaning of what we term *money–information markers*.

LST and Money

LST postulates that money is a special form of information that emerges in human societies. Such societies are the seventh level in an eight-level hierarchy of types of living systems ordered from simple expressions to complex ones. Together, all these types of living systems comprise a subset of all concrete (physical) systems. While there are many obvious differences, living systems at and across each of these levels have in common twenty critical processes (subsystems). Generally, the failure of any one of these critical processes terminates the system. Of the twenty processes, at least eleven are concerned with information processing. Money–information is among the forms of information processed by these subsystems.

The basic elements of all concrete systems, including the living ones, are matter, energy, and information. Fundamentally, information in concrete systems is the arrangement of various forms of matter and energy in three dimensions of physical space and order over time. For it to be preserved over time or to move in space (be communicated), information must be borne on information markers (relatively small bundles of matter–energy). Examples of forms of information markers are stone tablets, clay tablets, papyrus documents, paper documents, neural impulses, gestures, sound waves, radio and television waves, and electronic currents. Likewise, money–information must be carried on money–information markers, for example, coins, currency, credit cards, promissory notes, checks, money orders, bills, invoices, accounting entries such as accounts receivable, and electronic funds transfers.

Swanson and Miller (1986) have described accounting information systems in terms of LST. Such systems are components of the internal transducer process of organizations and societies. The internal transducer subsystem receives information markers from other subsystems within a system and transforms them to matter–energy forms that can be transmitted within the system. Accounting information systems contribute uniquely to the continuation of organizations and societies over time by providing a means of viewing as a coherent whole the many diverse forms of matter–energy that comprise those systems. They do this by measuring the diverse concrete flows on a unique accounting scale that incorporates the ratio monetary scale but is not encompassed by it (Swanson, 1987a and 1987b; Swanson and Miller, 1988). We discuss this scale in detail in Chapters 5 and 6. This spatiotemporal scale provides a cosmic measurement of the system in terms of specific exchange monetary value and time periods. It is unlikely that systems as complex as modern societies could have evolved without such a fundamental process.

Money and accounting are inextricably connected. Accounting cannot be comprehended without understanding the role of money, and it is unlikely that money can be understood disconnected from its accounting characteristics.

As introduced in Chapter 2, the evolution of accounting functional advances may be ordered based on the "fray-out" principle of LST. This principle states that living systems generally evolve from simple expressions toward complex expressions by specializing the functions of their components. Within components, evolution follows a similar pattern. Consequently, a hierarchy of accounting process may be constructed by conceptualizing its simplest expression and progressing step-by-step in the direction of more complex expressions (Swanson, 1982, pp. 50–55, 74–80; 1987a, p. 82). Table 2–1 provides such a hierarchy. On this hierarchy, money is the fourth emergent and thus may be expected generally to emerge chronologically between aggregation/classification and conceptual modeling.

Many writers have observed that various forms of advances in civilization typically do not occur in a smooth fashion; for example, see Einzig (1966, p. 16). Both advances and retrenchments occur. Some advances are isolated in local areas and, therefore, are developed independently much later in other areas. With this knowledge, we would not be surprised to find overlapping developments of the four hierarchical levels, that is, abstract recordkeeping, classification, aggregation, and money. Furthermore, we would not be surprised to find similar developmental processes occurring in different time frames and involving different specific artifacts. For example, Grierson (1977) traces independent developments of money in the Middle East and China.

In the following sections, we suggest that money–information markers in incipient forms (conveniently termed "primitive money" by Grierson, Einzig, and others) began to emerge with the invention of a recording system that used clay tokens to abstract accounting and economic information in the late prehistory period and culminated in the invention of coins in the first millennium B.C. The discussion traces incipient developments of counting, abstract recording, personal seals, and weights and measurements in a framework of four fundamental characteristics of money: (1) accounting unit; (2) mobility, or negotiability; (3) certification; and (4) value. In the artifacts record, the developments of these qualities are often imperceptibly and inseparably blended, crossing and recrossing each other like subtle threads in a complex web.

This development has created a complex phenomenon in which these characteristics are synthesized and finely tuned to create a form of communication that is more powerful than most forms used by society. This power is evident because "money information is more likely to cause a person to provide a product or service than ordinary communication" (Miller, 1978, p. 844). It is unlikely that an artifact with such complex intrinsic and relative characteristics as the coin was invented at a moment disconnected from a significant developmental process.

The evidence presented below is not concerned with the actual dating of developments but rather with their order and interrelationships. The time frame, however, provides the context of these developments and, consequently, is loosely identified. Counting may have begun with bone tallies at least as early as 10,000 B.C. (Schmandt-Besserat,1984, p. 52; Ifrah, 1987, p. 81). Abstract recording emerged about 8000 B.C. (Schmandt-Besserat, 1982, p. 872; 1986b, p. 33), and personal seals began to be used about 5500 B.C. in the Hassuma and Halaf cultures of Mesopotamia (Schmandt-Besserat, 1985). Cylinder seals date from the fourth millennium to the fifth century B.C. (Porada, 1962, p. 99), weights and measurements developed at least as early, and coins were produced after 700 B.C. (Kagan, 1982).

It may be reasonably hypothesized that the inception of money-related artifacts (money–information markers) occurred as follows:

1. Bone tallies and pebbles used for counting

2. Tokens used to count and account

3. Tokens used to count and account and as a medium of transaction

4. Tablets used to separate the accounting artifact from the transaction artifact

5. Precious metal artifacts used for long-distance exchanges

6. Coins

Money, the broader concept, would emerge during such an evolution; and the artifacts, money–information markers, would continue to evolve over time as documented in the numismatic literature (Kagan, 1982).

This hypothesis asserts the centrality of the accounting function of money and thus implies that the phenomenon that we call money should pose a major research question for accountants. The current accounting literature makes little reference to such research.

The Accounting Unit

A distinction should be made between a counting unit and an accounting unit. A counting unit is one belonging to a quantified conceptual numbering system that does not depend on any concrete system for its value. The value of a counting unit is defined with reference to this conceptual system itself. On the other hand, an accounting unit is a measurement unit of a convenient commodity used as a common denominator to establish specific relationships between the exchange values of other commodities. Consequently, an accounting unit is always defined with reference to a concrete system element. Grierson (1977, p. 16) views such a measurement unit as the fundamental characteristic of money.

The evolution of counting is postulated to occur in the following order: (1) one-to-one correspondence, (2) concrete (sometimes termed "quality" or "objective") counting, and (3) abstract counting (Danzig, 1959, p. 6; Kramer, 1970, pp. 4–5; Flegg, 1983, pp. 8–14; Schmandt-Basserat, 1984, p. 49; Smith, 1951, pp. 6–8). Obviously, the bijection, or matching, of one-to-one correspondence "suggests an abstract notion expressing a common property of the two collections, a notion *entirely independent of the nature of their elements*" (Ifrah, 1987, p. 14). Thus, the described development, notwithstanding the selected terms, is an evolution of abstract numbering that culminates in abstract counting.

The terms ordinal numbering and cardinal numbering also may be used to describe the developmental sequence of counting. Ifrah (1987, p. 24–25) argues that counting involves three actions: (1) assigning a rank to each object, (2) associating each object with all those considered before it, and (3) converting succession into simultaneity. Thus "the notion of whole number has two complementary aspects: cardinal, based only on correspondence, and ordinal, requiring both correspondence and succession."

Ordinal numbering (1st, 2nd, 3rd, etc.) is implicit, while not explicitly stated, in the idea of one-to-one correspondence. Moreover, ordinal numbering can occur without abstraction, for example, the time ordering of actors acting out creation myths of very ancient people (Boyer, 1968, p. 5; Seidenberg, 1962), and thus may be an earlier emergent than one-to-one correspondence. Both ordinal and cardinal (quantification) numbering can be absolutely abstract; that is, 1st, 2nd, and 3rd are no less abstract than 1, 2, and 3. Therefore, the evolutionary process from the most elementary form of numbering to the sort of quantification required by the modern interval and ratio scales of measurement may be usefully described on a matrix, as presented in Table 3–1.

This configuration highlights a connection between the evolution of counting and that of money–information markers. The incipient evolution of money–information markers might have contributed to the commonly postulated third

Table 3–1
An Evolution of Numbering

	Concrete System Elements	Artifactual Abstractions (Models)
Ordinal Numbering	Time ordering of creation rituals	Bone tallies, calendrical notations
		ONE-TO-ONE CORRESPONDENCE
Transition Numbering	Human counting systems-- (fingers, toes, multiple persons)	Administrative token system
	CONCRETE NUMBERING	ABSTRACT NUMBERING
	Trade of equal amounts of commodities	Abacus
	CONCRETE COUNTING	ABSTRACT COUNTING
Cardinal Numbering 1	Trade of differing amounts of commodities	Substitutions of differing amounts of administrative tokens representing different commodities
	CONCRETE COUNTING RATIOS	ABSTRACT COUNTING RATIOS
Cardinal Numbering 2	Trade on the basis of a common denominator	Administrative tokens representing common denominators
	ACCOUNTING UNITS	RUDIMENTARY MONEY- INFORMATION MARKERS 1
Cardinal Numbering 3	Accounting unit commodities used as medium of exchange e.g., weighed metals	Tokens representing absolute (undifferentiated) quantities of transaction value
	PRIMITIVE MONEY RUDIMENTARY MONEY- INFORMATION MARKERS 2	RUDIMENTARY MONEY- INFORMATION MARKERS 3
Cardinal Numbering 4	COINS Undifferentiated quantities of exchange value calibrated on various monetary scales	

evolutionary step of counting (abstract counting). Both "accounting units" and "rudimentary money–information markers 1, 2, and 3" (Table 3–1) are intermediary steps short of absolute abstract counting because quantity concepts are connected to specific concrete objects, either concrete system elements or abstracted but concrete models (representatives) of those elements. The same can be said of "primitive money" and "coins."

At this juncture, the evolution of money–information markers (with their multiple and intertwined characteristics) may be the dynamic that propels the evolution of the commonly postulated third step of counting (abstract counting). The tokens, representing real goods and services (concrete system elements) and coming to be valued accordingly (whether for coercion or incentive), provide a transitory vehicle for the abstract quantity "money" to be disconnected from the concrete system elements themselves used as accounting units, for example, grain in Sumer, and connected to representatives of those elements. This step constitutes a sort of concrete abstraction.

In a culture where trade of commodities and services occurred among private citizens, and incipient government (temples) coerced exchange of commodities and services with artifacts of a recording and control system, it is likely that the two systems eventually mixed. Such cross-pollination between methods of accounting for governmental/administrative systems and market systems have been important historical influences on the development of modern accounting for profit organizations (Most, 1972, p. 732). With the emergence of tablets and writing, this first abstract, though objective, counting would have continued to evolve into an absolute (undifferentiated) abstract counting.

The accounting unit is clearly recognized in an artifactual record of the preliterate cultures of the Middle East. This record consists of clay tokens first realized to function as a recording system by Pierre Amiet (1972) and studied extensively by Schmandt-Besserat (1974–1987). This system used clay tokens to account for administrative transactions from about 8000 B.C. to well after writing was used in all parts of the Middle East (Schmandt-Besserat, 1983). Schmandt-Besserat clearly asserts that the concept of an accounting unit existed in this system. "The choice of metrological units of grain for a more general use appears logical . . . because grain was the commodity most widely exchanged in the ancient Middle East. It played the role of currency and must have been, therefore, the most familiar accounting system"(1984, p. 57).

Burns (1965, p. 2) supports the notion of an early emergence of the accounting unit and the idea that the real good itself, for example, grain in Sumer, might not actually be exchanged in every transaction. Grierson (1977, pp. 17–18) says "money as a standard in fact lies behind money as a medium of exchange," and points out that the standard (e.g., grain) was not always used as the medium of exchange.

Schmandt-Besserat postulates that what we are terming "absolute abstract numbers" evolved from such accounting units or standards. "Until the Babylonian period, ca. 1800 B.C., the cuneiform signs of the elaborate sexagesimal

Sumerian system of numbers remained interchangeable with those for grain numeration. It seems likely, therefore, that in Sumer, abstract numbers derived from grain metrology . . . (which) provided a unique gamut of signs of increasing value which could conveniently be converted into the necessary series of numbers'' (Schmandt-Besserat, 1983, p. 120).

Notwithstanding the persistence of the connection between cuneiform signs for numbers and grain numeration in Sumer for about 1,300 years (3100 B.C. to 1800 B.C.), the abstract quantity "money" may have emerged in the token system about 3100 B.C., as Schmandt-Besserat points out: Abstract numbers appear related to the invention of writing. This assumption is supported by the reduction of shapes in the token system after 3100 B.C., which suggests that the tokens had then assumed numerical values'' (Schmandt-Besserat, 1983, p. 120).

The mobility of these tokens in economic actions suggests that the numerical values they were assuming were measurements of economic value—monetary value. Of the token system, Ifrah states, ''The system was the remote ancestor of our present monetary conventions and it was also a precursor of written accounting'' (1987, p. 90).

Mobility (Negotiability)

As cities began to emerge about 3500 B.C., the token recording system documented by Schmandt-Besserat underwent significant change. A great proliferation of markings occurred on the faces of the tokens and clay envelopes began to appear that contained tokens of shapes similar to the loose ones. The fact that the loose tokens and the envelope-sealed tokens continued in parallel use for some time is indicated by finding both in the same time periods and noting the differences of manufacturing techniques. The loose tokens were quite carefully formed and fired (apparently for endurance) while the envelope-sealed tokens were cursorily manufactured without firing. In later periods, after pictographic tablets emerged, the tokens became plain (no markings on the face).

The firing of the loose tokens to make them more durable, and the parallel use of both loose and envelope-sealed tokens might indicate that the loose tokens were used repeatedly, perhaps as an accounting unit in transactions. Such a use would necessitate a more durable token than one used simply as a record. The fired tokens, therefore, would be taking on the negotiability characteristic of money–information markers.

Initially, such information markers are abstractions of different kinds of commodities. At this stage it would be possible to exchange different kinds of tokens without claiming for use the actual commodities they represent. Such a transaction is new to the economy. As the accounting unit emerges as discussed above, the token's negotiability in the economy would be based more and more on its own perceived value in transaction, not on the commodity it represents. As tokens come to represent amounts disconnected from any specific commodity or service, monetary value emerges based on the negotiability of tokens themselves. What begins as an abstract record representing something of economic value becomes valuable in its own right by fiat.

Certification

From its emergence in the token system, the mobility characteristic is closely integrated with that of certification. The most basic accounting process is concrete system rearrangement. Possibly in ancient communities the certification process developed from the practice of what we term ritualistic recording. By this method, the ancient people performed ceremonies in designated public places to enter the record of certain individual rights (e.g., of private property and marriage) into the public domain. Any surviving member of the community who observed such ritual could testify to the contract (certify the contract) if later disputes occurred.

Because of the prominence of this recording method, the certification of particular artifacts by marking or other means would not be a major concern as long as economic transactions involved only community members and members of closely related communities. For negotiable tokens to have mobility beyond such relatively closed communities, however, methods of certification not dependent upon a back-up ritualistic recording system would be required. This need for innovative certification methods to extend the mobility of the rudimentary money–information markers might have been the dymanic that caused the decline of clay markers and the rise of metal markers.

Nippur, in the third millennium B.C., may provide an example of the confluence of important processes that involve the evolution of the accounting unit to a more mobile substance. Grierson (1977, p. 31) observes that "sums were both reckoned and paid in silver and barley . . . the silver being reckoned by weight, in mines and shekels, the barley . . . by volume." Here the connection is made between the earlier emergent grain accounting unit and the metal unit that provides increased mobility. This connection is an important step in the development of the certification process.

Schmandt-Besserat provides pictures of clay tokens that she believes represent metal (1986a, p. 40; 1983, p. 119). The existence of these tokens demonstrates that metal had economic significance in the clay system but was not significant as an accounting unit. Furthermore, Grierson (1977) states that the early coins were quite likely used for administrative purposes (e.g., payment of mercenaries), a function that would follow directly from the administrative uses of tokens asserted by Schmandt-Besserat (1982). An example of certification imposed upon an early economy and involving artifacts of several different materials in a particular system is recorded in the introduction to the laws of Ur-Nammu (2112–2095 B.C.): "The copper . . . , the (wooden) . . . (three lines missing), the copper . . . , the wooden . . . , (these) seven . . . , he standardized (143–144). He fashioned the bronze *sila*-measure, (145–149) he standardized the one *mina* weight, (and) standardized the stone-weight of a shekel of silver *in relation to one mina*'' (translated by J. J. Finkelstein in Pritchard, 1975, p. 32).

As the token system developed and its use replaced ritualistic recording, means of certifying the information in the record itself emerged. About 3250 B.C. clay envelopes holding tokens began to appear. The date coincides with the first monumental architecture and is generally believed to indicate the rise of state government. Seals were affixed to these envelopes. Schmandt-Besserat states: "The seals were engraved stones which, pressed upon clay, left a distinctive pattern representing an office or an individual's signature. Indeed, most of the envelopes recovered bear an imprint of one to four different seal impressions that probably represent the endorsement of several officers of the highly structured Sumerian bureaucracy, or of several parties" (1986a, p. 37). Such seals may be incipient procedures of societal certification of information in the record itself.

During the period 3350–3100 B.C., the use of seals proliferated. "Just about all Sumerians—even slaves—appear to have possessed personal seals" (Schmandt-Besserat, 1987, p. 47). Perhaps more important, the technology of certification was improved with the introduction of cylinder seals. Such seals made it possible to better detect any tampering with the record. At this early stage, already long-distance exchanges may have been influencing the method of certification. Schmandt-Besserat indicates that the artifactual record "of Eanna levels VI–IV constituted a foreign intrusion into Susiana, Syria and northern Mesopotamia . . . centers directly under the influence of the Sumerian temple" (1986b, p. 35). Reinfeld and Hobson (1963, p. 5) make the point that ancient Egypt, where coinage did not develop early, was a self-contained economy for the most part while Greece, where coinage appeared early, was made up of many independent city-states engaged in foreign trade.

As the accounting unit developed toward an abstract monetary unit and the accounting artifact used for record keeping was separated from the mobile artifact used to communicate economic information, the evolution of mobility and certification characteristics likely moved through a process similar to that exhibited in the artifacts now believed to be worker dockets (Weitemeyer, 1962). Generally, these receipts for work done were pyramidal clay objects bearing seal impressions mainly on the base that date in the Hammurabi and Samsuiluna reigns of the First Dynasty of Babylon. Most of the dockets are inscribed with various information. For example: "The inscription mentions on the first side: 1 lu hun-ga "one hired worker," on the second side the name of the man, and on the third side month and day" (Weitemeyer, 1962, p. 12).

The dockets formed part of a bookkeeping process that may have been constructed to expedite the long-distance communication of wage information. In this process, the seal (certification) played an important role, that of validating the information in the absence of the transmitting party.

Distance can be measured on the time dimension as well as in space. As with the transition from time-ordered numbering to space-ordered numbering, sealed dockets used to solve a space-distance problem may have been used to solve a time-distance problem. Such a solution may have occurred concerning harvest workers when the fulfillment of contracts made before harvest was documented by the use of dockets and "a certificate of fulfillment of a contract issued to a provider of hired harvesters" (Weitemeyer, 1962, p. 63). Again, in this system the seals serve the purpose of certifying the fidelity of the information content.

An important step in the development of the process of certification occurs when sealed but uninscribed dockets emerged. When the information carried on such information markers as the dockets became generic, the seal took on the added importance of constituting the message itself by virtue of its certifying that the docket was an authentic information marker carrying the generic information.

Weitemeyer describes this uninscribed docket system:

Uninscribed dockets furnished with all three characteristic features of the dockets made for hired workers (pyramidal shape, hole for string, and sealing) do exist. . . . The hired worker without specific qualifications was paid a fixed amount, and his name, specification of his status (hired worker), and even the date could be omitted on the docket if the seal impression of the overseer testified to the authenticity of the docket. This kind of uninscribed docket could have been issued by an illiterate overseer and the wages would then, it appears, have been handed to the bearer of the docket (Weitemeyer, 1962, p. 73).

This hypothesis may provide insights into another intricate connection that took place in the development of money. The cognitive powers of all individual persons are not the same. Almost certainly there always exists a need for simplifying the complex expressions of societal systems that are continually becoming more and more complex. A propensity for simplifying information and communication devices, as illustrated by the use of uninscribed dockets, may also be at work in the development of money. Thus, as the process of certification is improved, the exchange artifact becomes more mobile and, consequently, more widely used in a greater variety of exchanges. Coincidentally, the accounting unit is being used to determine value in these proliferating exchanges. As the volume of exchanges increases, the exchange artifacts become identified with the value of the accounting units; in some cases special purpose money emerges, and in others general purpose money develops.

Generally, advances in civilization occur by trial and error, formal or informal. If the fundamental characteristics of money, that is, accounting unit, mobility, certification, and indeed value, exhibit rudimentary development during the period that clay was used extensively as a record medium, it is reasonable to believe that somewhere somebody tried certifying generic tokens (those that Schmandt-Besserat suggests would have assumed numerical values) by means of seal impressions. Three such artifacts have been found—one flat disk with one seal impression on one face from Susa, Iran, IVth millennium B.C. (the Louvre, Paris, Museum Accession No. 85.1l), and two flat disks with one seal impression on one face from Sarafabad, Iran, IVth millennium B.C. (a private unpublished collection). In this connection it is interesting to realize that the earliest Greek coins had a design on only one side (Reinfeld and Hobson, 1963, p. 17).

As discussed above, Schmandt-Besserat shows that the tokens that developed into generic numeration devices were those that represented grain. She believes that these three flat disks represent a large measure of grain—larger than a bushel (personal correspondence, 1985). Consequently, these artifacts may be the earliest examples of a convergence of the characteristics of modern money on specific information markers.

Nevertheless, the mix was apparently unstable, because these information markers are not found extensively in the artifactual record. One reason may be a rapid advancement of the technology of certification for long-distance transactions, thus bringing about change during a relatively short period.

During this transition period, the technology for certification used metals for information markers as well as the long-used clay. In addition to the connection between the grain accounting unit and the metal accounting unit, Grierson describes the evolution of the use of metal for monetary purposes:

The original function of precise units of weight, as Professor Ridgeway long ago demonstrated, was for weighing precious metals, valuable substances imminently suitable for monetary purposes but not easily counted or measured. . . . The criterion of weight . . . gave a better guarantee of equality of proportion than measurements of length or area. But in due course the process of weighing ingot turned out to be cumbersome and time consuming; it could be shortened by making the metal up into pieces of uniform weight suitable for counting. When these were stamped with an official mark, coinage had come into existence (Grierson, 1977, p. 31).

To be useful, such weights were standardized and certified by some means, most probably the seal. Olmstead provides a phrase from an Assyrian document in the Nineveh archives that demonstrates this point: "Two pounds of silver, the principal, according to the pound of Carchemish, belonging to Addati, the 'governess' for the use of . . . the deputy of the chief of the city (Olmstead, 1960, p. 543). Powell (1981) traces the development of metals used for monetary purposes as follows:

From beginning to end, valuable metals used in commerce in ancient Mesopotamia seem to have been weighed, not counted . . . [T]he Mesopotamian weight system is also, at the same time, a monetary system. (pp. 217–218)

There is a never very clearly stated but subjectively ever present tendency among economic historians, if not among numismatists, to assume that, with the appearance of the first Aegean coins; everyone who traded with such coins stopped weighing and began counting. . . . [T]here is no way of knowing how long money continued to be weighed in the Aegean area after the introduction of coinage. (pp. 218–219)

Thus we might anticipate that whatever certification devices were used to validate weights continued to be used, as money–information markers made of metals emerged. Furthermore, the certification of weights connects the clay and metal mediums of money–information markers. Pritchard (1971, Illustrations 23 and 24) provides pictures of both clay and stone weights. As money calculated by weight emerged, certification was accomplished with existing technology—certified clay next in the form of weights instead of envelopes.

Because metals possessed economic exchange value in their own right by virtue of the scarcity attribute (which clay tokens did not possess), a certification of quality in addition to that of the quantity and weight became necessary. Powell (1981), discussing the meaning of the term *ginnu*, indicates that it can mean the stamp of the king denoting quality.

If this is the case, "then *ginnu* comes very close to denoting some type of coinage" (p. 224). During the time that the *ginnu* emerged (Sumerian—Old Babylonian periods), the "practice of trading metal in coils and upon occasion cutting off pieces of these coils provides evidence for the utilization of metal in a form analogous to the rod from which the flan or blank was cut." (p. 225). Such blanks may have been used to produce the first Aegean coins.

Thus certification of rudimentary money–information markers for long-distance exchanges may have evolved from the clay medium to the metal medium first by certifying weight only, later by certifying weights and quality in separate actions, and finally, in the coin, certifying both weight and quality together.

Value

The foregoing analysis clarifies the accounting information content of money. For accountants, this information should be a primary focus of research. What are the channels and nets over which monetary information about different processes is transmitted? Who are the receivers of this information? What is the communication of such information? How is the information transduced in society and what are the boundaries that allow or block its transduction? Can money–information be created by accepted accounting procedures outside of banks? What is the role of monetary information in the survival of a free society? Can a free enterprise system, and indeed a society, survive if a broad interpretation of the First Amendment of the U.S. Constitution is applied to money–information?

In modern times, the information content of money–information markers has been confused by the debate among economists over what value money represents. The idea of undifferentiated purchasing power appeals to a domain of investigation where theoretic purity can be maintained. As a result, economists often admit to information in the money flow only to the extent that units of money can be related to units of services and goods. That is, prices contain information; money–information markers, themselves, do not. To the extent that money–information markers constitute a scale of measurement, information about the object being measured is indeed obtained by comparing the scale to the object. Because this comparison is accomplished by exchanging the scale unit for the object unit, however, the exchange itself influences how many scale units might be exchanged for another such object. Therefore, in terms of un-differentiated purchasing power, the scale units vary; thus various combinations of prices must be compared in order to obtain useful economic information. By observing the relative movements of interrelated prices, the problem of the variant scale unit may be ameliorated and information about economic processes obtained.

Viewing money in the context of accounting process emergents suggests a different view (Swanson, 1987a; 1987b). Actually, it might not be so much a different view as a view from a different perspective. The economics view has proven quite useful for analytical science. The accounting view, we believe, may become every bit as useful for empirical science.

This view begins with acknowledging the empirical realities of the basic accounting measurement system commonly termed double-entry bookkeeping. Modern measurement theory accepts as a given the limitations inherent in a particular method of observation. Different methods use different sensors and clocks to assign numbers to observations. As a result, some methods allow fewer mathematical operations to be performed on the numbers than others.

The dual-entry system used by accountants observes the flows of various bundles of matter–energy as they pass through boundaries by exchanging various forms of money–information markers for these products and services. The money–information markers are stated in monetary units, such as yen, that are all alike. These monetary units taken together comprise a numeric system which is isomorphic (in this case, actually identified by definition) to arithmetic; that is, they constitute a ratio scale. Consequently, the manipulations that can be performed on monetary information are unlimited with respect to arithmetical operations.

However, the analytic view (that money measures undifferentiated purchasing power) highlights the phenomenon that different amounts of monetary units are given up for physically alike products and services in the marketplace. This phenomenon creates what seems to be a dilemma. While the system for assigning numbers creates a unique, comprehensive, objective, and quantified measurement of various matter–energy flows, it generates variant exchange values for phys-ically alike units of these flows. As a consequence, the system seems to lack a necessary quality of a measurement scale, that of the invariance of its units. This perceived dilemma is discussed in Chapter 5.

While such value is undifferentiated in terms of the various products and services exchanged, it is not fully abstract—these quantities constitute objective counting to the extent that they are money-information–marker constrained. Such values have no meaning divorced from the physical economic system in which they function. In the economic system, however, these markers are exchanged for goods and services. Consequently, their numerical value in exchange constitutes the specific exchange value of the goods and services of exchanges.

In sum, money–information markers bear measurements of the attribute specific exchange value in terms of monetary units. Such information may be used to map the complex physical flows of modern organizations and societies for policy and control studies.

Summary and Conclusion

Money is a special form of information that emerges in human societies. A hierarchy of fundamental accounting process emergents suggests that money–information markers may be expected to emerge generally during the period when abstract record keeping, classification, and aggregation emerge. We have discussed four fundamental characteristics of money–information markers (accounting unit, mobility, certification, and value) in relationship to incipient developments of counting, abstract recording, personal seals, and weights and measurements.

Prior to the first coins, the complex, interwoven characteristics of money were exhibited in differing degrees in various artifacts. We hypothesize that an accounting function is a critical dynamic in an evolution beginning with bone tallies and pebbles used for counting and culminating in coinage. Furthermore, the accounting function continues today to exert influence on the development of money–information marker forms. The developments of both accounting and money are inseparably connected. Consequently, the study of money–information markers should constitute an important part of accounting research. When such research becomes widespread, distinguishing between concrete system measurements and interpretations based on various decision and other types of models will be easier.

References

Amiet, P. *Glyptique Susienne, Memoires de la Delegation Archeologique en Iran.* Vol. 43, No. 1, Paris, 1972.

Boyer, Carl B. *A History of Mathematics.* New York: John Wiley, 1968.

Burns, A. R. *Money and Monetary Policy in Early Times.* New York: Sentry Press, 1927. Reprint. New York: Augustus M. Kelley, 1965.

Danzig, Tobias. *Number: The Language of Science.* 4th ed. New York: Macmillan, 1959.

Einzig, Paul. *Primitive Money.* 2nd ed. New York: Pergamon Press, 1966.

Flegg, Graham. *Numbers, Their History and Meaning.* New York: Schocken Books, 1983.

Grierson, Philip. *The Origins of Money.* London: The Athlone Press, 1977.

Ifrah, Georges. *From One to Zero: A Universal History of Numbers.* New York: Penguin Books, 1987.

Kagan. "The Dates of the Earliest Coins." *American Journal of Archaeology* Vol. 86, No. 3 (1982), pp. 343–60.

Kramer, Edna E. *The Nature and Growth of Modern Mathematics*. New York: Hawthorn Books, 1970.

Miller, J. G. *Living Systems*. McGraw-Hill, 1978.

Most, Kenneth. "Sombart's Proposition Revisited." *The Accounting Review* (October 1972), pp. 722–34.

Olmstead, A. T. *History of Assyria*. Chicago: The University of Chicago Press, 1923, 1960.

Porada, Edith. "The Seal Impressions." In Mogens Weitemeyer, *Some Aspects of the Hiring of Workers in the Sippar Region at the Time of Hammurabi*. Copenhagen: Munksgaard, 1962.

Powell, M. A. "*A Contribution to the History of Money in Mesopotamia Prior to the Invention of Coinage*." In Festschrift Lubor Matous. Herausgegeben von B. Hruska—G. Komoroczy, Bd. II = Az Eotvos Lorand Tudomanyegyetem Okori Torteneti tanszekeinek kiadvanyai 25 = Budapest: Assyriologia V., 1978 (appeared 1981).

Pritchard, James B., ed. *The Ancient Near East: An Anthology of Texts and Pictures*. Princeton, NJ: Princeton University Press, 1971.

_____. ed. *The Ancient Near East : A New Anthology of Texts and Pictures*. Vol. 2. Princeton, NJ: Princeton University Press, 1975.

Reinfeld, Fred, and Burton Hobson. *Picture Book of Ancient Coins*. New York: Sterling, 1963.

Schmandt-Besserat, Denise. "The Beginnings of the Use of Clay in Zagros." *Expedition* Vol. 16, No. 2 (1974), pp. 11–17.

_____. "The Earliest Uses of Clay in Anatolia." *Anatolian Studies* Vol. 27 (1977a), pp. 133–50.

_____. "The Earliest Uses of Clay in Syria." *Expedition* Vol. 19, No. 3 (1977b), pp. 28–42.

_____. "An Archaic Recording System in the Urak-Jemdet Nasr Period." *American Journal of Archaeology* Vol. 83, No. 1 (1979a), pp. 23–31.

_____. "Reckoning before Writing." *Archaeology* Vol. 32, No. 3 (1979b), pp. 23–31.

_____. "The Envelopes that Bear the First Writing." *Technology and Culture* Vol. 21, No. 3 (July, 1980), pp. 358–385.

_____. "The Emergence of Recording." *American Anthropologist* Vol. 84, No. 4 (December, 1982), pp. 871–878.

_____. "Tokens and Counting." *Biblical Archaeologist* (Spring, 1983), pp. 117–20.

_____. "Before Numerals." *Visible Language* Vol. 13, No. 1 (1984), pp. 48–60.

_____. Personal correspondence, 1985.

_____. "The Origins of Writing, An Archaeologist's Perspective." *Written Communication* Vol. 3, No. 1 (January, 1986a), pp. 31–45.

_____. "An Ancient Token System: The Precursor to Numerals and Writing." *Archaeology* Vol. 39, No. 6 (1986b) pp. 32–39.

_____. "Oneness, Twoness, Threeness, How Ancient Accountants Invented Numbers." *The Sciences* (July/August, 1987), pp. 44–48.

Seidenberg, A. "The Ritual Origin of Counting." *Archives for History of Exact Sciences* Vol. 2 (1962), pp. 1–40.

Smith, David E. *History of Mathematics, Vol. 1*. Boston: Ginn and Company, 1951.

Swanson, G. A. "A Living Systems General Theory of Accounting." Ph.D. dissertation, Georgia State University, 1982. University Microfilms order no. DEO 82–16502.

_____. "Accounting Information Can Be Used for Scientific Investigation." *Behavioral Science* Vol. 32 (1987a), pp. 81–91.

_____. "Using Burkhardt's Uniform Approach to Classical Physics and Miller's General Living Systems Theory to Analyze Accounting Information Systems." *Foundations and Applications of General Systems Theory* (Proceedings of the International Society for General Systems Research, Toronto, Ontario meeting, May 1987b) pp. VIII, 1–19.

Swanson, G. A., and Miller, J. G. "Accounting Information Systems in the Framework of Living Systems Theory and Research." *Systems Research* Vol. 3, No. 4 (1986), pp. 253–65.

_____. "Distinguishing between Measurements and Interpretations in Public Accounting Reports." *Behavioral Science* Vol. 33 (1988), pp. 1–30.

Weitemeyer, Mogens. *Some Aspects of the Hiring of Workers in the Sippar Region at the Time of Hammurabi*. Copenhagen: Munksgaard, 1962.

4
LIVING SYSTEMS THEORY AND ACCOUNTING

Important LST Definitions and Concepts

Living systems theory (Miller, 1965, 1978; Miller and Miller, 1981) is a conceptual framework that attempts to integrate scientific findings about the evolving hierarchical structure of levels of life, that is, (1) cells, (2) organs, (3) organisms, (4) groups, (5) organizations, (6) communities, (7) societies, and (8) supranational systems. The total set of all varieties of living systems comprise a subset of the set of all concrete systems (discussed in Chapter 2). Varieties of living systems differ in many obvious ways. Out of their common cosmological origin and their evolution, however, all living systems share many important and unique characteristics. It is reasonable, therefore, to attempt to construct a conceptual framework that recognizes and highlights the similarities in biological and social systems.

LST postulates that all living systems at each of the eight hierarchical levels named above have in common twenty functional subsystems (listed and briefly described in Table 4–1) that process inputs, throughputs, and outputs of various forms of matter, energy, and transmissions of information. These subsystems are critical in that the principles of physics require that their processes be carried out continuously if a system is to survive over time in the earth's environment. They ''are integrated together to form actively self-regulating, developing, unitary systems with purposes and goals''(Miller, 1978, p. 18).

This commonality is explained by the principle of fray-out. The term *fray-out* is used to describe a sort of evolutionary specialization by which higher-order living systems evolve from lower-level ones. It is important to recognize that LST is not merely a conceptual system of loose analogies. Rather, because these eight levels of life share a common developmental process, as expressed

Table 4-1
The Twenty Critical Subsystems of a Living System

SUBSYSTEMS THAT PROCESS BOTH MATTER-ENERGY AND INFORMATION

1. REPRODUCER, the subsystem that carries out the instructions in the genetic information or charter of a system and mobilizes matter and energy to produce one or more similar systems.

2. BOUNDARY, the subsystem at the perimiter of a system that holds together the components that make up the system, protects them from environmental stresses, and excludes or permits entry to various sorts of matter-energy and information.

SUBSYSTEMS THAT PROCESS MATTER-ENERGY

3. INGESTOR, the subsystem that brings matter-energy across the system boundary from the environment.

4. DISTRIBUTOR, the subsystem that carries inputs from outside the system or outputs from its subsystems around the system to each component.

5. CONVERTER, the subsystem that changes certain inputs to the system into forms more useful for the special processes of that particular system.

SUBSYSTEMS THAT PROCESS INFORMATION

11. INPUT TRANSDUCER, the sensory subsystem that brings markers bearing information into the system, changing them to other matter-energy forms suitable for transmission within it.

12. INTERNAL TRANSDUCER, the sensory subsystem that receives from subsystems or components within the system markers bearing information about significant alterations in those subsystems or components, changing them to other matter-energy forms of a sort that can be transmitted within it.

13. CHANNEL AND NET, the subsystem composed of a single route in physical space or multiple interconnected routes over which markers bearing information are transmitted to all parts of the system.

14. TIMER, the clock, set by information from the input transducer about states of the environment that uses information about processes in the system to measure the passage of time and transmits to the decider signals that facilitate coordination of the system's processes in time.

15. DECODER, the subsystem that alters the code of information input to it through the input transducer or internal transducer into a "private" code that can be used internally by the system.

56

6. PRODUCER, the subsystem that forms stable associations that endure for significant periods among matter-energy inputs to the system or outputs from its converter, the materials synthesized being for growth, damage repair, or replacement of components of the system, or for providing energy for moving or constituting the system's outputs of products or information markers to its suprasystem.

7. MATTER-ENERGY STORAGE, the subsystem that places matter or energy at some location in the system, retains it over time, and retrieves it.

8. EXTRUDER, the subsystem that transmits matter-energy out of the system in the form of products or wastes.

9. MOTOR, the subsystem that moves the system or parts of it in relation to part or all of its environment or moves components of its environment in relation to each other.

10. SUPPORTER, the subsystem that maintains the proper spatial relationships among components of the system, so that they can interact without weighting each other down or crowding each other.

16. ASSOCIATOR, the subsystem that carries out the first stage of the learning process, forming enduring associations among items of information in the system.

17. MEMORY, the subsystem that carries out the second stage of the learning process, storing information in the system for different periods of time, and then retrieving it.

18. DECIDER, the executive subsystem that receives information inputs from all other subsystems and transmits to them outputs for guidance, coordination, and control of the system.

19. ENCODER, the subsystem that alters the code of information input to it from other information processing sybsystems from a "private" code used internally by the system into a "public" code that can be interpreted by other systems in its environment.

20. OUTPUT TRANSDUCER, the subsystem that puts out markers bearing information from the system, changing markers within the system into other matter-energy forms that can be transmitted over channels in the system's environment.

Source: James G. Miller, Living Sytems, McGraw-Hill, 1978.

in the principle of fray-out, it is possible to make cross-level comparisons by constructing cross-level experiments and research designs that produce cross-level formal identities, for example, between organisms and groups or between organizations and societies.

In this manner, it is possible to integrate much of the scientific knowledge obtained by the social, biological, and physical sciences that relates to the concrete structures and processes at any of the levels. Anthropology, biochemistry, economics, genetics, medicine, pharmacology, physiology, political science, psychology, and sociology are almost entirely relevant, while many aspects of physical science and engineering are also relevant. Logic, mathematics, and statistics provide methods, models, and simulations, including the new approaches of cybernetics and information theory. Thus, LST may be used as a guide for integrating general scientific facts and methods into areas of applied science such as accounting information systems.

While LST is a general conceptual framework, the detail of its construction is such that it is a direct aid in constructing research studies, including those based on empirically testable hypotheses. For example, Table 4–1 identifies twenty critical functional subsystems. These subsystems are part of every type of system, from cell to supranational system. For instance, the *input transducer* is the sensory subsystem that brings markers bearing information into the system, changing them to other matter-energy forms suitable for transmission within the system. Components of living systems at each of the eight hierarchical levels of life carry out this function, for example, cell, specialized receptor site of cell membrane; organ, receptor cell of sense organ; organism, exteroceptive sense organ; group, lookout; organization, telephone operations group; society, foreign news service; supranational system, monetary exchange rates monitoring group of the World Bank.

While the structure of a system is the spatial location of matter-energy in such subsystems at a moment, the emphasis of the conceptual framework is on process. Each of these subsystems involves process. The subsystems are dynamic; they change over time. In fact, structure is continually changed by process over time. Only by taking both of these qualities into consideration can we map the state of a living system. Due to the detailed constructs and relationships of LST, it identifies a host of relationships that may be measured in a conventional scientific manner to help us understand the living systems that concern accounting information systems, for example, structural relationships—containment, number, order, position, direction, size, pattern, and density; process relationships—containment in time, number in time, position in time, direction in time, duration, and order in time; and spatiotemporal relationships—action, communication, direction of action, pattern of action, and entering or leaving containment.

Performance variables can be measured on each subsystem. For example, their equilibratory ranges, matter–energy specific exchange values (costs), variances, rates of transmissions, lags, efficiencies, error rates, omission rates, and so on, can be rigorously quantified. Using this information, we can build models to study input-output relationships, adjustment processes, feedback characteristics, degree of cohesiveness, and degree of integration under different environmental conditions.

Although all living systems must carry out all twenty critical subsystem processes to survive, they may do so through symbiotic or parasitic relationships with other living or nonliving systems. If a particular living system itself is capable of carrying out all critical subsystem processes, it is termed *totipotential*. Those that can carry out only some of the processes are *partipotential*. Partipotential systems disperse critical functions downwardly to systems at lower hierarchical levels, laterally to systems at the same level, or upwardly to systems at higher levels. The one subsystem that cannot be dispersed is the decider. This essential critical subsystem controls the entire system, causing the subsystems and components to interact. No living system would exist without such interaction under the control of a decider.

Living systems are relatively open systems, with boundaries that prevent potentially stressful or damaging inputs but are still permeable to other useful inputs, throughputs, and outputs of matter, energy, and transmissions of information. Many nonliving systems, on the other hand, are relatively closed. Because of the second law of thermo-dynamics, these systems progress from organization or negative entropy toward disorganization or increased entropy. By definition, systems constitute arrangements and order. Movement towards disorganization and disorder is, therefore, movement toward system dissipation.

While also subject to the second law, living systems because they are open systems are able to extend their organized survival for significant periods by obtaining inputs of matter and energy, including information, high in negative entropy and generating outputs of these elements higher in entropy. By importing matter, energy, and information of higher organization and breaking it down to repair the dissipation within the system (restore their own energy), living systems maintain a dynamic, fluctuous steady state of organization over time. As Miller explains, "In living systems many substances are produced as well as broken down; gradients are set up as well as destroyed; learning as well as forgetting occurs. To do this such systems must be open and have continual inputs of matter–energy and information. Walling off living systems to prevent exchanges across their boundaries results in what Brillouin calls 'death by confinement' " (Miller, 1978, p. 18).

In this context the term *steady state* is defined relative to three terms: (1) structure, (2) process, and (3) state. *Structure* is the arrangement of a living system's subsystems and components in three-dimensional physical space at a particular moment. Structure always changes over time. *Process* is all change over time of matter, energy, and information in a system. It includes both function and history. *Function* is reversible actions (which change structure) succeeding each other from moment to moment, while *history* is defined as less readily reversible actions that alter both structure and function. *State* is the arrangement and order of a living system's subsystems and components on a four-dimensional space-time continuum, that is, structure over time. State is dynamic; it always changes over time. State must therefore be observed over some period, and the critical information about state concerns change and relationships. Consequently, *steady state* is defined as a condition whereby changes in relationships among important system elements themselves and among these elements and those important elements in the system's environment are maintained within relatively narrow ranges over time.

It is important to recognize the coexistence of structure and process. The separation of functional (process) science from structural science inevitably limits the understanding of disciplinal scientists. Psychology and physiology are process sciences at the organism level, and sociology and political science are process sciences at the society level. Gross anatomy and neuroanatomy are structural sciences at the organism level, and physical geography is a structural science at the level of society.

A psychologist or neurophysiologist who cannot identify the anatomical structure that mediates an observed process is limited, and an anatomist can have only an incomplete view of a structure without comprehending its function. Consequently, whenever a process has been identified but the structure that carries it out is unknown, science should insistently attempt to identify its structure. Likewise, when a structure is believed to exist, science should identify the connections between such a structure and the processes it mediates.

Recognizing the coexistence of structure and process is often disregarded because such recognition is not considered urgent. This attitude apparently arises because in the academic world process or functional sciences are administered separately from, and communicate little with, their relevant structural sciences (e.g., gross anatomy at the level of the organism or physical geography at the society level).

The above statements apply to all levels of living systems. They apply not only to plants, animals, and human beings, but also to higher and more complex systems composed of human beings such as families, work groups, and other constituencies that make up corporations and other types of organizations, communities, societies, and supranational systems.

Living systems at the higher hierarchical levels, groups and above, may and often do contain nonliving inclusions termed *artifacts*. If such inclusions carry out essential processes, they are termed *prostheses*. Examples of such artifacts are beaver dams, buildings, books, machines, paintings, language, music, and the system of accounts of organizations.

Accounting Information Systems and LST

As discussed in previous chapters, accounting information systems have evolved over centuries as various levels of human organization have emerged. These information subsystems exist at all levels of human systems from the individual up. The major clients of modern accountants, however, are organizations. Consequently, the organization level with its suprasystems, communities and societies, is their main concern. Accounting for individual persons and groups has been largely ignored by the professional bodies. Organizational accounting for planning and control is termed internal or managerial accounting. External or financial accounting, largely for investment, taxation, and other accountability purposes, is generally believed to be community or societal accounting. International accounting, which is currently emerging at the supranational level, is an extension of societal accounting to multiple societies, involving multiple systems of accounting principles or standards and multiple numeraries.

The accounting function is clearly not matter–energy processing as described by LST. Also, nobody is seriously suggesting that accounting is management. Accounting and management, while related, are different functions. Consequently, accounting is not a component of any of the matter–energy processing subsystems identified by LST. Neither is it a component of the decider subsystem. Therefore, it may be a component of any of the information processing subsystems in Table 4–1 except the decider. An analysis of the functions of these subsystems clearly indicates that accounting is a component of the internal transducer. The *internal transducer* is the sensory subsystem that receives, from subsystems or components within the system, markers bearing information about significant alterations in those subsystems or components, changing them to other matter–energy forms of a sort that can be transmitted within it.

As a component of the internal transducer, the accounting information system services the other nineteen subsystems identified by LST. This concrete system always exists as a subsystem to its suprasystem; for example, societal accounting is a component of the internal transducer subsystem of a society, and corporate accounting is a component of the internal transducer subsystem of an organization.

The accounting information system services the twenty critical subsystem processes by monitoring the inputs, throughputs, and outputs of various forms of matter, energy, and transmissions of information. It accomplishes this by using an input-output model to map those flows as they move through various components of an organization. We discuss the characteristics of this model relative to measurement theory in Chapters 5 and 6. Here it is sufficient to recognize that the model quantifies information about those flows in terms of monetary units exchanged for the various forms of matter, energy, and information.

At the boundary of an organization, electronic sensors, meters, clocks, human observers, and so on, are used to monitor the movement of matter, energy, and information. The monitoring process assigns a specific quantity of monetary units to represent each particular set of these elements entering the organization. Once assigned, the quantity representing a particular set generally remains the same as long as that set remains in the organization. As it moves through the organization, a set is monitored as described below in the discussion of the twenty critical subsystems, and the quantity assigned to it is moved from one account to another, thus tracking its progress.

In the following sections we document the functions of accounting information systems in terms of living subsystem processes. The descriptions typically assume an organization-level perspective. Obviously, different types of organizations emphasize different functions such as distribution, manufacturing, or services. Consequently, the discussion is somewhat generic.

1. Reproducer

The reproducer subsystem gives rise to other systems similar to its own. For organizations, perhaps the purest form of reproducing occurs when an organization becomes a franchisor, creating several essentially identical subordinate, but largely independent, organizations. However, organizations reproduce in numerous ways. Different methods of reproduction involve various forms of control, from centralized to decentralized. A manufacturer may expand operations into another marketing territory by constructing another plant there like its main plant, complete with all essential parts. Two different organizations may consolidate, forming a new entity, or a single organization may organize semiautonomous subsidiaries. Whatever form reproducing takes, the accounting information system is involved.

The expanding manufacturer may select from several accounting monitoring procedures appropriate to the organizational and legal structures chosen. The firm may extend its own accounting system, treating the new plant as an integrated expansion of the old. In this procedure, the new plant accounts nest directly in the general ledger accounts; for example, the balance in the cash account of the new plant plus the balance in the cash account of the old plant equals the cash balance for the company as a whole. On the other hand, the firm may create a semiautonomous subsidiary, using branch accounting. This procedure enables management to view the operations of the new plant as a unified entity. Branch accounting nests all of the new plant accounts in one account termed *Home Plant*, which has a reciprocal account in the general ledger termed *Branch Plant*. Through these accounts the success or failure of the Branch Plant is viewed from an aggregate perspective. The former procedure allows highly centralized control, while the latter accommodates decentralized control.

Additional procedures are provided for managements that choose to relinquish various degrees of control in exchange for immediate additional resources. Three sets of procedures are provided to accommodate the entire spectrum of degrees of ownership: (1) cost method, (2) equity method, and (3) consolidation. Selection of the appropriate procedure is made on the judgment that the management of the parent company has, respectively, no significant influence, significant influence, or controlling interest in the management of the subordinate organization (AICPA, 1970b, 1971, 1972a; FASB, 1981). While this distinction is highly technical and detailed, the methods differ in that:

1. Cost method records the investment of the 'parent' in the subordinate organization at the time of the exchange of resources and does not again monitor the subordinate until the investment is given up, unless there is certain evidence that the market value of the subordinate's equity securities has diminished.
2. During the period of ownership, the equity method monitors the subordinate as a whole, recognizing increases and decreases in the assets in one account, termed *Investment in Subordinate,* and the corresponding gains and losses in the *Retained Earnings* account.
3. Consolidation nests the various accounts of the subordinate directly in the corresponding accounts of the parent organization.

When two existing organizations merge, accounting provides two generally accepted methods for viewing the combination: (1) pooling of interest, and (2) purchase (AICPA, 1959, 1970b, 1972b; FASB 1980a, 1980b). A given method is mandated by the characteristics of the merger. Pooling of interest treats the combination as if there is a continuation of management control; that is, two parts of a management whole are now integrated. The purchase method treats the combination as one organization buying the assets of the other.

Systems scientists may be interested to know that this last method includes, perhaps unwittingly, procedures to account for the system phenomenon described by the superadditive composition rule; that is, a system has at least one measure of the sum of its units that is larger than the sum of that measure of its units: $\phi (x+y) > \phi x + \phi y$, when ϕ is the square; $(x+y)^2 > x^2 + y^2$ by $2xy$. The value resulting from the interaction of a particular coalition of assets, liabilities, and equity is termed *goodwill* by accountants. Furthermore, the rule may be reformulated as a power function, in which case the results will vary with the nature of the power. If ϕ is $1/2$, the square root, then the sum of the parts is greater than the whole (the inequality is reversed). If ϕ is 1, an equality results. All of these different conditions (goodwill, equality, and negative goodwill) exist in firms and other organizations and can be mapped by the accounting information system.

In addition to those structures and processes involved in actual reproducing, accounting provides various decision models in the form of pro forma (projected) statements in the planning stages of the process. Thus, significant information about the processes of the reproducer subsystem is generated by accounting systems for transmission within organizations.

2. Boundary

The boundary holds together the components of the system, protecting them from environmental stresses and selectively excluding or permitting entry of various sorts of matter–energy and information.

Examples of boundary components are groups of guards, doorkeepers, walls, personnel or labor relations departments, purchasing departments, receiving and loading docks, library committees, loan committees, and credit departments. Some of these components are also components of other subsystems.

Accounting records the assets that belong to the organization, thus identifying its physical boundary. The accounting entity is a well-developed concept that sets boundaries primarily based on the control of management (AICPA, 1970a). For example, when inventory is ordered "FOB shipping point" from a supplier, the ownership, control, and liability associated with the inventory transfers to the buyer when the inventory leaves the supplier's shipping dock. Once the inventory is in the hands of the carrier, it is included in the assets of the buying company.

The accounting internal control system (AICPA, 1972b), which incorporates such procedures as "secured warehousing" techniques that produce information about authorized and unauthorized movement of assets and cash control techniques like bank statement reconciliations and the separation of the recording and handling functions, "protects" the organization's assets against unauthorized movement. Various audit techniques, including accounts receivable confirmations, computer hash totals, and input-output tests, are designed to preserve the fidelity of the accounting information flow itself. Thus, the accounting information flow contains significant information about the boundary of the organization. It changes this information to forms that can be transmitted for use by other subsystems, including the decider (management).

3. Ingestor

The ingestor brings matter–energy across the organization system boundary from the environment. Examples of ingestor components are buyers, public utilities, dock workers, commercial vendors, selection committees, receptionists, and recruiters.

The accounting system monitors and provides management control of this process, using such devices as purchase orders, invoices, shipping bills, and other transaction documents. For example, management decides to increase inventory. Purchase orders are drawn up, authorizing the purchases, and sent to the suppliers, constituting offers to buy. The suppliers send invoices, indicating their acceptance of the offers. Upon receipt, the invoices are held to be compared with shipping bills. When the goods arrive, the shipping bills are compared to the goods themselves, and any missing or damaged goods are noted. The corrected shipping bills are then compared to the invoices and corrections are made. The corrected invoices are entered into accounts, indicating increases in various items of inventory and liability. Various reports are generated from the accounts for use by various other components of the organization such as sales and warehousing departments.

4. Distributor

The distributor carries inputs from the environment and outputs of various subsystems around the system to each component. Examples of distributor components are supply officers, helicopter or airplane pilots, elevator operators, waiters, car or truck drivers, and railroads.

The accounting system monitors the movement of inventory, funds, and so forth through an organization, making extensive use of such source documents as petty cash vouchers, materials requisition forms, and job order cost sheets and such account classifications as petty cash, raw materials, work-in-process, finished goods, and cost of goods sold. From this system, reports on the timely movement of inventory items are generated to be transmitted to various levels of management. Major movements and the dissipation of noninventory items, including equipment and plant assets, are documented in subsidiary records such as depreciation and maintenance schedules and the equipment subsidiary ledger.

5. Converter

The converter changes certain inputs to the system into forms more useful for the special purposes of the system. Examples of converter components are electric generating plants, oil refineries, steel mills, packing plants, and various machines such as cotton gins and metal presses.

The accounting system monitors the converter processes as part of its cost accounting system. Depending on management requirements for the information, the process may be monitored continuously, or it may be reviewed from time to time. A review might be made in the context of the application of a management accounting decision model. For example, the electric motor on a hydraulic press converts electricity to movement of matter that is converted into pressure by a pump that applies the press to the product to be shaped. Information about the efficiency of this conversion process may be obtained from the accounting system. The cost of the electricity is monitored along with the other production costs. A standard cost system can estimate variances in prices of electricity and in the amounts of electricity used. How efficiently purchases are made in the energy market is reflected in the price variance, and the internal efficiency of use is gauged by the use variance. When executives must decide between two different processes, the information from the accounting system can be used in a decision model that compares the two processes on costs per product made to determine which one is more efficient or more economical.

6. Producer

The producer forms enduring associations of matter and energy for, among other things, product output. Examples of producer components include production workers in factories, cooks, repair and maintenance personnel, and automatic assembly lines.

Common accounting information systems include extensive procedures for monitoring and controlling the production process. These procedures are collectively called cost accounting (Horngren, 1982; Morse, 1981). They include special inventory control accounts, for example, raw materials, work-in-process, factory overhead, finished goods and cost of goods sold, and production reports such as departmental production reports, job cost sheets, and manufacturing statements. Here, as in the converter subsystem, standard cost systems provide variance analyses (analyses of deviations from established standards) for applying ''management by exception'' principles. The information gathered by the cost-accounting system about the changes occurring in production is combined and summarized in various ways for transmission to virtually all of the other components of the organization, for example, to marketing for product pricing, to top management for external reporting, and to purchasing for raw-product acquisition.

7. Matter–Energy Storage

Matter–energy storage retains in the system various sorts of matter and energy over time. Examples of matter–energy storage components are groups responsible for warehouses, garages, parking areas, reservoirs, and stockrooms, including buildings and equipment involved.

The accounting system monitors the storage function with inventory accounting procedures such as keeping perpetual inventory records (input-output records of all inventory items) and taking physical inventory (tallying the inventory items and comparing the tally with the records of these items). Other inventory accounting procedures deal with the monetary amounts at which the inventory should be reported outside the organization. Because the value of inventory to the organization is the monetary amount it can command when sold, these inventory valuation procedures generally require that some sorts of decay of this value be recognized even though the inventory has not yet been sold. Additionally, numerous assumptions may be made about the costs of like items sold over time. Because prices change over time, a pool of like items may have different item valuations. To determine the cost of the entire inventory, one may assume first-in/first-out flow, or the opposite, last-in/first-out, among other possible assumptions, as long as the same assumption is applied consistently from year to year. All of these valuation procedures are arithmetic manipulations of the basic accounting information that is originally encoded by metering or observing the physical flows of inventory. The manipulations generally can be reversed to arrive at the original information. Only this original information reflects directly the actual storage function.

8. Extruder

The extruder transports matter and energy out of the system in the form of saleable products and wastes. Examples of extruder components are personnel that operate garbage, trash, express, and delivery trucks; packing and shipping departments; discipline committees; and college officials who preside over the graduation of students.

The extruder process is monitored by the accounting system in much the same way as the ingester is monitored. Sales orders, invoices, shipping bills, and so on are used to document the movement of inventory across the boundary of the organization when products (matter) are sold. Documents like engagement letters, time sheets, and meter slips are used to trace the export of services (energy). The information on these source documents is processed into a set of accounts from which it is summarized in various reports that are transmitted to various components of the organization, including such decider components as planning and budgeting.

9. Motor

Among other things, the motor moves the system or parts of it in relation to its environment. Examples of motor components include crews, pilots, drivers, operators, and maintenance personnel for such machines as ships, aircraft, spacecraft, trucks, and buses.

Travel vouchers and transportation logs are used by the accounting system to track and provide some management control over employees' travel and the movement of products and equipment. Relocating a large component, such as an office or a factory, from one place to another might be done by a moving-van company, an example of the motor function being outwardly dispersed, in LST terms, to another organization. In such a case, the move would be shown by an invoice from the moving-van company, which would be entered into the accounting record.

10. Supporter

The supporter provides proper spatial relationships among components of the system to enable proper functioning. Accounting for both branches and subsidiaries (as discussed under ''Reproducer'') can provide some information on crowding. Various accounts in the general ledger, for example, office buildings, factory, or building rent, provide information about the support function. Certain departmental accounting procedures and transfer pricing concepts (Madison, 1979; Shaub, 1978) deal with methods of allocating joint costs. Some of these allocation techniques obscure the information about physical flows. However, such allocations can be reversed and reallocated on the basis of the physical flows. If this is done, these procedures can enhance the flow of information about the supporter function.

11. Input Transducer

The input transducer brings information markers (communications, money, and time-lagged money) into the system and transforms them into forms suitable for transmission within the system. Examples of input transducers are market research departments; specialists that acquire information on the state of the economy, politics, and the community; sales departments that take orders for the company's products or services; legal departments that arrange to obtain licenses to use patents; and cashiers. The accounting role in this subsystem is to record money–information marker flows, sales orders, and so forth that are to be entered into the accounts. For example, the person or machine that records the cash receipts on a cash register slip or daily sales report is an input transducer and part of the accounting system.

12. Internal Transducer

The internal transducer receives information markers from components within the system and transforms them into forms suitable for transmission to other components. Components of the internal transducer include all departments that have the responsibility for internal reports of various sorts concerning the matter–energy and information flows as well as needs, attitudes, and efficiencies. Examples include inspectors; spokespersons for components, such as committee chairpersons and department heads; bookkeepers; payroll departments; accountants; and operations analysts. Within this subsystem human beings or nonliving sensors such as meters, scales, and clocks are used for data collection to monitor the flows in organizations and other social systems of such elements as materials, energy, communications, money, and personnel, and to report them to management or other components. The accounting information system is a component of this internal transducer subsystem that monitors flows as they relate to various forms of money–information markers. Within this subsystem, the accounting system extracts summary reports from the financial accounts, the money values and units of materials and energy from job order forms and inventory records, wage costs from personnel records and time cards, and numerous other sorts of monetary data from other internal sources and transforms them into ''internal'' management reports.

13. Channel and Net

The channel and net consists of routes in physical space for the transmission of information markers (including money information markers) for communications. These channels and nets connect all the subsidiary organizations, groups, departments, and other components of an organization across echelons as well as at a given echelon. Physical channels include the air, which conveys sound, microwaves, and radiowaves; telephone wires; and roads and passages of various sorts over which markers like letters, books, and human beings pass. The accounting system uses communication routes formed by human beings and mechanical devices as well as electronic channels. For instance, couriers carry sensitive accounting documents, while large amounts of information pass over the electrical lines connecting remote computer terminals with a central processing unit. Extensive use is made of channels for bills, checks, electronic funds transfers, reports, and so on. Not only does the accounting system use the channel and net extensively, but in its function as transducer, it monitors the channel and net in terms of cost.

14. Timer

The timer is the clock of a living system. Set by information from the input transducer about states of the environment, it uses information about processes in the system to measure the passage of time and transmits to the decider signals that facilitate coordination of the system's processes in time. The accounting information system monitors this subsystem in terms of costs. Additionally, it provides, in forms useful for decision making, information about the timing of money–information marker and matter–energy flows between a living system and its environment.

15. Decoder

The decoder alters the code of information input to it through the input or internal transducers into a private code that can be used internally. Components of the decoder include translators of foreign languages, security, and other secret codes; telegraphers; experts in reporting upon mathematical, statistical, economic, technical, or scientific findings; and employees who decode orders for merchandise. In the accounting system, a major decoding function occurs when the monetary flows, sales orders, and so on, are translated into debit-credit notation for entry into the journals and ledgers (the system of accounts) (AICPA, 1970a). An account is a certain physical space divided into left and right sides in which amounts may be entered. To enter an amount on the left side is to debit the account; a right-side entry credits the account. By entering all debits as positive and all credits as negative in the computer, the resulting computerized system will retain the basic "double-entry format" that Fra Luca Pacioli first published during the Renaissance in Italy and that has continued to this day as the fundamental accounting equation (Canning, 1929; Littleton and Yamey, 1956). Whether a debit entry increases or decreases a particular account's balance depends on the category of the account (e.g., assets and expenses are increased by debiting, and liabilities, owner's equity, and revenues are increased by crediting). Using accounts to classify basic flows in whatever degree of detail management desires maintains in debit-credit notation the record of the basic organizational flows. In addition to using the decoder function, the accounting system includes the flows devoted to the decoder subsystem in the accounts, thus monitoring it in terms of monetary units.

16. Associator

The associator forms enduring associations among items of information in the system. The associator in organizations generally is dispersed downwardly to organism components in whose nervous systems the connections among items of information are made.

Individuals within an organization can experience associative learning without the organization itself forming a new association. An organization forms a new association to one item of information when its response to subsequent transmissions of that item or a similar one, from the environment or from within the organization, is altered.

This means that no association at the organization level occurs unless components of the organization's decider subsystem are influenced to change its future structure or processes in some way. It is conceivable that a management information system using sophisticated computerized data analysis and a learning program may do some associating at the organization level if the system directly controls certain processes or structures. While cybernetic control of processes based on negative feedback principles is in general use, a system to change a living process or structure "automatically" (bypassing a human decider) may not yet exist, though artificial intelligence systems are on the horizon.

Decider subsystems in complex organizations receive information about the environment and components of the organization through numerous information processing subsystems. These subsystems transform and reduce the information in various ways. Thus the information received by the decider is, in virtually all cases, blurred or filtered information; that is, some aspects of the information are obscured or lost.

Under these conditions a degree of organizational associative learning may occur in components of information processing subsystems. Such association may occur when the filtering process delivers information to deciders in a form that permits only one rational conclusion. In this case the decision is effected by the filtering process. Consequently, the association results from the filtering process itself and the action of the decider is completely predictable. Thus the changed responses result from the filtering process and not from organism-level associations.

The accounting information system organizes money–information marker inflows and outflows, thereby associating them in a manner peculiar to the particular organization of which it is a part. This process effectively places limits on the domain of decisions that could result from the total information flowing into the accounting system, and may, in the manner discussed above, dictate certain decisions or behaviors. For example, when the net income of a department or plant is used as a criterion to evaluate its manager for promotion, the manager will predictably seek to increase revenues and decrease expenses. By changing the classification of research and development costs from an asset to an expense, the system of classification predictably changes the response of the organization to research and development costs from efforts to increase them to efforts to decrease them, other things held constant. In addition to performing such organizational associations, the accounting system monitors the costs of the various input, throughput, and output flows of the associator subsystem.

17. Memory

The memory stores various sorts of information in the system for different periods of time. Among the components of the memory subsystem of organizations are individual human beings, filing departments, bookkeeping departments, computers, books, microfilm, libraries, and photographs. Over time, the accounting system maintains journals and ledgers of accounts containing information about matter–energy flows. The accounts are divided into two categories: temporary (or income statement accounts) and permanent (or balance sheet accounts). The temporary accounts generally maintain separate inflow and outflow records. The inflows and outflows are typically netted one against the other in the permanent accounts. As new flows are recorded in the temporary accounts, a process of adjustments connects the temporary and permanent accounts and updates the system with reference to time. It thus provides a history of the state of the organization on specific exchange values in terms of monetary units.

18. Decider

The decider subsystem receives information inputs from all other subsystems and transmits to them information outputs that control the entire system. Components of this executive subsystem include the chairman of the board, president, major, council member, vice president, department head, plant manager, and supervisor. A decider subsystem structured into echelons is characteristic of all types of organizations. As previously discussed, the accounting information system provides a variety of management reports to deciders at all levels to control the twenty various subsystem processes of organizations.

Today, the accounting profession generally considers decision usefulness to be the overriding criterion by which accounting choices of ideas, methods, and applications should be judged (FASB, 1978), even though accountants do not believe it is their role to make organizational decisions regarding policy, either strategic or tactical. The accounting system supplies information on which to base such decisions; management (the decider) makes the decisions.

19. Encoder

The encoder alters the private code of information used inside the system to a common public code that can be interpreted by other systems in the environment. Examples of encoder components are groups that write and edit speeches, publications, letters, contracts, reports, and estimates; translate from one language to another; or act as lawyers or lobbyists. In the accounting information system, the debit-credit notation of the accounts must be encoded into reports that are understandable by management. A further encoding procedure necessary for distributing financial statements outside the organization is the adjustment of account balances in accordance with Generally Accepted Accounting Principles (AICPA, 1953). An example of such an adjustment is that required to change the reported marketable equity securities held by an organization from the balance that reflects the price the organization paid to a current market value if it should be lower (determined by reference to the currently quoted stock market prices).

In the United States, Congress and the president have the authority to set accounting principles and procedures. This authority is generally delegated through the Securities and Exchange Commission to the accounting profession. The structure and process of this delegation evolves as society undergoes change (Skousen, 1980). Currently, the delegation is to the Financial Accounting Standards Board. This board is financed by and its members are selected by the Financial Accounting Foundation. The FASB "Statements of Financial Accounting Standards" have the force of law. This particular set of statements, however, does not cover all specific types of accounting transactions; and, therefore, various other pronouncements and sources are considered part of GAAP, for example, AICPA Statements of Position, AICPA Industry Accounting and Auditing Guides, and FASB Technical Bulletins.

20. Output Transducer

The output transducer changes information markers within the system into other matter–energy forms that can be transmitted over channels in the system's environment. Examples of output transducer components include public relations departments, labor negotiators, salespersons, missionaries, publications, telephone operators, billing departments, and public address systems. The accounting system is involved in condensing and preparing financial statements and reports in standard form for public distribution outside the organization in much the same way that it transduces information within the organization.

Summary

As described above, the accounting information system monitors the inputs, throughputs, and outputs of various forms of matter, energy, and transmissions of information within each of the twenty critical subsystem processes of organizations. Obviously, accounting information systems are vital, though often imperfect, components of organizations and other social systems. Their integrated monetary information flows enable managements to view certain aspects of these living systems as coherent wholes. They do this by tracking selected basic flows, namely, the concrete elements of living systems.

References

American Institute of Certified Public Accountants (AICPA), Accounting Procedures Committee. *Accounting Research Bulletin No. 43*. New York: AICPA, 1953.

――――. Accounting Principles Board (APB), *Accounting Research Bulletin No. 51*. New York: AICPA, 1959.

――――. APB. *Basic Concepts and Accounting Principles Underlying Financial Statements of Business Enterprises*. (Accounting Statement No. 4) New York: AICPA, 1970a.

――――. APB. *Business Combinations*. (Opinion No. 16). New York: AICPA, 1970b.

――――. APB. *The Equity Method of Accounting for Investments in Common Stock*. (Opinion No. 18) New York: AICPA, 1971.

――――. APB. *Disclosure of Accounting Policies*. (Opinion No. 22) New York: AICPA, 1972a.

――――. Auditing Standards Board, *Statement of Auditing Standards No. 1*. New York: AICPA, 1972b.

Canning, J.B. *The Economics of Accounting*. New York: Ronald Press, 1929.

Financial Accounting Standards Board (FASB). *Objectives of Financial Reporting by Business Enterprises* (SFAC 1). Stamford, CT: FASB, 1978.

――――. *Elements of Financial Statements of Business Enterprises* (SFAC 3). Stamford, CT: FASB, 1980a.

――――. *Accounting for Preacquisition Contingencies of Purchased Enterprises* (SFAS No. 38). Stamford, CT: FASB, 1980b.

――――. *Criteria for Applying the Equity Method of Accounting for Investments in Common Stock*. (Interpretations of FASB No. 35) Stamford, CT: FASB, 1981.

Horngren, C. J. *Cost Accounting*. Englewood Cliffs, NJ: Prentice-Hall, 1982.

Littleton, A. C., and B.S. Yamey, *Studies in the History of Accounting*. Homewood. IL: Richard Irwin, 1956.

Madison, R.L. "Responsibility Accounting and Transfer Pricing: Approach with Caution." *Management Accounting* (1979), 25–29.

Miller, J.G. "Living Systems: Structure and Process." *Behavior Science* 10 (1965), pp. 337–379.

――――. *Living Systems*. New York: McGraw-Hill, 1978.

Miller, J. G., and J. L. Miller, "Systems Science: An Emerging Inter-Disciplinary Field." *The Center Magazine* (1981), pp. 44–45.

Morse, W. J. *Cost Accounting*. Reading, MA: Addison-Wesley, 1981.

Shaub, J. J. "Transfer Pricing in a Decentralized Organization." *Management Accounting* 42 (1978), pp. 33–36.

Skousen, K. F. *An Introduction to the SEC*. 2nd ed. Cincinnati, OH: Southwestern, 1980.

5
A THEORY OF CONCRETE
PROCESS MEASUREMENT

Introduction

In Chapter 3, we describe evidence in the archeological and anthropological records that artifacts that we term money–information markers developed early in human civilization. To preserve information in concrete systems over time or to communicate it, we must use relatively small bundles of matter–energy termed *information markers*. Money–information markers carry a special form of information characterized by these four qualities:

1. It is quantified in terms of an accounting unit.
2. It is mobile (negotiable).
3. Its authenticity is certified.
4. It measures the specific exchange value of elements of concrete processes.

These four qualities converge on money–information markers to produce the holistic quality *medium of exchange*, which itself cannot be fully reduced to them. Money–information markers are society-level living system emergents.

In modern societies, money–information markers are legal tender that can be directly exchanged among the components of society, for example organizations and individual persons, for various sorts of matter–energy and information. In relatively free market societies, these exchanges are negotiated by the participants in each exchange. Societies with relatively centralized economic control often standardize the ratios of monetary units to goods and services (prices) by a political process and enforce such ratios in individual exchanges. In both cases, the flow of money–information markers as a medium of exchange directly reflects the flows of the different forms of matter–energy and information of societies, both within and among certain components, such as corporations, and among societies themselves, such as between Japan and England. This process uses the relational attribute specific exchange value (prices) as a means to express all sorts of concrete flows or processes of human systems in terms of a common denominator of monetary units like marks. Such monetary units make it possible to construct a very useful money–information system that describes at a cosmic level major aspects of the economy of any human system.

How money–information markers are used by accounting information systems to measure concrete processes is discussed in this chapter. Because modern accounting systems mingle measurements of concrete processes with estimates based on various different interpretations of those measurements, we must distinguish among procedures used for gathering those two different types of data. The components used to measure concrete processes form a system within a system, a cohesive core of related procedures, ideas, structures, and processes that constitutes the skeleton of accounting information systems. Our description of accounting procedures emphasizes this core and consequently neglects other aspects of common accounting information systems.

Measurement

Measurement theory makes it possible to build quantitative models and simulations of concrete processes that can be manipulated in ways that are impossible or impractical in the case of the concrete system itself. Such manipulations provide insights that may produce new and useful information about concrete systems.

Scientific disciplines do not always agree in detail as to what constitutes measurement. They generally agree, however, that measurement is a methodology for abstracting information from concrete or conceptual systems into another conceptual system being constructed to study those systems. This abstracting process assigns numbers to objects of measurement according to standardized (publicly agreed upon) rules in a manner that numbers representing objects can be manipulated according to the understood mathematical laws of a particular number system, usually termed a *scale*. Such scales are themselves quantitative conceptual systems. The main purpose of measurement theory is to provide a means of public observation to minimize the biases of different individual observers.

Measurement theory requires evidence that the structures of the methods of assigning numbers to systems under investigation be isomorphic to some understood numerical structure. Two systems are isomorphic if their structures are the same in the relationships and operations they permit. By establishing isomorphism between a system that allows useful manipulations of the numbers and the systems of assigning numbers to observations, scientists can analyze the empirical data by applying to it operations that are understood.

Classical measurement theory requires that systems for assigning numbers be isomorphic to the numerical system termed *arithmetic*. This connection requires that in respect to a property of interest, attributes measured exhibit at least four qualities, that is, that they be (1) reflexive: $x = x$ for all values of x; (2) symmetrical: if $x = y$, then $y = x$; (3) transitive: if $x = y$ and $y = 2$, then $x = 2$; and (4) additive: if $a + b = z$ and $a = c$ and $b = d$, then $c + d = z$. Researchers concerned with the physical and biological sciences have found that many concrete processes may be modeled using such a number system. Furthermore, mathematicians have formulated many laws that allow a myriad of useful manipulations of models based on this system. According to this view, the domain of measurement is enlarged as new methods of extracting empirical data that meet these criteria are devised.

On the other hand, modern measurement theory allows the system for assigning numbers to be isomorphic to numerical systems other than arithmetic. According to this theory, the limitations inherent in a particular kind of observation dictate certain rules that limit the mathematical operations that can be performed on the assigned numbers. Thus, the characteristics of the empirical data drive the rule-making process. Two general standards underlie this theory: (1) mathematical systems must be invariant (how can assigned numbers be changed without losing any of their empirical content?) and (2) the rules must be consistently applied. This theory distinguishes at least four widely accepted levels of measurement, each with its own set of rules and scale (Stevens, 1946, 1951).

While various aspects of measurement theory have been applied to accounting numbers (e.g., Ijiri, 1967), the idea that the observation system drives the rule-making process has not been applied directly to accounting measurement. Instead, efforts have generally concentrated on such approaches as showing that accounting numbers do or do not constitute measurements or that they are measurements on a particular type of scale. A direct application of this idea provides evidence that basic accounting data are, in fact, measurements of concrete system variables of interest to social actors.

Modern theory accepts as a given the limitations inherent in a particular method of observation. Different methods use various forms of sensors and clocks that, in turn, assign numbers to observations in different ways. Consequently, some methods allow fewer meaningful mathematical operations on the numbers than others.

Measurement versus Surrogation in Concrete Systems

Our taxonomy of systems—concrete, abstracted, and conceptual—introduced in Chapter 2 is useful in that it focuses attention on the fundamental differences among these systems. This focus prepares us to view the action of assigning numbers to objects as somewhat dependent upon the type of objects involved and to acknowledge that it may be useful to distinguish among methods of assignment. Is there a traceable connection between a concrete system element and an element of a conceptual system believed to represent it? Is a procedure used to abstract information conventional or private? If a procedure is repeated by an observer not privy to an obtained set of information, will the information abstracted be the same within reasonable error limits?

Measurement theory provides a basis for developing methods for abstracting information from concrete systems. In Chapter 2, we distinguish between measured abstracted systems and surrogated abstracted systems. This distinction is important. Nevertheless, it generally has not been taken into serious consideration by social scientists and accountants.

Observers select measured abstracted systems by comparing elements of a concrete system with some sort of scale or standard contained in the concrete system. That is to say, they assign numbers based on the relationships established by the scale because they observe similar relationships among elements of a concrete system of interest to them. To observe these similarities, the scale—being a conceptual system—must be borne on information markers that may be located in spatiotemporal proximity to the object being measured. It is the locating of information markers in proximity to other matter–energy forms that distinguishes the comparison to a scale aspect of measurement from other methods of assigning numbers.

Examples of information markers that bear scales are rulers, weights and balances, various forms of meters and clocks, including combinations such as speedometers, thermometers, and money–information markers as described in Chapter 3. Examples of measured abstracted systems are the physical dimensions of a box measured by comparing its length, breadth, and height to a metric scale, temperature measured by observing the expansion and contraction of a column of mercury along a standard calibration such as that designed by Celsius, and specific exchange value measured by counting the number of monetary units (such as yen) carried on money-information markers exchanged for goods and services.

On the other hand, observers select quantitative surrogated abstracted systems by comparing elements of a concrete system with a conceptual system composed of units that cannot be identified individually with specific information markers. The absence of a standard within a concrete system (i.e., in terms of identifiable information markers) makes it difficult to establish any assurance that a surrogated abstracted system corresponds in any important way to elements of a concrete system.

Examples of quantitative surrogated abstracted systems are the Stanford-Binet measure of intelligence, obtained by ranking individual persons on performance measurements and assuming a direct connection between intelligence and performance; the Rorschach test of personality, also obtained on the basis of performance; and current market value, obtained by assigning to concrete elements, which were not exchanged in a particular period, averages or other statistical values derived from the specific exchange values of other similar elements exchanged in the period.

In each of these examples, observers select conceptual systems that are composed of units that can be traced to specific information markers, ratio scale units borne on tests and inventories for the first two examples and monetary units borne on money-information markers for the last one. The tests and inventories purport to measure intelligence and personality, however, when in fact they measure performance on the particular instruments used. There is no traceable connection between the fundamental explanatory units of the concepts of intelligence or personality and performance in terms of concrete system elements. The connection must be established by the ingenuity of the authors of the instruments. This action is purely conceptual. Although many other persons may be persuaded that the connection is reasonable, there exists no unit of a scale carried on information markers that can be located in spatiotemporal proximity to a cluster of fundamental explanatory units of intelligence or personality so that an independent observer, without persuasion, would assign the same values as do other such observers within reasonable error limits.

In a similar fashion, current market value purports to measure output (exit) values of concrete elements that have not exited a system. The measurements are not taken on these elements themselves, however, because they have not actually exited. The monetary values calculated are based on measurements made on other such elements by exchanging certain quantities of monetary units borne on money–information markers for those other elements. In this situation, the attribute measured is specific exchange value, and the measured relationship holds only between the specific elements and markers involved in the exchanges. Consequently, the connection between the average monetary specific exchange value of those elements and similar ones that have not been exchanged is not traceable and must be established by the ingenuity of the theorist proposing it. Establishing this relationship is an action of surrogation, not measurement.

Our focus emphasizes comparing scales and objects. This emphasis is important because common accounting measurement theory emphasizes the aspect of assigning numbers to objects (Ijiri, 1967, 1969; Sterling, 1970, 1979; Chambers, 1969). This latter emphasis allows *all* assignments of numbers to concrete objects and processes to be treated as measurements, a treatment that reduces measurement to a sort of quantified surrogation. Such a view allows measurements taken on concrete elements to be mingled freely with numbers assigned to concrete elements based on interpretations of the measurements. For example, accounting statements, which are based mainly on specific exchange values, may include contingent liabilities—liabilities presumed to exist but for which no time-lagged money–information marker has been exchanged. Along with the common eclectic theoretic approach to accounting, the emphasis on the assignment of numbers aspect of measurement theory has allowed firms to publicly report obscured information about the measurements taken on their concrete processes.

The measurement focus on assigning numbers is not unique to accounting. The social sciences often assign numbers to the perceptions of individuals with little attention to whether the interrelationships among those perceptions are isomorphic to the measurement scale being used. In many cases, such actions are not significant in a practical sense and may be dealt with as measurement error. We believe, however, that this focus, when combined with the theoretical focus of the social sciences on abstracted systems such as roles, creates a serious problem for these sciences and thus for accounting information systems. On the other hand, it also creates opportunity for accounting information systems because once accounting measured data are separated from interpretive data, the measurement data may be used by these sciences to investigate social systems.

Miller distinguishes between concrete systems and abstracted systems (1986). He also defines conceptual systems. Because individual researchers have differing personal philosophies of science, the distinction he makes may be confusing. A personal bent on the question of whether science is purely epistemological or is in some degree ontological influences an individual's concept of concrete systems. Miller's definitions of these concepts assumes a purely epistomological stance. All of the systems he defines may or may not be ontologically real. He constructs LST, a conceptual system designed primarily to study concrete systems, from the viewpoint of an interesting subset of such systems, the living ones. According to LST, living systems construct conceptual systems (words, symbols, etc.) and may do so in nearly infinite variation. The particular conceptual system variation he chooses to emphasize is one that has been developing in empirical science (mainly the physical and biological sciences) and that concerns physical processes and structures existing in Euclidian space and time. This variation of conceptual systems he terms concrete systems.

It is important to realize that this definition of concrete systems itself is a conceptual system and as such purports to describe important relationships abstracted from human experience. These relationships have been abstracted over time by many different scientists using conventional measurement procedures and accepted disciplinal research designs. What Miller defines as abstracted systems, for example, roles such as the presidency, are also conceptual systems abstracted from human experience. These latter kinds of abstractions, however, are relationships set by the general perceptions of an observer or group of observers. That is to say, what Miller terms *abstracted systems* are *conceptual systems* that are constructed without establishing a traceable connection between their elements and those of *concrete systems*. There exists no unit of a scale borne on information markers in a concrete system that can be located in spatiotemporal proximity to a cluster of fundamental explanatory units of the presidency so that it may be measured. Because conceptual systems based on such abstractions are not constructed by formal research and measurement procedures involving measurable elements of concrete systems, no formalized traceable connections exist between the two types of conceptual systems that Miller describes as abstracted and concrete.

Scientific research may be conducted in terms of abstracted systems. There is no question, however, that such systems are observed to inhere in concrete systems and could not exist in the absence of concrete system processes. The social sciences as yet have not exploited significantly the conceptual systems based on the idea of concrete systems for investigating groups, communities, organizations, societies, and supranational systems. Therefore, we believe that investigations based on measurements of concrete processes should become a major emphasis of social science research.

The focus of social sciences on the assignment of numbers aspect of measurement (instead of the comparison to a scale aspect) in tandem with general theory based on the idea of abstracted systems (rather than the idea of concrete systems) has given rise to methods and procedures that never actually test empirically the propositions of such general theories. The growth of such disciplines of thought is more analogous to the growth of general philosophy than of science. Philosophy is certainly an important human exercise, as is art. We believe, however, that if the social sciences are to make advances in stride with the physical and biological sciences, they must devise means of empirically investigating social systems. Social scientists can no more presume to understand social systems than physical or biological scientists can presume to understand the systems that concern them.

When social scientists attempt to measure concrete processes by assessing the perceptions of individual persons about those processes, they nullify the main purpose of measurement—to minimize the bias of private observation. To presume that collecting many casual private observations and statistically manipulating the resultant data provides information about concrete social processes ignores the mechanistic aspect of measurement.

When objects and processes are compared to a scale, the data are biased by the scale and not by any particular observer, barring measurement error. The demand of measurement theory that isomorphism be established between the scale and the system for assigning numbers encourages observations about primitives of near-decomposable explanatory systems. The degree to which the primitives (the structural givens of an explanation) persist over time determines the degree of predictive power of an explanation. To establish isomorphism, elements that have relationships that persist must be identified.

This process provides a significantly different result from that offered by summarizing individually biased data. When the common ignorance is summarized, the information generated is a summary of common ignorance. For some purposes, for example, political campaigning, opinions are important. However, if the purpose of investigation is to discover how social systems work so that we may avoid nuclear disaster, such information does not contribute very much to our investigation. Assigning numbers in a way that simply quantifies casual perceptions of individual persons, even experts, is not measurement, if the comparison to a scale aspect of measurement is acknowledged. Perceptions are important for many reasons, but empirical science is ultimately concerned with the concrete processes without which perceptions could not exist.

The Monetary Scale

The accounting scale is a four-dimensional spatiotemporal scale. As such, it is not fully defined by the monetary scale. This characteristic is a unique scaling quality. Consequently, it is important to discuss the accounting scale in two parts. First, we demonstrate that the monetary scale that is incorporated in the accounting scale is fully analogous to other scales accepted by the scientific community. Afterward, the aspects unique to the accounting scale (which concern the time dimension) may be discussed without confusing the characteristics that are spatial with those that are temporal.

Accounting information systems observe flows of various forms of matter–energy and money–information markers as they pass through the boundaries of its suprasystem or the boundaries of a component of that system. They accomplish this observation by exchanging various forms of money–information markers (which are themselves bundles of matter–energy) for various other forms of matter–energy commonly called goods and services. For example, when a piece of equipment is brought under the control of the decider subsystem (management) of an organization (accounting entity), currency money–information markers (such as coins, paper money, electronic monetary transfers, and checks) or time-lagged money–information markers (such as promissory notes and accounts payable) are given in exchange. These markers are stated in monetary units, such as francs, that are all alike.

Such monetary units taken together comprise a numeric system that is iso-morphic (in this case, actually identified by the defined calibration of the scale) to arithmetic, that is, a ratio scale. Consequently, we would expect that the mathematical manipulations allowable by this system for assigning numbers to objects are unlimited with respect to arithmetic operations. However, some accountants, economists, and others (such as Abdel-Magid, 1979) have suggested that this is not the case because different numbers of monetary units are exchanged for alike products and services in the marketplace. This situation creates what seems to be a dilemma. On the one hand, the monetary scale is ratio; and on the other hand, the exchange values of its units vary in relation to alike units of objects being measured.

This dilemma is the result of a fallacy. In no other situation are the units of a scale said to be variant because they vary in relationship to units of the objects of measurement. For example, the pressure in one acetylene tank is 90 pounds per square inch, and in another tank of the same volume it is 120 pounds per square inch. In no case do we say that the measurement unit (pounds per square inch) is variant because in one measurement action a pound per square inch is 1/90 of a tank and in the other it is 1/120 of a tank. The quality of invariancy applies to one pound per square inch as compared to another pound per square inch. The scale is internally invariant with respect to its own units. Furthermore, typical scales may be expanded by simply adding alike measurement units. Such expansion does not make the scale variant.

The monetary scale does not consist of specific exchange values (purchasing power). It consists of monetary units. The fallacy that creates the dilemma is a confusion of the attribute being measured with the measurement unit. When the pressure of an acetylene tank is measured as described above, all of the attributes of the acetylene are not being measured, only its pressure in that container. The specific exchange value of the acetylene is an attribute, as is its pressure in the tank, and the quantity of both attributes may change. By confusing specific exchange value with monetary units, a dilemma that is empirically unresolvable is created. By recognizing that the monetary scale consists of monetary units, however, the dilemma is resolved, and a well-behaved conceptual system that is analogous to other recognized measurement scales emerges.

The monetary scale is invariant with respect to its units. It is a ratio scale; that is, zero has meaning, and each alike unit measures the same amount of statistical space. For example, cross-sectional exchanges of alike monetary units are always made one for one. No rational person exchanges a certain number of marks for a smaller or larger number because the latter was used in an exchange for a different amount of a certain commodity. Time series exchanges of alike monetary units cannot be made. Nobody yet has learned how to be in the past or future at a present moment. Consequently, monetary information, carried on money-information markers, measures various flows of matter-energy such as materials, personnel, energy, and communications. The measurements are made on a ratio monetary scale in terms of monetary units and measure the relational attribute specific exchange value.

The basic accounting system uses this invariant monetary scale to measure the specific exchange values (the attribute) of various forms of matter and energy. Consequently, the accounting scale is not variable but, rather, measures a variable, specific exchange value that may differ from transaction to transaction.

The monetary data gathered by the basic accounting system are, therefore, measurements of obviously different physical forms of matter and energy on a common attribute, specific exchange value, in terms of monetary units. These measurements make it possible for deciders to view the relationships and interactions of the internal and environmental elements of their systems on a common attribute. Because these data meet the criteria for measurement and as such are numbers assigned to observed concrete systems, they may be used as well for scientific investigations that are concerned with rearranging various bundles of matter and energy by human organisms, groups, organizations, communities, societies, and supranational systems.

This assertion does not imply that functions exist at a general level to transform anything like an erg of energy or a pound of matter to a given monetary unit. In a practical sense, such functions probably do not exist; and it is unlikely that they can be formulated due to the many interrelated influences on specific exchange values. Monetary values measure specific exchange values. Consequently, in the absence of a constant relationship between such inherent attributes and the relational attribute specific exchange value, a constant relationship between monetary values and measurements of inherent attributes cannot be established. The basic accounting system, however, may be used to measure other attributes of the bundles of matter–energy that are being exchanged, because the system observing those flows is already in place. Measuring those other attributes simply depends on providing appropriate sensors, clocks, and scales.

The desire for a convenient means of restating measurements of specific exchange values into measurements of intrinsic physical attributes should not be allowed to obscure the unique usefulness of specific exchange value. Science has been able to expand dramatically its investigations of concrete systems by devising sensors and clocks that are combined with machines that calculate derived measurements of process as it occurs over time, for example, speedometers and radar speed detectors. These devices take into consideration numerous interrelated influences to measure directly (for practical purposes) a complex attribute of interest. In a similar way, measuring specific exchange values captures many interrelated influences on the complex behavior of economic exchange.

Many community, society, and international decisions can be properly based on such complex behavior. For example, when entrepreneurs organize various forms of materials, personnel, energy, communications, and money into a firm, the primary variable of concern is the specific exchange value of these elements, not reducing the measurements of this value to measurements of intrinsic physical attributes. The values of the intrinsic physical attributes of interest to organizers are contained in the exchange values. If an organization can be put together in a manner that satisfies the financial demands of the specific exchange values involved, it will succeed; if not, it will fail.

In summary, the monetary scale is a component of a spatiotemporal accounting scale that measures spatial relationship. This scale is fully analogous to other such scales used for scientific investigations. However, it is a component of a more comprehensive accounting scale. The next section discusses this comprehensive accounting scale.

The Accounting Scale

In terms of measurement theory, the means of assigning numbers to concrete processes of organizations and other social systems used by accounting information systems measures those processes on a unique scale. It is important to realize that this scale cannot be fully described on three dimensions of physical space. Incorporating time, a fourth dimension, is an integral part of it.

This unique scale measures obviously different physical elements on the common attribute specific exchange value to produce a view of an organization as a coherent whole, the *cosmic view*. On this scale, values have no cosmic meaning divorced from the time dimension. As discussed in the previous section, the monetary scale is used by accounting information systems to measure concrete system elements on the attribute specific exchange value in physical space. Such measurements are simultaneously classified into particular time frames according to when the measurements are made, filling out a four-dimensional cosmic scale.

While classical measurement theory requires that a scale be isomorphic to the numerical system termed *arithmetic*, modern measurement theory allows scales that consider characteristics of empirical data that are not isomorphic to arithmetic. Under the guidance of modern measurement theory, numerous scales have been constructed. Four are widely recognized: (1) nominal, (2) ordinal, (3) interval, and (4) ratio.

The cosmic scale uses the monetary scale as well as numerous other ratio scales such as pounds and gallons. Additionally, it may from time to time use weaker scales. In the accounts themselves, it typically uses a nominal scale to record the physical attributes of various matter–energy forms. Such measurements may be provided to various deciders inside and outside an organization on specific items or on aggregates of such items. When the purpose of the measurement is to aggregate obviously different items on the common attribute specific exchange value to provide a cosmic measurement of an organization or other social system, the accounting measurement method incorporates the time dimension as an integral part of the measurement scale itself. Consequently, no accounting measurement has cosmic meaning in the absence of the time frame of the measurement; and thus the accounting measurement scale incorporates the monetary measurement scale but is not fully defined by it.

What do we mean by the phrase "incorporates the time dimension as an integral part of the measurement scale"? The determination of income (aggregate increases or decreases in a system) by accounting information systems has evolved from measuring a set of discrete variables to measuring continuous variables. Under a pool-of-wealth concept, the resources committed to a particular business venture were measured at its start and, after a discrete period of time, the resources that remained at its conclusion were measured. A derived measurement of income was calculated by comparing the latter with the former. As the corporate legal structure emerged and organizations began engaging in continuously overlapping business ventures, accountants began to devise ways to measure these continuous variables.

Obviously, measuring overlapping and interacting continuous variables became quite complicated and confusing. Consequently, accountants simplified the process by connecting measurements to different time locations instead of to different business ventures. Thus, modern accounting measurement became particularly *time-intensive*. The meanings of measurements change, not with their assignment to particular ventures, but rather with their assignment to periods.

This period consciousness operates in virtually every accounting classification decision. The information that a transaction belongs to an identifiable accounting entity existing in three dimensions of physical space is not enough. The time location must also be designated. Furthermore, how the time location is designated is important. The dominant perception by far is that a transaction belongs to a period, not an instant. Such time considerations demonstrate that accountants in fact, although probably unconsciously, view the accounting domain as a four-dimensional space-time continuum consisting of three dimensions of physical space and one of time.

The notion of the accounting period is sometimes termed the *periodicity concept*, which may be a subtle misnomer. Periodicity refers to recurrence; and, indeed, some accounting theorists have suggested that the accounting period is defined by dominant accounting cycles. There is little doubt, however, that the modern accounting period generally is arbitrarily defined as one year. The fundamentally important aspect of the meaning of the term *period* with reference to the accounting information system is "a portion of time," that is, extended time. The inflected forms of the word *period* do not include this meaning. We understand instantaneity, but we have no parallel inflection of the word period. Perhaps we could term the idea "periodaneity," and, thus, a measurement would be made either instantaneously or "periodaneously."

The empirical and mathematical operations used to calculate commonly derived accounting measurements assign numbers to periods, that is, changes over time. Derived measurements at an instant are calculated as residuals of previous process. Thus the assignment of numbers to process ("periodaneous" measurement) is the fundamental or primary measurement of this method.

Such a measurement methodology reflects the concern of accountants and other business actors for providing reliable accounting measurements on concrete processes that over time may be orderly, disorderly, or somewhere in between. In this environment, the probability that a single measurement taken on a continuous variable represents in any fashion the population of such measurements approaches zero. Accountants have found, however, that aggregating such variables into cosmic wholes over certain periods provides information to deciders.

Therefore, the accounting scale (which provides a cosmic measurement) is actually instantaneously (three-dimensionally) ratio *and* periodaneously (temporally) a unique measurement concept that incorporates characteristics of both the ordinal and interval scales. The ordinal scaling operation exhaustively subclasses assumed equivalent units of a scaled property into mutually exclusive subclasses that are ordered by a relationship such as "greater than." This relationship holds between subclasses. The relationship within subclasses is *assumed* equivalence. This assumption is made because the characteristics of the empirical data make it more reasonable than the alternative, that we can quantify more precisely the property being measured.

The interval scaling operation extends the requirement of equivalence from within the subclasses to the relationships among subclasses. In doing so, it replaces assumed equivalence with measured equivalence. That is to say, equivalence is now determined by reference to the calibration of the continuous number system underlying the scale. If the property being measured on different objects can be described by the same scalar quantity, the objects belong to the same subclass. Each subclass, whether it is empty or occupied, is the same distance from the next ordered subclass as from the previous one. Furthermore, the distances between subclasses can be divided infinitely to produce additional subclasses, thus ensuring a different subclass for every different object up to the degree of precision required.

The temporal aspect of the accounting measurement scale does not fit either of these descriptions fully. On this scale, all values assigned to a period are assumed to have equivalent temporal value. This equivalence is similar to the assumed within subclass equivalence of the ordinal scale. The accounting measurement scale also requires between-subclass equivalence. This equivalence, however, is not similar to that of the interval scale. The distance between periods (subclasses) is not infinitely divisible. Instead, it is zero. The end of one period is the beginning of the next. Thus, with reference to time, the accounting measurement scale is a sort of connected ordinal scale, ordered by the unidirectionality of the second law of thermodynamics, which assumes no time differential within a period and allows none between periods. It is a true continuum discretely divided by single instants into equal-length periods (subclasses).

The significance of this analysis for mathematical model building is at least twofold; that is, (1) all point measurements with reference to the temporal dimension are fictions because no point measurements are made on the accounting measurement scale itself, and (2) state equations that describe a system as moving from state to state, changed by process, treat the accounting measurement as secondary to the fiction. The opposite treatment should be given. On the accounting measurement scale, what is termed the *state* (actually ''structure'' in LST) is merely a convenient assumption constructed to fit certain decision models believed to be useful by bankers and other societal deciders and to account for residual flows in an input-output model. The *process* is what the accounting measurement scale measures, and it does this by aggregating inflows and outflows in designated periods. Thus the emphasis of the accounting measurement scale is process, and we are interested primarily in changes in process over time rather than changes in structure.

We believe that modern measurement theory provides the basis to rigorously identify this unique cosmic accounting scale and to develop methodologies and mathematical models that exploit its characteristics for rigorous empirical research. Such measurements can be used to infer characteristics of complex roles from empirical data, providing an alternative to selecting proxy variables (surrogates) for such roles.

To apply modern measurement theory to accounting information, the following three actions should be taken:

1. Identify how concrete processes are observed and recorded by the accounting information system.

2. Determine what measurement (relational) qualities such data exhibit; for example, they are or are not reflexive.

3. Formulate mathematical laws (rules) for manipulating such data.

In this and the next chapter, we attempt to take the first two actions to a useful degree of specificity, although certainly not to consummation. The last action is a process that begs the attention of researchers in the disciplines of analytical science.

Summary

In this chapter we have discussed the accounting measurement procedure with particular reference to measurement theory concentrating on the accounting scale. We continue the discussion in the next chapter and concentrate on the accounting model used to map the concrete processes of organizations.

References

Abdel-Magid, M.F. "Toward a Better Understanding of the Role of Measurement in Accounting." *The Accounting Review* Vol. 54, No. 2, (April 1979), pp. 346–357.

Chambers, R. J. *Accounting, Finance, and Management*. Chicago: Arthur Andersen, 1969.

Ijiri, Y. *The Foundations of Accounting Measurement: A Mathematical, Economic, and Behavioral Inquiry*. Englewood Cliffs, NJ: Prentice-Hall, 1967.

_____. "Theory of Accounting Measurement," *Studies in Accounting Research* #10. American Accounting Association, 1969.

Miller, James Grier. "Can Systems Theory Generate Testable Hypotheses?: From Talcott Parsons to Living Systems Theory." *Systems Research* Vol. 3, No. 2 (1986), pp. 73–84.

Sterling R. R. *Theory of Measurement of Enterprise Income*. Houston, TX: Scholars Book Company, 1970.

_____. *Toward a Science of Accounting*. Houston, TX: Scholars Book Company, 1979.

Stevens, S. S. "On the Theory of Scales of Measurement," *Science* 103 (1946), pp. 677–80.

_____. "Mathematics, Measurement, and Psychophysics." In S. S. Stevens, ed., *Handbook of Experimental Psychology*. New York: Wiley, 1951.

6
AN ACCOUNTING MODEL
OF CONCRETE PROCESSES

Introduction

For centuries, accountants and other social actors have been concerned with the concept of income, that is, a measurement of the net increases or decreases of an organized economic activity over time on a common attribute. As the societal prosthesis money developed (discussed in Chapter 3), it became possible for accountants to provide such a measurement on the attribute specific exchange value.

At first, the measurements were made on obviously physical products—trading artifacts. As time progressed, services of individuals were measured, and with the development of debt instruments, accounting documents such as promissory notes themselves were included in the set of accounting measurements.

As a result of these developments, modern accounting documents do more than model a concrete system composed of goods and services. They actually become an integral part of the exchange process itself while concurrently modeling the process. Thus physical products, physical services, and physical accounting documents (money–information markers) reflecting a particular type of abstraction, that is, the flow of money both current and time-lagged, became part of the systems on which income is measured.

The money–information markers that were integrated into the exchange system were not only currency markers composed of such media as coins, paper money, and gold bullion, but also markers that provided delays in exchanging currency markers, termed time-lagged money information markers, such as promissory notes. Some forms of this latter type of markers consist of the accounting records themselves, for example, Accounts Receivable of the organizations party to a contract to delay currency marker flows. In this marker medium, the abstract characteristics of money–information markers are emphasized, and it is easy to fail to remember that all money–information markers have concrete characteristics as well as abstract ones. Because accounting documents such as Accounts Payable are in a medium that may be used for absolute abstractions as well as concrete abstractions (as explained in Chapter 3), it is easy to introduce into the accounts other sorts of abstractions, such as quantities based on interpretations, that do not measure concrete flows in the manner described in Chapters 3 and 5. As a result, interpretive abstractions based on the eclectic theory of GAAP often are mingled with measurement abstractions in the accounts.

Despite the introduction of interpretive abstractions into accounting information, the basic measurement methodology remains intact. While the profession has not overtly propagated the concept in its recent pronouncements or textbooks, it implicitly recognizes the logic of that methodology by persisting generally to use double-entry bookkeeping and historical cost valuations in the basic accounting records.

We believe that the highly complex economic environment of our modern world would be served well by overtly recognizing that the double-entry bookkeeping method is part of a basic dual-entry accounting measurement methodology and building theory within this methodology rather than ignoring it.

Chapter 5 discusses the accounting measurement of concrete processes, emphasizing how money–information markers are used to accomplish this action. What constitutes the accounting scale and how measurement and surrogation differ are important components of that description of the measurement action. In this chapter, we emphasize the logic of the system of accounts for recording accounting data, clarifying its characteristics as a system that maps the circuitous relationship between matter–energy flows and money–information marker flows. This mapping action measures concrete processes. We build our discussion around identifying an unbiased global measurement of the double-entry bookkeeping method that we term net matter–energy flows (NME).

Measurement and Bias

Measurement theory is a major progenitor of modern methods of empirical scientific investigation. Despite its crucial contribution to their activities, many modern investigators define measurement so broadly that its basic function (to minimize individual researcher bias) may be circumvented and thus nullified.

Some modern accounting theorists have accepted such a broad definition of measurement that it is unnecessary to consider the traceable connection between concrete processes and accounting numbers. Neglecting to investigate this connection has contributed to the current state of affairs in the accounting profession where leading accountants admit that the meaning of the ''net income'' amount is so ambiguous that it can be described only as a score bounded by GAAP.

Understanding what measurements are produced by a particular measurement methodology is important. When structures and processes are compared to a scale, the numbers assigned to a conceptual system describing those objects are biased by the scale instead of by an observer within limits of measurement error. This bias is the result of premeditated efforts to remove individual biases from any quantitative conceptual system being constructed. It is a public bias agreed upon by convention. While we know it is there and analytic science attempts to reduce it with reference to the investigatory purposes of a discipline, we generally do not pay much attention to this global bias with reference to a particular investigation. Instead, what is termed measurement bias is concerned with the intrusion of logics of other conceptual systems (such as interpretations) on the logic of the measurement scale and other constraints of the measurement methodology being used.

Consequently, an unbiased measurement is a value that is logically consistent with the scale and other methodological constraints of a measurement methodology being used. This idea is unambiguous, and thus a derived value can be rigorously demonstrated to be an unbiased measurement with reference to a particular measurement methodology.

Unbiased Accounting Measurement

In an environment ruled by the veneration of eclectic theory, it is difficult to entice colleagues to consider an assertion that an unbiased accounting measurement exists. To do so is like claiming in a democracy that a particular political proposition is most "right." In fact, to accept the dictum that central political control is most "right" is to reject democracy; to accept the assertion that an unbiased accounting measurement exists is to reject the eclectic theoretic approach that overtly acknowledges a "one bias, one vote" principle.

Notwithstanding the dialectic opposition of the assertions of unbiased accounting measurement and the eclectic theoretic approach, specific theories of the eclectic approach need not be disregarded to accept the unbiased measurement assertion. To reject the eclectic approach is not the same as rejecting those specific theories. Rather, to reject the eclectic approach is to remove from each particular special theory the discipline-approved right to vie freely for claims that the numbers assigned to accounting reports based on it have the same degree of generalizability as those based on any other theory. For its numbers to be most generalizable, a special theory must concern the mapping methodology itself unbiased by interpretation. All other special theories concern interpretations within various decision models—sometimes sets of related models, sometimes a single model.

Acknowledging that unbiased accounting measurement exists in the sense that we are describing it is the first step in distinguishing between measurements and interpretations in accounting information. Recording and reporting, although related, are different functions driven by different theoretical considerations. Recording concerns measurement of concrete processes. Reporting is concerned with both measurement and interpretation; it is an internal transducer interface between the other critical subsystems and the decider subsystem. Measurements are the results of applying measurement theory. Interpretations are the results of applying decision models to measurements.

Does the Double-Entry Bookkeeping Measurement Method Converge on an Unbiased Global Measurement?

Does the double-entry bookkeeping method converge on an unbiased global measurement? We believe that it does. In this section we derive such a measurement after discussing generally how the observation method works.

A Synopsis of the Observation Method

Notwithstanding the introduction of interpretative numbers into accounting information, modern accountants generally have not yet begun to disregard the dual-entry measurement methodology handed down to them from centuries of development within the economic exchange environment. Out there, it is clear that in every exchange, an individual person or other living system receives an identifiable input of goods, services, or money–information markers and gives up similarly distinguishable items. No mystery exists in the marketplace as to the fundamental characteristic of double-entry bookkeeping or whether double-entry is the consummate form of this measurement method.

The essence of double-entry bookkeeping is the systematic recording of the only two component actions of a transaction (exchange), that is, the inflow and the outflow. This dual entry on each exchange is made on the basis of actual observation, always in terms of monetary units and sometimes in terms of additional other kinds of measurement units.

Double-entry is the consummate form of this measurement method because at the boundaries of living systems (e.g., organizations) only two interesting actions can occur that directly influence the system's survival—generally the system can either take in inputs or give out outputs of matter–energy and transmissions of information. Double-entry maps both the inputs and outputs of this dichotomous universe and, consequently, is the consummate form of this measurement method. Numbers may be assigned by this method on different scales for different attributes of interest, capturing many differentiated characteristics of economic flows, but such assignments will always represent only two actions— inflows and outflows. In this general view, the actions included in the inflow-outflow universe are the only interesting actions of the boundary subsystem because the negative universe of actions, that of exclusion, is not measured easily nor with any degree of certainty. An observer can never be certain that all items excluded by the boundary are accounted for by any identifiable set of observations. These boundary characteristics explain why organizations persist in using dual-entry methodology.

The reason they use the full double-entry bookkeeping method is further explained by its characteristics as a mechanistic methodical thought system that allows perceptions to be manipulated only as quantities (thus providing data for quantitative modeling) and as a model closed by a residual of net inputs (providing a global measurement of system-generated net increases and decreases).

Organizations may be described in the context of LST as living systems. Being relatively open systems, they extend their survival by processing inputs of various forms of matter–energy, including information transmissions, which are high in negative entropy for repair and growth, and by producing outputs higher in entropy. Such systems maintain dynamic steady states over time by negative feedback. That feedback includes accounting information.

The accounting information system, a component of the LST-defined internal transducer subsystem, measures the concrete processes of organizations by monitoring the inputs and outputs of various forms of matter–energy. It is important to realize that these matter–energy forms include relatively small bundles, called information markers, on which information is borne. Money is a special form of information flow or communication. It is an emergent of advanced human societies. In such societies, accounting is concerned particularly with money–information markers.

Negative feedback works through the combined feed relationships among variables in a system to return a perturbed system element to its original state. It promotes stability. For example, when a disturbance moves a ball from the center of a bowl, it is returned to its original position by the negative feedback of the combined influences of the concave form of the bowl and gravity. Positive feedback is destabilizing. For example, if a ball resting at the center of an inverted bowl is moved slightly, the combined positive feedback of the convex structure and gravity moves it ever more rapidly away from the center. The accounting information system can participate in both negative and positive feedbacks.

Although the Conceptual Framework of the Financial Accounting Standards Board does not recognize the concept of conservatism as a quality of accounting information, conservatism permeates both the statements of FASB and the opinions of its predecessor, the Accounting Principles Board. In accounting reports the application of this concept works as a negative feedback. For example, recongnizing contingent liabilities before they actually occur increases expenses in a period, thus reducing net income. Lower net income signals management to draw back from a set of actions rather than to proceed with them. Conservatism suggests that such contingent liabilities be recognized but does not allow the recognition of the opposite of such liabilities, contingent receivables.

Consequently, in addition to any negative feedback working on organizations in the relationships among societal elements themselves, accounting information systems likely bias their reports in favor of negative, rather than positive, feedback. Thus, accounting information systems may be important in maintaining dynamic steady states by organizations. Whether or not accounting information systems bias information toward negative feedback, the money–information marker flows that they monitor are part of a cross-level (e.g., between the organization level and the society level of living systems) feedback that is used by a particular management and by various other decider subsystems of an economy to regulate survival.

Three important aspects of this method of observation may be clarified, as follows:

1. Observations are always made at the boundary of the organization or a component. In business terms, an arms-length transaction between independent parties determines the specific exchange value of a transaction. Such arms-length transactions occur when organizations make exchanges at their boundaries with other organizations and persons. It is this exchange that is observed by the accounting information system. If measurements of internal flows are to be made, departments and other components are created with prescribed boundaries at which the measurements are made.

2. Dual measurements on every transaction (exchange) are always recorded. That is to say, both the inflow and outflow of an exchange are recorded. These flows consist of matter–energy or money–information markers. The quality of the flow is designated by an account title, and the quantity is stated in terms of the money–information marker flow.

3. Money–information markers are introduced directly into the exchange process itself, and this facilitates the dual measurement; that is, the markers are actually exchanged for matter–energy forms and other money–information markers.

As a general rule, this method uses money–information markers as the medium through which all matter–energy exchanges are transacted. As a result, a transaction consists of a transfer of matter–energy to or from a particular organization and a transmission of money–information markers in the opposite direction. The money–information markers consist of two general types: currency, current transfers of value, and time-lagged, delayed transfers of value. The system also permits the exchange of currency and time-lagged money–information markers in a transaction. This permission effectively makes currency the final medium of exchange.

The system assigns a particular monetary value to every bundle of matter–energy being transferred, thus measuring its specific exchange value. This specific exchange value is the attribute on which the accounting information system provides a view of the organization as a cohesive whole. Both the transfers of matter–energy and the transmissions of money–information markers are recorded, using various sorts of sensors and clocks, and processed into various report forms by the accounting system. This dual recording system provides certain checks and balances within an articulated system of accounts.

Exceptions to the general rule may be viewed as though they obeyed the rule. This is accomplished by judgmentally determining a best estimate of the specific exchange value and decomposing the exceptional transaction into multiple transactions as if the medium of money–information markers were used. For example, a direct trade of a truck for a drill press would be viewed as if the truck were sold and the money received used to buy the press.

This observation method assigns numbers to various forms of concrete processes, including both matter–energy flows and money–information marker flows. In the final analysis, however, the money–information markers are the expeditors of trade. Consequently, the fundamental measurement objects of this observation method are matter–energy flows. A global measurement unbiased by interpretive quantities must be an aggregate of measurements made on those objects themselves. We have chosen the global measurement net matter–energy flows to demonstrate the principle of accounting measurement unbiased by interpretive quantities. Although money–information markers are forms of matter–energy, from this point on it is useful to clearly distinguish between these forms and all other matter–energy forms. Therefore, we term all other forms of matter–energy simply *matter–energy*, forms that constitute markers bearing money–information simply *money–information markers,* and the two taken together simply *concrete elements* or *concrete processes.*

The Derivation of Net Matter-Energy Flows (NME)

The system of accounts for recording the dual measurements made on transactions is described at a general level by the following identity:

$$MIMO - MIMI \equiv MEI - MEO \qquad (6-1)$$

where:

MIMO is aggregate money–information marker outflows during a particular period

MIMI is aggregate money–information marker inflows during a particular period

MEI is aggregate matter–energy inflows during a particular period

MEO is aggregate matter–energy outflows during a particular period

For example, an organization gives up money–information markers valued at $50,000 for a piece of equipment. The dual measurements are recorded as follows:

$$MIMO - MIMI = MEI - MEO \qquad (6-2)$$
$$50,000 - 0 = 50,000 - 0$$

These terms representing general classifications of accounts are decomposed into many specific accounts by accountants according to management needs. At this point, it is convenient to discuss the general case.

A reminder of the four-dimensional characteristic of the accounting measurement scale may be useful at this point. The purpose of a global measurement such as NME certainly is to present a cosmic view of an organization—a cohesive view of obviously different forms of matter–energy elements. Consequently, periodanious measurements (discussed in Chapter 5) should be made.

This concept is applied by recognizing that the general classifications (*MIMO*, *MIMI*, *MEI*, and *MEO* of identity [6–1]) represent accumulations, that is, totals, over a particular accounting period. That is to say, for cosmic measurement purposes an account is not a vector of entries of individual transactions although a vector of entries is in fact aggregated to arrive at a particular total. The account is the total for a particular period. Decompositions of such totals likely lack cosmic meaning although they may, and certainly do, have other useful meanings.

Let X represent the total value of a classification such as *MIMO*. On one hand, let x represent a set of values x_1, x_2, $x_3 \ldots x_n$, each consisting of the total accumulation over an accounting period in each account comprising a classification. On the other hand, let t represen a set of all individual inflow-outflow values t_1, t_2, $t_3 \ldots t_n$ recorded over an accounting period in every account comprising a classification. Then

$$X = \sum_{i=1}^{n} x_i \qquad (6\text{–}3)$$

and also

$$X = \sum_{j=1}^{m} t_j \qquad (6\text{–}4)$$

Obviously, both sums equal the total value of a particular classification. However, the formulation $X = \Sigma t_j$ does not signal the disaggregation limitation of the accounting scale. In formula (6–3) X and x_i are cosmic measurements (they are aggregates [totals] over a specified accounting period). Only X is a cosmic measurement in formula (6–4), because the individual t_j are not aggregates over a specified accounting period. In this example, they equal a cosmic aggregate because they are aggregated over an accounting period. However, they could be aggregated over any arbitrarily chosen period as well.

While we may use the operational convenience of aggregating individual transactions to arrive at *MIMO*, and so forth, we must remember that only the aggregate of such transactions over an accounting period that has been proven to provide useful information has meaning for viewing the organization as a cohesive whole.

We use the symbol $\| \ \|$ to denote absolute amounts, that is, amounts on a ratio scale that are stripped of any positive or negative meaning. Thereby, we formalize a partial suspension of the rules for manipulating amounts on a particular scale.

To formalize the constraint of the fourth dimension on the accounting scale, we can use the rules that apply to the three-dimensional monetary scale (a ratio scale) with one suspension. We must suspend allowing the disaggregation of obvious aggregates within an accounting period. Therefore, let a symbol termed *period aggregate*, TT, denote such suspensions; then

$$X = \sum_{j=1}^{m} T t_j T \qquad (6-5)$$

Transactions are processes, and all processes occur over time. The accounting information system reports the specific exchange values of processes per accounting period. Therefore, in each of the foregoing equations and identity (6–1), time is taken into consideration using implicit denominators of the amount 1. This means that x_i and X are rates of change representing flows per accounting period. For a particular report, the accounting period may be designated as a month, quarter, year, or any other period proven to provide useful information on a particular question. For general statement purposes, however, the accounting period is arbitrarily designated as one year. These variations can be incorporated in the period aggregate symbol; for example, we can designate a quarter period as $^{.25}T,T$ and the annual period as $^{1.0}TT$.

Organizations process outflows of various forms of matter–energy and time-lagged money–information markers in an effort to entice inflows of similar elements of greater monetary value and thus make a profit. Sometimes the effort fails and they incur a loss. This exchange system creates a circuitous relationship between matter–energy and money–information marker flows.

System-generated increases or decreases occur first in the money–information marker flows. Consequently, at any particular instant, it is likely that all money–information markers have not completed the cycle of exchange back to matter–energy, and thus currency and time-lagged money–information markers exist in the system.

This circuitous exchange system is continuous over time. Furthermore, it does not distinguish overtly in every exchange what money–information markers represent system-generated increases or decreases. Consequently, a conceptual system is needed to calculate such increases or decreases.

Double-entry bookkeeping is a mechanistic methodical thought system that takes measurements on the continuous circuitous exchange system and restates these measurements in terms of discrete periods. It accomplishes this restatement by arbitrarily dividing the time continuum into discrete periods and accumulating the various inflows and outflows that occur within a particular period. By adding the difference between the aggregated inflows and aggregated outflows to the smaller of these two types of flows, double-entry bookkeeping closes the thought system mechanistically. This closure creates a set of relationships among the inflow-outflow elements that allows useful manipulations of the accounting data.

Consequently, equation (6–2) is actually an interlocking system of equations (a balancing equation) composed of two equations that both describe net matter–energy flows, *NME*: equation (6–6) below from the money–information marker view, and equation (6–7) below from the view of the matter–energy flows themselves.

$$MIMO - MIMI = NME \qquad\qquad (6\text{–}6)$$

$$MEI - MEO = NME \qquad\qquad (6\text{–}7)$$

Equations (6–6) and (6–7) clearly isolate net matter–energy flows without violating the relationships of identity (6–1). These measurement-established relationships constitute the logic of the double-entry bookkeeping method itself. Therefore, the variable NME is an unbiased variable with reference to that logic. It is derived fully from accounting measurements within a closed methodical mechanistic thought system without reference to the logic of interpretive thought systems. As such, *NME* is an unbiased global accounting measurement. Such a measurement may be used, among other applications, to evaluate variables such as net income that also are derived from accounting measurements; but the logics of the derivations are based on various interpretations of those measurements.

Again, equation (6–2) is actually an interlocking two-equation system that restates measurements taken on a continuous system into measurements based on discrete periods. Analyses made on discrete variables at first glance may be believed to be less useful for dynamic analysis than those made on continuous variables. Indeed, methodical mechanistic thought systems are sometimes viewed as devices that can produce only static analysis. These perceptions are not necessarily true. In fact, by requiring that two entries of equal amounts be the only pattern for introducing new data into the interlocking two-equation system, a recording system based on a balancing equation is constructed that allows us to map fully dynamic systems. While remaining coupled to other variables, any variable in the system may change its relationship to any other variable, but not without interacting with one or more other variables.

A dynamic balance is maintained in this interlocking two-equation system by making all entries according to the following double-entry rule:

In every case, record both the inflows and outflows of each transaction, entering all increases in any term of the equation (e.g., *MIMO*) as positive (+) and all decreases as negative (−).

Caveat: Increases and decreases are not respectively synonomous with inflows and outflows due to the inverse functional relationship of the left-side and right-side expressions of the balancing equation with respect to inflow-outflow. For example, the sale of a machine for $100,000 is entered in the following manner:

$$MIMO - MIMI = NME = MEI - MEO \tag{6-8}$$
$$0 - (+100,000) = -100,000 = 0 - (+100,000)$$

where both *MIMI* and *MEO* are increased to record the inflow of currency money–information markers and outflow of a form of matter–energy.

Although we are interested in the aggregates of measurements over a prescribed accounting period, the fundamental measurements are taken on transactions themselves. This action makes it possible to set the lengths of accounting periods differently for analyses involving different purposes. The aggregate of various transactions can be calculated for a period of any length.

Because both the inflows and outflows of a particular type of money–information marker or matter–energy are recorded in the same or related accounts, residuals of particular types of elements as well as the global residual *NME* can be calculated from the accounts. This characteristic provides data for detailed analyses of specific aspects of organizations. Furthermore, it provides a means for mapping the dynamic state of organizations, using the two aspects of state—structure and process.

LST defines structure as the arrangement of the concrete elements and components of a system at a particular moment. Consequently, structure is modeled as a set of residuals (the net of inflows and outflows under the control of a system at a moment). Process is all action over time. As an organization progresses over time, its set of residuals is discretely changed by each transaction of the entity. An aggregate of these transactions over an accounting period is a cosmic measurement.

The relationships involved may be described by the following equation:

$$R_t + I_T = R_{t+1} \tag{6-9}$$

where R_t is a vector of residuals that includes all accounting classifications of net inflows and outflows at moment t, I_T is a vector that includes all changes in these classifications over time T where $T = t + 1 - t$, and R_{t+1} is a vector of residuals that includes all accounting classifications of net inflows and outflows at moment $t + 1$. Consequently, as transactions occur, classifications (accounts) contained in the general categories *MIMO*, *MIMI*, *MEI*, and *MEO* are changed by this recording process.

Before demonstrating how this interlocking dual-measurement and time-sensitive system maps the processes of an accounting entity to provide the derived measurement NME, the general terms should be expanded to produce a more specific, and thus useful, system. The suprasystem of organizations may be viewed as a pentamerous market, where market is defined as any competitive exchange environment, consisting of (1) goods, (2) services, (3) owner documents (MIM, or money–information markers), (4) creditor documents (MIM), and (5) socialization documents (MIM). The terms *goods* and *services* refer to the extremities of a market continuum consisting of various mixtures of matter

Figure 6–1
Goods-Services Market Continuum

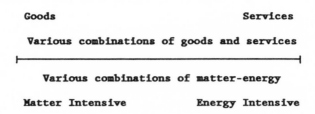

Figure 6–2
Time-Lagged Money–Information Marker Market Continuum

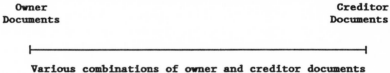

Private prior claims on control
(process) and negative income.
Private residual claims on
structure and income.

Private prior claims on
income and structure.
Private residual claims on
control (process) and
negative income.

and energy as illustrated in Figure 6–1. The common perception determines identification with either the goods or services markets by a particular combination. The terms *owner documents* and *creditor documents* refer to the extremities of a market continuum consisting of time-lagged money–information markers of various mixed characteristics as shown in Figure 6–2. Socialization documents provide no private claims and represent a contribution to or extraction from the organization-level control by the society level of living systems. Of course, all of these elements are exchanged through the medium of currency money–information markers. Goods and services may be further distinguished usefully as materials, personnel, energy, and communications. Additionally, organizations engage in market transactions to generate inflows greater than outflows; thus, a time-lagged money–information classification is needed to record system-generated increments and decrements. The following balancing equation incorporates these more specific classifications:

$$Cr + 0 + S + Sy + Mo = NME = Ma + P + E + Co,\qquad(6\text{–}10)$$

where the normal direction is outflow for the terms of the left-side expression and inflow for the right but all terms can assume both positive and negative values, *NME* is measured by the left-side expression in terms of money–information markers and by the right side in terms of matter–energy, and

Cr is creditor money–information markers

O is owner money–information markers

S is socialization money–information markers

Sy is net system- (organization-) generated increments and decrements

Mo is currency money–information markers

Ma is materials

P is personnel

E is energy

Co is communications

The term *currency money–information markers* (Mo) is a special case. Actually, $Ma + P + E + Co - Mo$ composes the concrete system of matter, energy, and information; and $Cr + O + D + S$ describes the system in terms of time-lagged markers.

Caveat: The term $-Mo$ denotes a negative net output, hence a net input. Consequently, the normal directive of all terms in the expression $Ma + P + E + Co - Mo$ is inflow.

As stated above, in the accounting measurement method, money flows in the direction opposite to the other flows, hence, the negative $(-)$ relationship of the Mo term. Perhaps an unbiased measurement of the concrete system is $Ma + P + E + Co - Mo$ because it incorporates all of the basic elements of this system, that is, matter, energy, and information. However, the function of currency money–information markers as the final medium of exchange endows them with the characteristic of potential matter–energy flows. Although the formulation of the concrete system as $Ma + P + E + Co - Mo$ is unbiased with reference to the constituted relationships (i.e., the balancing equation [6–2] is not violated), the placement of Mo with the matter–energy flows $(Ma + P + E + Co)$ introduces the assertion that *potential* matter–energy is a proper subset of matter–energy. Many intervening influences, for example, inflation, interest, and dividend payments, in the circular process of the exchange of matter–energy elements deny this assertion. Consequently, the formulation of equation (6–10) is used to avoid such an implication.

The exclusion of currency money–information markers from the measurement of matter–energy processes is consistent with Marx's notion of potential money capital; that is, "If the surplus-value derived from one circular course of capital is not sufficient, it must be accumulated until, after many such circular courses, it has attained the requisite dimensions. Meanwhile it is immobilized in the shape of treasure, and forms in this shape potential money capital, i.e., *money susceptible of serving as capital, but which does not yet serve as such*" (Eastman, 1932, p. 228; Italics by authors). Currency money–information markers are money susceptible of serving as matter–energy system processes, but which do not yet serve as such.

Table 6–1 illustrates how this dual-measurement recording system maps the processes of an organization to provide the derived measurement net matter–energy flows, *NME*. It illustrates the effects of the following incipient chronological transactions of an organization:

a. Owners invest $10,000 cash in the organization.

b. Equipment is purchased for $5,000 cash.

c. Inventory is purchased for $7,000 on open account.

d. Inventory costing $2,000 is sold for $4,000 cash.

e. Salaries of $1,000 are incurred and paid.

f. Inventory costing $1,500 is sold on open account for $3,000.

In every case, when the inflows and outflows are entered according to the double-entry rule as increases or decreases in classifications of money–information markers or matter–energy, the change in *NME* is generated. The aggregate of such changes over a specified accounting period is the NME for the period, a global cosmic measurement. If the transactions of Table 6–1 represent all of the transactions of a specified accounting period for the classifications indicated, $9,500 is a cosmic measurement. It provides a coherent measurement of these organization processes.

Many subclassifications of inflows and outflows are useful for economic decisions. Such subclassifications nest in the more general classifications of Table 6–1. Transactions (a), (b), (c), and (f) of Table 6–1 are illustrated in Table 6–2 using common accounting subclassifications.

The Utility of NME for Referencing Accounting Reports to Raw Accounting Measurements

Obviously, NME is not the only useful accounting-derived measurement. It is uniquely useful, however, for referencing accounting reports to an unbiased estimate of the raw accounting measurements of the economic inflows and outflows of organizations. This is so for the following reasons:

1. It does not arbitrarily change the interrelationships of the accounting variables constituted by the measurement method itself.

2. It avoids mismatching past, current, and future exchange values (prices). All exchange values are measurements of current period processes.

3. In an environment characterized by conglomerate corporations, multinational inclusions, an increasing not-for-profit segment, and a blurring of the boundaries between industries belonging to the monetary and real economies, it avoids the many arbitrary decisions involved in classifying various costs or revenues as "belonging" or "not belonging" to "operations."

4. It clearly dichotomizes accounting measurement information into statements of the money-information marker view and the matter-energy view of the same economy,

Table 6-1
Mapping Organization Concrete Processes in Terms of Monetary Units

*	MIM (+ = Outflow)										ME (+ = Inflow)								
	Cr	+	O	+	S	+	Sy	+	Mo	=	Ma	+	P	+	E	+	Co	=	NME
Beginning	0	+	0	+	0	+	0	+	0	=	0	+	0	+	0	+	0	=	0
Process (a)	0	+	(+10,000)	+	0	+	0	+	(-10,000)	=	0	+	0	+	0	+	0	=	0
Aggregate	0	+	10,000	+	0	-	0	+	10,000	=	0	+	0	+	0	+	0	=	0
Process (b)	0	+	0	+	0	+	0	-	(+5,000)	=	(+5,000)	+	0	+	0	+	0	=	+5,000 △
Aggregate	0	+	10,000	+	0	+	0	-	5,000	=	+5,000	+	0	+	0	+	0	=	+5,000 △
Process (c)	(+7,000)	+	0	+	0	+	0	+	0	=	(+7,000)	+	0	+	0	+	0	=	+7,000 △
Aggregate	+7,000	+	10,000	+	0	+	0	+	5,000	=	+12,000	+	0	+	0	+	0	=	+12,000
Process (d)	0	+	0	+	0	+	(+2,000)	+	(-4,000)	=	(-2,000)	+	0	+	0	+	0	=	-2,000 △
Aggregate	+7,000	+	10,000	+	0	+	2,000	+	9,000	=	+10,000	+	0	+	0	+	0	=	+10,000
Process (e)	0	+	0	+	0	+	2,000	-	(+1,000)	=	0	+	(+1,000)	+	0	+	0	=	+1,000 △
Aggregate	+7,000	+	10,000	+	0	+	2,000	+	8,000	=	+10,000	+	1,000	+	0	+	0	=	+11,000
Process (f)	(-3,000)	+	0	+	0	+	(+1,500)	+	0	=	(-1,500)	+	0	+	0	+	0	=	-1,500 △
Aggregate	+4,000	+	10,000	+	0	+	3,500	+	8,000	=	+8,500	+	1,000	+	0	+	0	=	+9,500

*Explanation of terms: MIM - money-information markers, ME - matter-energy, Cr - credit documents, O - owner documents, S - socialization documents, Sy - system generated increments and decrements, Mo - currency money-information markers, Ma - materials, P - personnel, E - energy, Co - communications, and NME - net matter-energy flows.

Table 6-2
Mapping Organization Concrete Processes with Commonly Used Accounting Classifications

*	MIM (+=Outflow)					=	ME (+=Inflow)		=	NME
	A/P +	CS +	R/E +	A/R +	Cash	=	Inv +	P/E	=	
Balance	0	0	0	0	0	=	0	0	=	0
Trans. (a)	+0	(+10,000)	0	0	(-10,000)	=	+0	0	=	0
Balance	0	10,000	0	0	10,000	=	0	0	=	0
Trans. (b)	+0	0	0	0	(+5,000)	=	+0	(+5,000)	=	+5,000 Δ
Balance	0	10,000	0	0	5,000	=	0	5,000	=	+5,000
Trans. (c)	+(+7,000)	0	0	0	0	=	+(+7,000)	0	=	+7,000 Δ
Balance	+7,000	10,000	0	0	5,000	=	+7,000	5,000	=	+12,000
Trans. (f)	+0	0	+(+1,500)	(-3,000) +	0	=	+(-1,500)	0	=	-1,500 Δ
Balance	+7,000	10,000	1,500	3,000	5,000	=	+5,500	5,000	=	+10,500

*Explanation of terms: MIM - money-information markers, ME - matter-energy, A/P - accounts payable, CS - common stock, R/E - retained earnings, A/R - accounts receivable, Inv - inventory, P/E - plant and equipment, NME - net matter-energy flows.

thus ameliorating the problem of ambiguous accounting reports that results from confusing the two.

5. With reference to the relationships constituted by the measurement method, it provides a pragmatic and unbiased referent that may be used to determine the effects of various interpretive assumptions underlying the many accounting classifications and adjustments used to construct public accounting reports.

6. It avoids the arbitrary construction of such residuals as "human capital" by concentrating attention on variations of processes rather than variations in stocks (residuals).

7. And possibly most important, it focuses attention on the purpose of all organization-level living systems, including business firms, governmental entities and not-for-profit organizations—to increase the economic security and welfare of a multi-echelon decider subsystem that designs and attempts to control the various components of the system to accomplish this ultimate purpose. Generally, the greater the decider-controlled concrete processes, the better is the security and welfare provided for the decider subsystem members. This means that the greater the aggregate processes composed of such things as people, machines, buildings, communications systems, and energy controlled by management, the greater will be the survival potential of an organization.

The current focus on sales volume does not take into account the potential growth forgone to outsiders (creditors, owners, and government) for permission to exist in the economic environment. GAAP—defined Net Assets focuses on residuals rather than process and such residuals are biased away from a measurement of concrete processes. GAAP-defined Net Income is so ambiguous that it cannot be used as a global cosmic measurement of increased or decreased control of processes. By refocusing attention on matter–energy inflows (generally the expenses and merchandise purchases on an income statement and "Land, Building, and Equipment" on a balance sheet) instead of sales, we can take into account the potential growth forgone to outsiders on the one hand and supplied by outsiders on the other hand.

8. It recognizes that the terms *debit* and *credit* have meaning other than to describe their arbitrarily decided positions in journal and account entries as left and right, respectively. Debits always mean inflows of such concrete processes and credits always mean outflows. Of course, these statements apply to concrete process analysis. GAAP adjustments may confuse this obvious structure of the measurement methodology with conceptual locations such as residuals, which are viewed as belonging to the system but are not process. Such residual accounts increase and decrease on a different pattern from the inflow-outflow pattern.

Many managers and some accountants have disputed the usefulness of debit-credit notation now that the logic of relationships can be maintained by computer programming. In light of the common attitude among accountants that the main use of debit-credit notation is to easily maintain the logic of the system of accounts, this assertion seems reasonable. The main purpose of debit-credit notation, however, is to assure the observer that no element of a transaction is being omitted in the observational recording process. Such a use by managers when they are contemplating transactions may actually enhance management skills because it imposes a holistic consideration on each specific transaction.

Apparently, each of the many different accounting adjustments prescribed by generally accepted accounting principles has informational purpose for at least some of the economic actors. The assertion that the NME should be disclosed publicly does not deny the usefulness of any of the commonly used accounting derivations. Neither does it suggest that NME should be substituted for any other derivation. What it implies strongly is that the economic actors need a point of reference to sort out which adjustments to the raw accounting measurements serve their individual information needs and which do not. To illustrate that NME is referentially useful for this purpose, the next section examines some effects of the matching principle on the calculation of net income using the variable NME as a point of departure.

The Matching Principle with Reference to the Variable NME

As demonstrated above, the interlocking two-equation system maps the money–information marker and matter–energy element inflows and outflows of an organization. To arrive at the widely used accounting derivation net income, accountants adjust NME by various inclusions and eliminations based on different interpretive assumptions about what best describes the results of operations (processes) of organizations. Because the matching principle is a fundamental assumption of modern accrual accounting, it is used here to demonstrate the effect of an assumption on net income using NME as a referent.

The principle involves two aspects: (1) revenues matched to time (termed the revenue realization principle), and (2) expenses matched to their related revenues. The revenue realization principle states that all revenues (system-generated increases) realized (generated) in an accounting period should be recognized in (reported as belonging to) the period. The second aspect of the matching principle requires that all expenses contributing to the realization of particular revenues be matched with (offset against) those revenues in the period of revenue recognition. Of the two, the revenue realization principle is the first aspect applied and has particular implications for accounting measurements of concrete processes. Consequently, it is discussed in depth and the second aspect is neglected.

The realization concept is stated with reference to matter–energy element outflows, not to money–information marker inflows. It specifically states that revenues are realized (and thus should be recognized) in the period that the goods and services are transferred outwardly, not necessarily when the cash is transmitted inwardly. When goods or services are provided prior to the receipt of cash, time-lagged money–information markers, such as Accounts Receivable, are constructed to record the exchange value increase from revenue recognition in the period of matter–energy element outflows.

Despite the anchoring of the realization concept to matter–energy element flows, the exchange cycle is viewed as money–information markers → matter–energy elements → money–information markers instead of matter–energy elements → money–information markers → matter–energy elements. This is confusing because money–information markers, not matter–energy elements, are the medium of exchange. Because money is legal tender and its value is set at a higher level, not by the exchanging parties, it facilitates the trade of goods and services, not the reverse.

This reflexive view follows naturally from an organization's originant template. Typically, money–information markers are committed to management control to be exchanged for matter–energy assets that can be manipulated to produce increased money–information markers and the increase is distributed to the economic actors (other organizations and individuals, but ultimately, individuals) in the form of money–information markers. In fact, from the position of the individual (organism level), money–information markers are exchanged through the medium of matter–energy elements in an effort to produce increased money–information markers. Indeed, in the societal frame, organizations that fail to provide money–information markers to meet their contractual obligations are decomposed and their components redistributed among other organizations and individuals. Consequently, organizational decider subsystems must manage money–information markers in a manner that satisfies society–level constraints.

On the other hand, all organizations are fundamentally concrete systems and their extended survival over time depends on their ability to import matter–energy and information higher in negative entropy than their exports. The ingenious combining of matter–energy elements is precisely the quality that makes it possible for organizations to produce the increase in money–information markers required to pay their dues to society. Information about the inflows and outflows of these matter–energy elements is essential to management for evaluating the effectiveness and efficiency of the system for both strategic and control purposes. Consequently, the revenue realization concept, which connects the accrual accounting system to these matter–energy elements, is first an internal (organization-level) accounting function and only secondarily an external (society-level) function. The common perception is just the opposite.

The recognition that the matter–energy elements and money–information markers cycle begins at different points for organization-level (internal) and society-level (external, environmental) management purposes imputes distinctly different meanings to the information provided by accounting records about matter–energy flows and money–information marker flows. Information about matter–energy flows gives a view of the expansion and contraction of the organization itself, whereas money–information marker flows reveal what costs or benefits the societal suprasystem is exacting from, or contributing to, the organization.

The proper exchange cycle at the organization level is matter–energy elements → money–information markers → matter–energy elements. Nevertheless, the revenue realization principle, as commonly applied, does *not* measure system-generant differentials in terms of matter–energy element inflows but rather in terms of matter–energy element outflows. This forces into the measurement of net income any money–information markers that have not completed the cycle, even though the principle basically calls for measuring the system-generant differentials in terms of matter–energy inflows-outflows. As it relates to measurement, the consequence of the judgment to break the cycle sequence at the point of money–information instead of matter–energy inflows is to treat all system-generant increases in monetary assets like increases in matter–energy assets, that is, as system inflows. Actually, in terms of matter–energy flows, the opposite treatment should be given.

Increases in monetary asset accounts are time-lagged money–information marker inflows. Equation (6–2) describes the net matter–energy flows of an organization from the view of both matter–energy and money–information markers. The normal vector of this system description points toward the interior of the system and includes matter–energy *inputs* (matter–energy asset *increases*) and money–information marker *outputs* (monetary asset *decreases* and liability and owners equity *increases*). As it is commonly applied, the revenue realization principle has the effect of inverting the monetary-asset treatment, which would in fact measure NME; that is, it adds increases in all monetary assets to matter–energy assets instead of subtracting them from increases in liabilities and owners equity.

If the cycle sequence is broken at the point of matter–energy inflows instead of money–information inflows, the relationships of equation (6–2) would be preserved by measuring matter–energy inflows by the money–information marker outflows of the transactions. Furthermore, the money–information increases would be measured by using the same mechanics, that is, increases in money–information marker outflows.

This last point may be intuitively explained. Recall that currency money–information markers are the final medium of exchange. Time-lagged money–information marker inflows transmit currency to other organizations and individuals (e.g., a note payable is returned to the organization when it is paid), thus giving up their potential use in exchange for matter–energy assets during some designated or indefinite period. On the other hand, time-lagged money–information marker outflows do just the opposite. Currency that remains unused has the same effect on the matter–energy *processes* of organizations in a particular period as money–information marker inflows.

Notwithstanding the inaction of increased residual currency as it relates to the system processes of a particular period, it measures immediate potential matter–energy flows (i.e., a potential that could have been exercised in the period); and it is generally a result of actions of the period. To take these considerations into account, the term *Mo* of equation (6–10) is transposed to construct equation (6–11) below:

$$Cr + 0 + S + Sy = Ma + P + E + Co - Mo = I \qquad (6\text{–}11)$$

where *Mo* retains its outflow designation. Equation (6–11) is not an unbiased measurement with reference to the measurement method itself. Although we have not violated the mathematical operations allowed by the ratio scale, we have used a closed system to converge on an element other than the one used to close the system. Any element or combination of elements can be thus obtained. This is the advantage gained by artificially closing a system. Such a use of the system, however, is biased by a purpose other than to close the system with a residual. Thus equation (6–10) yields *NME* as in (6–12) below, and equation (6–11) yields a measurement of net total flows (*I*) including net money currency inflows as in (6–13) below.

$$Cr + O + S + Sy + Mo = Ma + P + E + Co = NME \qquad (6–12)$$

$$Cr + 0 + S + Sy = Ma + P + E + Co - Mo = I \qquad (6–13)$$

This formulation captures all matter–energy element changes and changes in period potentiality without distorting the period process measurements with the future period potentiality of noncurrency (time-lagged) money–information markers. This formulation both violates the construct logic of the accounting measurement method (although not the construct logic of the equation) and, as stated above, introduces the assertion that period potential, that is, currency, is more closely associated with matter–energy elements than with time-lagged money–information marker elements.

By treating all monetary assets in a similar fashion, the revenue realization principle as commonly applied violates even further the construct logic of the accounting measurement method by introducing the assertion that future period potentiality is the same as achieved matter–energy flows. The removal of this violation from the accounting reports undoubtedly would affect such fraud as that exemplified by the landmark 1938 *Dennis* v. *McKesson and Robbins* law case. In this case, auditors certified several millions of dollars' worth of fictitious receivables and inventory. If increases in receivables are treated as time-lagged money–information marker inputs (reductions in time-lagged money–information marker outputs), the net result signals the various societal deciders that process has decreased. This signal is opposite to that sent when Accounts Receivable are treated as assets rather than offset against liabilities and owners equity.

With reference to NME, the effect on net income of the matching principle as commonly applied is demonstrated in Tables 6–3 and 6–4 using the transactions of Table 6–2. The effects of other commonly used assumptions may be demonstrated in similar manner.

Summary

Chapters 5 and 6 have developed a theory of the accounting measurement of concrete processes. Chapter 7 provides extended examples of how this theory

Table 6–3
The Effects of the Revenue Realization Concept on Net Income with Reference to NME (First of Two Tables)

	A/P	+	CS	+	R/E	-	NME		A/R	+	Cash	-	Total Assets	
*							Inv	+ P/E +						
Beginning	0	+	0	+	0	-	0	+ 0 +	0	+	0	-	0	
Trans.(a)	0	+	(+10,000)	+	0	-	0	+ 0 +	0	+	(+10,000)	-	+10,000	Δ
Balance	0	+	10,000	+	0	-	0	+ 0 +	0	+	10,000	-	+10,000	
Trans.(b)	0	+	0	+	0	-	0	+ (+5,000) +	0	+	(-5,000)	-	0	Δ
Balance	0	+	10,000	+	0	-	0	+ 5,000 +	0	+	5,000	-	+10,000	
Trans.(c)	(+7,000)	+	0	+	0	-	(+7,000)	+ 0 +	0	+	0	-	+7,000	Δ
Balance	+7,000	+	10,000	+	0	-	+7,000	+ 5,000 +	0	+	5,000	-	+17,000	
Trans.(f)	0	+	0	+	(+1,500)	-	(-1,500)	+ 0 +	(+3,000)	+	0	-	+1,500	Δ
Balance	+7,000	+	10,000	+	1,500	-	+5,500	+ 5,000 +	3,000	+	5,000	-	+18,500	

* Explanation of terms: NME - net matter-energy flows, A/P - accounts payable, CS - common stock, R/E - retained earnings, Inv - inventory, P/E - plant and equipment, A/R - accounts receivable, Total Assets - a typical Balance Sheet accounting of the flows, a variable that is the result of aggregating monetary assets and matter-energy assets, Δ - change in Total Assets. This table isolates the effect of changing the construct logic of the accounting measurement method.

110

Table 6-4
The Effects of the Revenue Realization Concept on Net Income with Reference to NME (Second of Two Tables)

*	Total Assets (Δ)		EX		NI		NI		From Table 6-3 NME		EF
Beginning	0	–	0	–	0		0	–	0	–	0
Trans.(a)	10,000 Δ	–	(+10,000)[a]	–	0		0	–	0	–	0
Aggregate (Balance)	10,000	–	10,000	–	0		0	–	0	–	0
Trans.(b)	0 Δ	–	0	–	0		0	–	(+5,000)[b]	–	-5,000
Aggregate (Balance)	10,000	–	10,000	–	0		0	–	5,000	–	-5,000
Trans.(c)	7,000 Δ	–	(+7,000)[c]	–	0		0	–	(+7,000)	–	-7,000
Aggregate (Balance)	17,000	–	17,000	–	0		0	–	12,000	–	-12,000
Trans.(f)	1,500 Δ	–	0	–	1,500		1,500	–	(-1,500)[d]	–	3,000
Aggregate (Balance)	18,500	–	17,000	–	1,500		1,500	–	10,500	–	-9,000

* Explanation of terms: Total Assets - as described in Table 6-3, EX - exclusion of transactions that change Total Assets but are not GAAP-classified as affecting net income, NI - net income from transactions, NME - net matter-energy, and EF - the effect of the common application of the matching concept with reference to NME. The EF of -9,000 indicates that NME is understated in NI by 9,000.

a GAAP does not recognize owner contributions as a component of net income.

b GAAP does not distinguish between money-information marker assets and matter-energy assets in the aggregate Total Assets, NME does.

c GAAP does not recognize the effect of a purchase of Inventory until it is sold, NME recognizes it immediately.

d When Inventory is sold, NI increases by the profit and NME decreases by the Inventory cost.

111

may be applied to accounting recording and reporting procedures, and Chapter 8 discusses how concrete process measurements may be allocated internally according to living systems process analysis (LSPA).

Reference

Eastman, Max, ed. *Capital, the Communist Manifesto, and Other Writings by Karl Marx.* New York: The Modern Library, 1932.

7
ACCOUNTING MEASUREMENT OF CONCRETE PROCESSES APPLIED TO ORGANIZATIONS

Introduction

Accounting is an applied discipline. Few accountants are interested in theories that cannot be shown to have practical applications. We believe that the theory of accounting measurement of concrete processes can be applied to the empirical data collected by accountants to map important aspects of modern organizations and to produce better-understood public reports. Applications of the theory developed in Chapters 5 and 6 are illustrated in this chapter.

Before providing two extensive illustrations of detailed applications, we discuss the question of how this theory would change common accounting procedures. Following the illustrations we suggest how concrete process information might be disclosed in public reports.

How Would LST Change Accounting Information-Gathering and Reporting Procedures?

In terms of theoretic continuity and the utility of the information provided, the application of LST would cause dramatic and major changes in accounting information. Almost paradoxically, no aspect of the required procedural changes is totally unfamiliar in the accounting literature. Some of the procedural and theoretical ideas have been put forward by one or more accounting writers in various usually specific contexts. Here we bring them together in a functional arrangement that follows from clearly distinguishing, according to LST, the measurements of concrete flows from their interpretations.

An LST view of accounting information systems suggests the following changes in information-gathering and reporting procedures:

1. Implement three-dimensional double-entry bookkeeping. All three dimensions are physical. They are: (1) time locations periodaneously, (2) physical attributes measured quantitatively, and (3) specific exchange value measured in monetary units. Measurements of all three of these attributes are currently recorded by the accounting information system. It is a relatively simple procedure to extend the information from the source documents and journals to the accounts themselves. Using computers, it involves elementary coding and addressing procedures. This procedure would increase the flexibility of accounting information for analytic purposes, both managerial and scientific.

Because monetary units are used to measure specific exchange value and this attribute on a particular object can change with each exchange of the object, functions relating the relational attribute specific exchange value to measurements of intrinsic attributes of an object, for example, size, weight, and so on, can be written only for particular exchanges. Consequently, information about important intrinsic attributes of exchanges (such as, number of people, tons of materials, kilowatts of energy, and hours of communication) should be recorded in tandem with the monetary measurements. Likewise, changes in values over time, both intrinsic and relational, may be important; thus the time frame should be similarly identified.

2. Record all inflows and outflows in separate accounts. Currently, the temporary accounts are recorded in this manner. Endurance of organizations depends not only on results of operations but also on all other investing and financing actions. The permanent accounts should be separated to improve the analytical detail of these flows.

3. Distinguish accounts that record measurements of concrete flows, both matter–energy and money–information markers. This can be done by coding. This information makes it possible to distinguish between measurements of the concrete elements of organizations and interpretations, based on various decision models, introduced into the accounts. The classifications can be as detailed as the decision requirements of the economic actors, but should provide at least the detail suggested in procedure 4 below.

4. When possible, require that public accounting statements report the following aggregated inflows and aggregated outflows: materials, personnel, energy, communications, currency money–information markers, credit MIM, owner MIM, and socialization MIM. Because these classifications represent combinations of matter–energy flows, consensus should ultimately determine the actual types of flows to be classified in each category. All of these flows, however, are clearly concrete flows measured at the boundary of an organization or component. Information from the commonly used set of accounts can be restated into these classifications, as illustrated in this chapter. However, the system of common accounts can be changed easily to identify in the recording process itself the concrete flows using the same general procedures now used by accountants, that is, classification and aggregation.

Implementing the procedures suggested in (1) through (4) is quite possible.

The rapid advancement in computer technology over the last few years makes it possible to account for large amounts of information with relative ease. Furthermore, this technology makes it possible, and in fact necessary, to process information in a precise and ultimately quantifiable manner. By combining precision with the ability to process large masses of information, modern computer technology can solve important multivariant problems. Such solutions may be pursued in a traditional, problem-oriented manner or by a modern systems approach involving on-line, real-time, and artificial intelligence capabilities. The basic procedural changes we suggest in (1) through (4) are needed to gain the greatest benefit from our modern information processing capabilities.

5. Estimate and report the aggregate measurement error on those accounts in procedure 4 that is accepted by auditors in their assessment of materiality. Economic actors know that no measurement is absolute. There is always some probability that error exists in the reported measurements. Various writers have suggested that some expression of measurement error limits should be reported. Mostly, however, writers have confused the different questions of measurement error on the one hand and the uncertainty associated with stochastic events on the other. Auditors decide what error limits are acceptable when they calculate sample sizes. Measurement error is taken into consideration in those calculations, and such limits should be aggregated and reported.

6. Define systematically and operationally accounting assumptions such as the income realization principle, the matching concept, and conservatism (the idea that certain potential losses should be recognized but only realized gains should be recognized). Operational definitions of accounting assumptions in the context of LST would provide a basis for categorizing the influence of these assumptions on various accounting variables such as net income. Such categories could be presented in an "interpretations" section of, or footnote to, accounting statements. These disclosures would help dispel the belief that accountants sometimes resort to "creative accounting" when calculating net income.

7. Provide estimates generated by the accounting information system for the twenty critical subsystem processes identified by LST. This can be done by connecting information generated by living systems process analysis to accounting information, as we discuss more fully in Chapter 8. Such an action would add to living systems process analysis the view of the organization as a coherent whole. Alternatively, the analytic power of accounting information would be increased significantly by providing details of critical processes commonly so intermingled in an organization that they are obscured and sometimes forgotten.

How the Theory of Accounting Measurement of Concrete Processes May Be Applied—under Full Measurement Conditions

In Chapter 6, we develop small examples of how the relationships described in identity (6–1), that is,

$$MIMO - MIMI \equiv MEI - MEO, \tag{7-1}$$

can be used to map the concrete processes of organizations. There we use individual transactions to demonstrate the recording method. However, we clarify the characteristic of the accounting measurement methodology that only *aggregates* of such transactions over an accounting period proven to generate useful information provide a view of an organization as a *coherent whole*, a cosmic view.

Furthermore, in our ivory tower of theory, we simply assume that each term of identity (7–1) can be fully measured in every organization. Under this assumption, we may use empirical data to calculate net matter–energy flows (*NME*) at will. The variable *NME*, then, may be an ideal single referent for assessing management's individual accounting biases introduced to public reports of economic activity and allowed by GAAP.

This assumption is valid for many organizations, for example, any organization that uses the specific identification method of inventory valuation (including automobile dealers) and retailers that use automated inventory controls driven by point-of-sale input to integrated computer systems. Illustration 1, below, demonstrates the application of the theory of accounting measurement of concrete processes under conditions that measure all four terms of equation (6–2) of Chapter 6, that is,

$$MIMO - MIMI = MEI - MEO, \tag{7-2}$$

where *MIMO* is money–information marker outflows, *MIMI* is money–information marker inflows, *MEI* is matter–energy inflows, and *MEO* is matter–energy outflows.

In equation (6–11) of that chapter, we differentiate the terms of equation (7–2) as follows:

$$Cr + 0 + S + Sy + Mo = NME = Ma + P + E + Co \tag{7-3}$$

where the normal direction is outflow for the terms of the left-side expression and inflow for the right-side but all terms can assume both positive and negative values; NME is measured by the left-side expression in terms of money–information markers and by the right-side in terms of matter–energy; and *Cr* is creditor money–information markers, *0* is owner *MIM*, *S* is socialization *MIM*, *Sy* is system- (organization-) generated increments and decrements, *Mo* is currency *MIM*, *Ma* is materials, *P* is personnel, *E* is energy, and *Co* is communications. Further differentiation of each term into its component inflows and outflows supplies terms consistent with an account structure that provides maximum information for different types of analyses required for economic decisions, that is,

Table 7–1
A Chart of Typical Accounts

Cash (Ca)	Sales (Sa)
Notes Receivable (N/R)	Rent Revenue (Ro)
Accounts Receivable(A/R)	Interest Revenue (I/Rv)
Interest Receivable (I/R)	Insurance Receipts (Is/Rc)
Merchandise Inventory (Inv)	Subsidies & Contributions (S/C)
Furniture & Equipment (F&E)	Cost of Sales (CoS)
Land (L)	Salaries & Wages Expense (S/W)
Notes Payable (N/P)	Rent Expense (Ri)
Accounts Payable (A/P)	Tax Expense (T/E)
Taxes Payable (T/P)	Utilities Expense (U)
Common Stock (C/S)	Interest Expense (I/E)
Preferred Stock (P/S)	Insurance Expense (Is/E)
Retained Earnings (R/E)	Telephone Expense (Tel)
Dividends (D)	

$$(CrO + OO + SO + MoO + SyO) - (CrI + OI + SI + MoI + SyI) = NME$$
$$= (MaI + PI + EI + CoI) - (MaO + PO + EO + CoO), \qquad (7\text{–}4)$$

where the terms are as previously defined except that the added symbol O means outflow and the added symbol I means inflow of the matter–energy or money–information marker elements represented by a term. Illustration 1 is based on this differentiation. We present this illustration to distinguish between measurements made on concrete processes and interpretations imposed by accounting adjustments.

> *Illustration 1.* Given: A firm has completed its incipient accounting period of operations and reports its accounting data according to the classifications of the chart of typical accounts stipulated in Table 7–1. To enhance management analysis of the data, however, the company maintained separate accounts for the inflows and outflows of permanent as well as temporary accounts.

The Trial Balance in Table 7–2 lists these accounts. (A *trial balance* is a listing of all account balances so that all debit balances are in a leftward position and all credit balances are in a rightward position. The debits and credits are summed separately to show equality.) The accounts have been adjusted to include all matter–energy and money–information marker flows that occurred within the period. For example, on Table 7–2, no Salaries and Wages Payable are outstanding, so the company has paid all wages earned during the period. Also, the company has accepted credit documents in the amount of $8 instead of currency during the period, as evidenced by Interest Receivable In. All of these documents, however, have been given up in exchange for currency as evidenced by Interest Receivable Out in the amount of $8. Furthermore, the tax expense of $62 has been recorded even though $12 has not yet been paid.

Table 7–2
Trial Balance and Concrete Process Classification (CPC)

	Debit	Credit	CPC
Cash In (Cai)	1685		MoI
Cash Out (Cao)		1670	MoO
Notes Receivable In (N/Ri)	150		CrI
Notes Receivable Out (N/Ro)		75	CrO
Accounts Receivable In (A/Ri)	563		CrI
Accounts Receivable Out (A/Ro)		475	CrO
Interest Receivable In (I/Ri)	8		CrI
Interest Receivable Out (I/Ro)		8	CrO
Merchandise Inventory In (Invi)	457		MaI
Merchandise Inventory Out (Invo)		200	MaO
Furniture & Equipment In (F&Ei)	28		MaI
Furniture & Equipment Out (F&Eo)		0	MaO
Land In (Li)	9		MaI
Land Out (Lo)		0	MaO
Notes Payable In (N/Pi)	0		CrI
Notes Payable Out (N/Po)		20	CrO
Accounts Payable In (A/Pi)	385		CrI
Accounts Payable Out (A/Po)		457	CrO
Taxes Payable In (T/Pi)	50		CrI
Taxes Payable Out (T/Po)		62	CrO
Common Stock In (C/Si)	0		OI
Common Stock Out (C/So)		111	OO
Preferred Stock In (P/Si)	0		OI
Preferred Stock Out (P/So)		15	OO
Dividends In (Di)	20		OI
Retained Earnings In (R/Ei)	0		SyI
Retained Earnings Out (R/Eo)		0	SyO
Cost of Sales In (CoSi)	200		SyI
Sales out (Sao)		723	SyO
Salaries & Wages In (S/Wi)	65		PI
Salaries & Wages Out (S/Wo)		0	PO
Rent Expense In (Ri)	100		MaI
Rent Revenue Out (Ro)		1	MaO
Tax Expense In (T/Ei)	62		SI
Subsidies & Contrib. Out (S/Co)		10	SO
Telephone Expense In (Teli)	13		CoI
Utilities Expense In (Ui)	32		EI
Interest Expense In (I/Ei)	2		CrI
Interest Revenue Out (I/Rvo)		8	CrO
Insurance Expense In (Is/Ei)	7		SI
Insurance Receipts Out (Is/Rco)		1	SO
Totals	3836	3836	

All amounts are aggregates of transaction data and include only
adjustments that are used to include in the record of a particular
accounting period all concrete processes occurring within that period,
e.g., the adjustment for unrecorded salaries. No adjustments that
attempt to match expenses to related revenues are included.

The logic of the Trial Balance reports all inflows of matter-energy and
money-information markers as debits and all outflows as credits.
CAVEAT: Inflows and outflows are not the same as increases and
decreases in the accounts. All accounts on this Trial Balance only
increase--inflows by debit entry, outflows by credit entry.

The first step of a concrete process analysis is to classify each account according to important global classifications such as those of equation (7–4). The extreme right column of Table 7–2 provides these classifications. Table 7–3 sorts the accounts into concrete process classifications. This arrangement explicitly indicates related accounts and thus may be a useful exercise prior to placing the classifications on a Trial Balance.

The logic of the Trial Balance in Table 7–2 is clearly based on process. The typical accounting trial balance is simply a list of all accounts, and accountants recognize that both periodic (process) accounts and permanent (residual structure) accounts are listed. By dividing each permanent account into "in" and "out" components, as the temporary accounts are typically constructed by accountants, we convert the entire set of accounts into process accounts. Having removed the mixed characteristics of the accounts on the trial balance, *debit* means process in (inflows to the organization processes), and *credit* means process out (ouflows from the organization processes). The meanings of these words are always the same.

The common format of debits to the left and credits to the right on accounts is arbitrary. The meanings of the terms debit and credit are not left and right, respectively. The meanings are inflow and outflow and those meanings make debit-credit notation useful. In every exchange, the inflows to organizational processes are equal to the outflows. Because the common balance sheet accounts net inflows and outflows, inflows may either increase or decrease an account. Consequently, account increases and decreases are not necessarily equal in every transaction. Process accounts only increase, and increases in debit accounts always equal increases in credit accounts. The maintenance of debit-credit equality in every transaction is a convenient way to ensure that an entire transaction is recorded.

After the individual accounts have been classified according to useful global classifications of concrete processes, the trial balance information should be sorted into those classifications. Table 7–4 provides a Trial Balance that does this and also aggregates the information into the classifications of equation (7–2). Netting these aggregates converges on NME. The Trial Balance illustrated in Table 7–4 provides the basic accounting information for CPA, concrete process analysis.

The purpose of Illustration 1, however, is to distinguish between this measurement information and the interpreted version presented by accountants in public reports. Table 7–5 presents a worksheet showing how the information on the concrete processes trial balance of Table 7–4 may be adjusted to GAAP disclosure requirements. The first set of columns contains the information of Table 7–4. The second set of columns provides adjustments based on the typical GAAP requirements described at the bottom of the table and keyed to the amounts in those columns. The third set of columns contains information in accordance with GAAP disclosure requirements. The last two sets of columns sort the GAAP

Table 7-3

Accounts of Expanded Chart Sorted into Concrete Process Classifications

MIMO					MIMI				NME	MEI				MEO			
(GrO + OO + SO + MoO + SyO)				-	(GrI + OI + SI + MoI + SyI)				=NMIM=	MaI + PI + EI+ CoI)				-	(MaO + PO + EO + CoO)		
N/Ro	C/So	Cao	Sao		N/Ri	C/Si	Cal			Invi	S/Wi	Ui	Teli		Invo	S/Wo	
A/Ro	P/So Is/Rco	R/Eo			A/Ri	P/Si Is/Ei	R/Ei			F&Ei					F&Eo		
I/Ro	S/Go				I/Ri	D1	T/Ei	CoSi		Li					Lo		
N/Po					N/Pi					Ri					Ro		
A/Po					A/Pi												
T/Po					T/Pi												
I/Rvo					I/Ei												

information into sets that appear on two of the three generally required annual statements.

Tables 7–6 and 7–7 present the information from the last two columns respectively in statement form. Table 7–8 presents a cash flow summary of the GAAP information, which is a third generally required annual report. The NME of Illustration 1 is $503, the Net Income from Operations is $68, the "bottom line" Net Income is $33, the Total Assets amount is $313, the Net Assets amount (Total Owners' Equity) is $139, the Net Cash Flows from Operating Activities amount is $(54), and the Change in Cash is $15.

None of these accounting variables (believed to be the most used variables) come close to describing the NME of the organization. Each of the accounting adjustments makes sense within the logic of certain decision models, but all users of financial information are not making the same decision. Furthermore, the latitude allowed by GAAP for selecting accounting procedures makes it possible for internal deciders (managers) to manage each of these accounting variables within limits over time. Consequently, distinguishing between the concrete process measurements summarized in NME and the interpreted variables disclosed by accountants may be useful. If disclosed, NME may provide a summary measurement that may be used to evaluate and compare the meanings of those other variables. Furthermore, certain cosmic measurements (e.g., the classifications of equation [7–4]) may provide useful information about the fluctuant steady-state characteristics of organizations. Such information may provide certain prediction power as discussed in Chapter 2.

A Practical Application of the Theory of Accounting Measurement—under Partial Measurement Conditions

Illustration 1 assumes that all four terms of equation (7–2) are measured by the accounting information system. While it holds for some firms, this condition does not hold for all organizations. For organizations that measure all four terms, NME is possibly the best single cosmic measurement that can be used as a referent unbiased with reference to the measurement method to judge the relative characteristics of GAAP-defined accounting variables.

It turns out, however, that NME is often esoteric despite its fully concrete composition. It is illusive because all four terms of equation (7–2) cannot always be measured by the accounting measurement method. Due to the circuitous pattern of matter–energy and money–information marker flows, the MEO measurement is contained in the MIMI measurement (cash or accounts receivable inflows). However, this boundary measurement itself cannot distinguish between the MEO component and the increment-of-value component commonly called profits.

Obviously, to the organization the specific exchange monetary value of the MEO component is its value as MEI. In relatively simple organizations, this inflow value can be traced through the organizational subsystems and assigned

Table 7–4

Trial Balance Accounts Sorted by Concrete Process Classification and Converging on Net Matter–Energy

MONEY-INFORMATION MARKER OUTFLOWS (MIMO)	Debit	Credit
Creditor documents out (CrO)		
Notes Receivable Out (N/Ro)		$ 75
Accounts Receivable Out (A/Ro)		475
Interest Receivable Out (I/Ro)		8
Notes Payable Out (N/Po)		20
Accounts Payable Out (A/Po)		457
Taxes Payable Out (T/Po)		62
Interest Revenue Out (I/Rvo)		8
Owner's documents out (OO)		
Common Stock Out (C/So)		111
Preferred Stock Out (P/So)		15
Socialization documents out (SO)		
Subsidies & Contributions Out (S/Co)		10
Insurance Receipts Out (Is/Rco)		1
Currency information markers out (MoO)		
Cash Out (Cao)		1670
System generated increments out (SyO)		
Sales Out (Sao)		_723_

TOTAL MONEY-INFORMATION MARKER OUTFLOWS (MIMO)		$3635

MONEY-INFORMATION MARKER INFLOWS (MIMI)		
Creditor documents in (CrI)		
Notes Receivable In (N/Ri)	150	
Accounts Receivable In (A/Ri)	563	
Interest Receivable In (I/Ri)	8	
Notes Payable In (N/Pi)	0	
Accounts Payable In (A/Pi)	385	
Taxes Payable In (T/Pi)	50	
Interest Expense In (I/Ei)	2	
Owner documents in (OI)		
Common Stock In (C/Si)	0	
Preferred Stock In (P/Si)	0	
Dividends (Di)	20	
Socialization documents in (SI)		
Tax Expense In (T/Ei)	62	
Insurance Expense In (Is/Ei)	7	
Currency information markers in (MoI)		
Cash In (Cai)	1685	
System generated decrements in (SyI)		
Cost of Sales (CoSi)	_200_	

TOTAL MONEY-INFORMATION MARKER INFLOWS (MIMI)		3132

NET MONEY-INFORMATION MARKER FLOWS: OUT (IN)		$503

MATTER-ENERGY INFLOWS (MEI)		
Materials in (MaI)		
Merchandise Inventory In (Invi)	457	
Furniture & Equipment In (F&Ei)	28	
Land In (Li)	9	
Rent Expense In (Ri)	100	
Personnel in (PI)		
Salaries & Wages In (S/Wi)	65	
Energy in (EI)		
Utilities Expense In (Ui)	32	
Communications in (CoI)		
Telephone Expense In (Teli)	13	

Table 7–4 (Continued)

	Debit	Credit	
TOTAL MATTER-ENERGY INFLOWS (MEI)			$704
MATTER-ENERGY OUTFLOWS (MEO)			
Materials out (MaO)			
Merchandise Inventory Out (Invo)		200	
Furniture & Equipment Out (F&Eo)		0	
Land Out (Lo)			0
Rent Revenue Out (Ro)		1	
Personnel out (PO)			
Salaries & Wages Out (S/Wo)		0	
TOTAL MATTER-ENERGY OUTFLOWS			201
NET MATTER-ENERGY FLOWS: IN (OUT)	____	____	$503
TRIAL BALANCE TOTALS	$3836	$3836	

to *MEO*. In such organizations it should be thus assigned. Organizations are typically complex, however, and within them specialized functions separate many *MEI* components and rearrange them into unique configurations. As a result of this process, any tracing of *MEI* to *MEO* becomes quite arbitrary and is generally controlled by interpretive decision models (conceptual systems based on logic other than that of the measurement method itself).

For practical purposes, therefore, we substitute for *NME* itself the *NME* component that is measured directly and always at the boundary. This component is *MEI*. It can be isolated by the following transposition of equation (7–2):

$$MIMO - MIMI + MEO = MEI \qquad (7-5)$$

Some components of *MEO*, however, have traceable specific exchange monetary values and some do not. To describe this condition, we differentiate the term *MEO* in equation (7–5) into the terms *traceable MEO* (*TMEO*) and *non-traceable MEO* (*NTMEO*) as follows:

$$MIMO - MIMI + (TMEO + NTMEO) = MEI \qquad (7-6)$$

To use all of the information available from the measurement method, we net traceable *MEI* against *MEI* to obtain gross matter–energy inputs net of measured matter–energy outflows (*GMEINO*).

$$MIMO - MIMI + NTMEO = MEI - TMEO = GMEINO \qquad (7-7)$$

If the unknown (unmeasured) *NTMEO* is recorded at the full exit specific monetary exchange value (a measured value obtained by the MIMI of the trans-

Table 7–5
Worksheet for Converting Concrete Process Amounts to GAAP Adjusted Amounts

	Concrete Processes Trial Balance		Adjustments		GAAP Adjusted Trial Balance		Income Statement		Balance Sheet	
	Debit	Credit	Debit	Credit	Debit	Credit	Debit	Credit	Debit	Credit
MIMO										
CrO										
N/Ro		75	75							
A/Ro		475	475							
I/Ro		8	8							
N/Po		20	0			20				20
A/Po		457	385			72				72
T/Po		62	50			12				12
I/Rvo		8				8		8		
_OO_										
C/So		111	0			111				111
P/So		15	0			15				15
_SO_										
S/Co		10				10		10		
Is/Rco		1				1		1		
MoO										
Cao		1670	1670							
SyO										
Sao		723				723		723		
MIMI										
CrI										
N/Ri	150			75	75				75	
A/Ri	563			475	88				88	
I/Ri	8				8					
N/Pi	0			0						
A/Pi	385			385						
T/Pi	50			50						
I/Ei	2				2		2			
_OI_										
C/Si	0			0						
P/Si	0			0						
Di	20				20				20	
_SI_										
T/Ei	62		[a]15		77		77			
Is/Ei	7				7		7			
MoI										
Cai	1685			1670	15				15	
SyI										
CoSi	200		[a]106		306		306			
MEI										
MaI				[a]106						
				[b]50						
Invi	457			200	101				101	
F/Ei	28			[d] 3	25				25	
Li	9			0	9				9	
Ri	100				100		100			
_PI_										
S/Wi	65				65		65			
_EI_										
Ui	32				32		32			
CoI										
Teli	13				13		13			

Table 7–5 (Continued)

	Concrete Processes Trial Balance		Adjustments		GAAP Adjusted Trial Balance		Income Statement		Balance Sheet	
	Debit	Credit	Debit	Credit	Debit	Credit	Debit	Credit	Debit	Credit
MEO										
MaO										
Invo		200	200							
F&Eo		0	0							
Lo		0	0							
Ro		1				1		1		
TOTAL	3836	3836								
Extraordinary Loss			[b]50	[e]15	35		35			
Warranty Expense			[c]70		70		70			
Est. Warranty Liab.				[c]70		70				70
Depreciation Expense			[d]3		3		3			
			3107	3107	1043	1043	710	743	333	300
GAAP Net Income							33			33
							743	743	333	333

(a) Adjust merchandise inventory account to GAAP inventory valuation.
(b) Adjust for flood loss of merchandise inventory of $50.
(c) Adjustment to recognize estimated liability of $70 under warranties.
(d) Adjustment to recognize depreciation of $3 on the furniture and equipment.
(e) Adjustment to report extraordinary loss (recorded in (b) above) net of tax of 30%.
(f) Adjustments to consolidate inflow/outflow into net account balance as generally reported according to GAAP (all amounts in the adjustment columns without item numbers).

actions) as a money–information marker outflow from process to an internal residual classification termed system-generated increments (SyO), the measurement method converges on the cosmic measurement GMEINO. Substituting SyO for $NTMEO$, we have

$$MIMO - MIMI + SyO = GMEINO = MEI - TMEO \qquad (7\text{–}8)$$

This treatment records the $NTMEO$ in Sy when in fact it did not actually increase Sy by an entire transaction amount—only the profit portion.

Having constructed the time-lagged money–information marker SyO, we can describe the left side of the equation straightforwardly as net money–information marker flows ($NMIM$). $NMIM$ equals $GMEINO$. Consequently, if system-generated increments and decrements are entered only on measured amounts, we have in the $NMIM\text{-}GMEINO$ a cosmic measurement of concrete processes.

However, our confidence in this measurement, although unbiased with reference to the measurement method itself, is threatened by behavioral consider-

Table 7–6
GAAP Income Statement

Revenues:		
Sales	$723	
Insurance Receipts	1	
Subsidies & Contributions	10	
Rent Revenue	1	
Interest Revenue	8	
TOTAL REVENUES		$743
Expenses:		
Cost of Goods Sold	$306	
Depreciation Expense	3	
Rent Expense	100	
Salaries & Wages Expense	65	
Utilities Expense	32	
Telephone Expense	13	
Insurance Expense	7	
Interest Expense	2	
Warranty Expense	70	
Tax Expense	77	
Total Expenses		675
Net Income Before Extraordinary Items		$ 68
Extraordinary Loss		35
NET INCOME		$ 33

ations. This measurement is subject to accounting record manipulation by including items in *TMEO* or excluding them by keeping internal records or failing to do so. Such manipulation might be controlled by the consistency principle now applied to accounting reports. Any change in the composition of *TMEO* would be considered an accounting principle change and thus would need to be disclosed properly. However, such required disclosure would be difficult, if not impossible, to police.

If less than full measurement of *NME* is accepted, the next most comprehensive measurement that cannot be internally manipulated, that is, is based only on measurements made at the boundary of an organization, is *MEI*. While using this measurement disregards the information content of *TMEO*, we have more confidence in it because it is not easily manipulated by bookkeeping changes instead of economic process.

Disregarding any information that may be available about *TMEO*, we return to equation (7–5) and develop a means for analyzing concrete processes under conditions of the missing information. As already discussed, the *MIMO* term

Table 7–7
GAAP Balance Sheet

Assets:

Cash	$ 15	
Notes Receivable	75	
Accounts Receivable	88	
Merchandise Inventory	101	
Furniture & Equipment (net of $3)	25	
Land	9	
TOTAL ASSETS		$313

Liabilities & Owners' Equity:

Liabilities:

Notes Payable	$20	
Accounts Payable	72	
Taxes Payable	12	
Est. Warranty Liability	70	
TOTAL LIABILITIES		$ 174

Owners' Equity:

Common Stock	$111	
Preferred Stock	15	
Retained Earnings	13	
TOTAL OWNERS EQUITY		139

TOTAL LIABILITIES & OWNERS' EQUITY	$313

---

decomposes into $CrO + OO + SO + MoO$, the $MIMI$ term to $CrI + OI = SI + MoI$, and the MEI term to $MaI + PI + EI + CoI$. Although not always in this detail, the three terms $MIMO$, $MIMI$, and MEI are commonly identifiable directly from published accounting reports. MEI can be combined with the other commonly disclosed amounts in a manner that captures much of the information content of NME.

The MEI term is the matter–energy inflows measured by the money–information marker transmissions of exchanges. The Mo term of equation (7–3) is the net currency money–information marker outflows occurring during an accounting period. For liquidity purposes, this net amount is usually negative; that is, inflows of currency exceed outflows slightly. As discussed previously, this increment is typically generated by period processes and is potential NME that could have been converted during the period. The Mo term is typically the net currency that remains in the circuitous system unconverted to MEI.

If we accept the proposition that immediate potential MEI is different from time-lagged potential MEI, then the actual MEI and the immediate potential MEI taken together constitute the gross system generated increments or decrements. The management of time-lagged money–information markers, however, may

Table 7–8
GAAP Cash Flows Statement

Cash Flows from Operating Activities:

Net Income	$ 33	
Add:		
Depreciation Expense	3	
Increase in Accounts Payable	72	
Increase in Notes Payable	20	
Increase in Taxes Payable	12	
Increase in Est. Warranty Liab.	70	
Subtract:		
Increase in Notes Receivable	(75)	
Increase in Accounts Receivable	(88)	
Increase in Merchandise Inventory	(101)	
Net Cash Flows from Operating Activities		$ (54)

Cash Flows from Investing Activities:

Purchase of Furniture & Equipment	$ (28)	
Purchase of Land	(9)	
Cash Used by Investing Activities		(37)

Cash Flows from Financing Activities:

Issuance of Common Stock	$ 111	
Issuance of Preferred Stock	15	
Payment of Dividends	(20)	106
Increase in Cash		$ 15

---

add to or take away from *MEI* or *Mo*. Consequently, these terms should be taken into consideration. If management has succeeded in enticing from the time-lagged money–information markets more currency money–information markers into its processes than it gave these markets, some of the *MEI* or *Mo* or both is the result of this success, not of the matter–energy processes themselves.

Therefore, we may determine a measurement of gross system-generated increments or decrements as follows:

$$(MaI + PI + EI + CoI) - (MoO - MoI) = GI \qquad (7\text{–}9)$$

and

$$GI - (CrO + OO + SO) + (CrI + OI + SI) = GSG \qquad (7\text{–}10)$$

where *GI* is gross inflows (which includes net currency money–information markers), *GSG* is gross system-generated increments or decrements (which includes net time-lagged money–information markers), and the other terms are as previously defined. These equations configure the accounting information in a manner that does not violate identity (7–1) and make it possible to calculate three critical ratios that may be used to analyze an organization as a coherent whole at the high level of aggregation typically reported publicly.

The three critical ratios are as follows:

$$\frac{GSG}{GI}, \text{ the gross system generant to the gross inflows;} \qquad (7\text{–}11)$$

$$\frac{GI}{MEI}, \text{ the gross inflows to matter–energy inflows; and} \qquad (7\text{–}12)$$

$$\frac{GSG}{MEI}, \text{ the gross system generant to matter–energy inflows.} \qquad (7\text{–}13)$$

These ratios are critical because they are orderly information reductions of critical cross-level (between organization-level and society level-living systems) feedback processes. The following relationship holds between the three ratios:

$$\frac{GSG}{GI} \cdot \frac{GI}{MEI} = \frac{GSG}{MEI} \qquad (7\text{–}14)$$

The term GSG/GI contains information about the relationships between the organization's matter–energy processes and its societal suprasystem. This information is borne on various sorts of money–information markers and is transmitted through the channels and nets of the time–lagged information phases of a pentamerous market. The term GI/MEI contains information about the organization's management of treasure to maintain steady-state relationships, both internally and with its environment. The term GSG/MEI contains the combined information of the first two ratios and describes the concrete endurance of the organization over time, that is, its matter–energy growth and decay. Taken together, these ratios may be used to map the results of management actions as they relate to the maintenance of a fluctuous steady state within a fluctuant range that generally is biased purposefully toward growth and away from decay. The meanings of each ratio are discussed further below.

The ratio GSG to GI is above 1.0 when the organization as a whole is a net exporter of money–information currency markers to the time-lagged money–information marker phases of the market. That is to say, owners, creditors, and society beneficiaries as a group are receiving net benefits from the organization. Below 1.0, the GSG/GI ratio indicates that the organization is a net importer of money–information currency markers; that is, the organization is being fed (maintained) by the owners, creditors, and society benefactors as a group.

More specifically, when GSG/GI is below 1.0, net outflows of the time-lagged money–information markers of Cr, O, and S, taken as a group, have contributed to MEI or Mo or both. When it is above 1.0, the organization has forgone MEI or Mo or both for net inflows of the time-lagged money–information markers of Cr, O, and S, taken as a group. For example,

$MaI + PI + EI + CoI = MEI$, $MEI - (MoO - MoI) = GI$,
$GI - (Cr + O + S) = GSG$, where $+$ Cr, O and S are outflows,
      (a) $100 + 75 + 50 + 25 = 250$, $250 + 10 = 260$,
           $260 - (50 + 10 - 15) = 215$,
      (b) $100 + 75 + 50 + 25 = 250$, $250 + 10 = 260$,
      $260 - (-50 + 10 - 15) = 315$
    (a) $\dfrac{GSG}{GI} = \dfrac{215}{260} = 0.83$, $0.83 < 1.0$,

therefore the net outflows, 45, of Cr, O, and S markers have contributed to the MEI amount of 250 and the Mo amount of 10.

    (b) $\dfrac{GSG}{GI} = \dfrac{315}{260} = 1.2$; $1.2 > 1.0$,

therefore the organization has forgone a potential increase of 55 in MEI to achieve net inflows of Cr, O, and S markers of 55.

The Mo monitoring ratio GI/MEI is below 1.0 when Mo (treasure) has been decreased to contribute to MEI or inflows of Cr, O, or S. When it is above 1.0, Mo has been increased, forgoing contribution to MEI or net inflows of Cr, O, or S. For example,

$MaI + PI + EI + CoI = MEI$, $MEI - (MoO - MoI) = GI$,
$GI - (Cr + O + S) = GSG$
    (a) $100 + 75 + 50 + 25 = 250$, $250 + 10 = 260$,
      $260 - (50 + 10 - 15) = 215$
    (b) $100 + 75 + 50 + 25 = 250$, $250 - 10 = 240$,
      $240 - (50 + 0 - 15) = 205$
    (a) $\dfrac{GI}{MEI} = \dfrac{260}{250} = 1.04$, $1.04 > 1.0$,

therefore Mo (treasure) was increased, forgoing a potential increase of MEI to 260.

    (b) $\dfrac{GI}{MEI} = \dfrac{240}{250} = 0.96$, $0.96 < 1.0$,

therefore Mo was decreased to maintain MEI at 250 despite
the failure to increase O by 10 as occurred in (a).

The ratio of GSG to MEI connects the analysis directly to matter–energy flows, ignoring changes in Mo. As a result, this ratio gets to the very heart of an organization's endurance over time, that is, the relative amount of its generated increase or decrease that contributes to matter–energy growth or decay. The

GSG/MEI ratio is above 1.0 when the organization is forgoing some certain amount of growth in deference to "building treasure," owners, creditors, or socialization. When it is below 1.0, the organization is growing some certain amount as a result of the benefits of owners, creditors, contributions by society, or the recirculation of treasure.

More specifically, when *GSG/MEI* is below 1.0, net outflows of *Cr*, *O*, and *S* markers and changes in *Mo* contributed to *MEI*. When it is above 1.0, *MEI* was forgone in favor of net inflows of *Cr*, *0*, or *S* markers or changes in *Mo*. For example,

$Ma + P + E + Co = MEI, MEI - (MoO - MoI) = GI,$
$GI - (Cr + O + S) = GSG$
(a) $100 + 75 + 50 + 25 = 250, 250 + 10 = 260,$
   $260 - (50 + 10 - 15) = 215$
(b) $100 + 75 + 50 + 25 = 250, 250 + 10 = 260$
   $260 - (-50 + 10 - 15) = 315$

(a) $\dfrac{GSG}{MEI} = \dfrac{215}{250} = 0.86; 0.86 < 1.0$

therefore net money-information marker flows have contributed 35 to *MEI* of 250.

(b) $\dfrac{GSG}{MEI} = \dfrac{315}{250} = 1.26; 1.26 > 1.0,$

therefore in this case, since *Mo* and *O* did not change, the organization has forgone potential increase of 65 in *MEI* in favor of either inflows of credit documents or payment of interest and inflows of socialization documents.

In Illustration 1, we begin with concrete process measurements and show how accountants adjust such measurements to GAAP-defined reports. Illustration 2, below, reverses the action. Actual accounting data are taken from the annual reports of J. C. Penney Company and W. T. Grant, Inc., and restated in terms of concrete system processes.

If the usefulness of our theory of the accounting measurement of concrete process is to be tested, analyses similar to those shown in this second illustration must be used. It is unlikely that any extensive studies can be based on reorganizing the accounts themselves, as is assumed in Illustration 1. Why would society reorganize an accounting system to conform to a theory not yet proven to be useful? We believe that the concrete process analysis, CPA, demonstrated in Illustration 2 provides a method to extensively and effectively demonstrate at a general level the usefulness of the measurement theory.

Illustration 2. Given: Information taken from the annual reports of J. C. Penney Company and W. T. Grant, Inc., as reported in *Moody's Industrial Manual*. To illustrate the restatement procedure, we use data for J. C. Penney Company for the years 1964 and 1965. A worksheet similar to that shown in Table 7–9 is used to determine the sources and uses of funds and to prove the articulation of the

Table 7–9
Sources and Uses Worksheet, J. C. Penney Company, 1965

Assets	1965	1964	Source(1) Change	Use(0)
U.S. Government Securities	$ 61,000,000	$ 8,000,000	$53,000,000	0
Prepaid Taxes, Rents, Etc.	11,000,000	9,000,000	2,000,000	0
Accounts Receivable	107,000,000	227,000,000	(120,000,000)	1
Merchandise Inventory	311,000,000	285,000,000	26,000,000	0
Land	24,000,000	16,000,000	8,000,000	0
Furniture and Fixtures	182,000,000	169,000,000	13,000,000	0
Improvements to Leased Property	15,000,000	11,000,000	4,000,0000	0
Accumulated Depreciation	109,000,000	102,000,000	(7,000,000)	1
Liabilities & Equity				
Accounts Payable	152,000,000	57,000,000	95,000,000	1
Notes Payable	0	79,000,000	(79,000,000)	0
Accrued Taxes	0	10,000,000	(10,000,000)	0
Other Accrued Items	0	60,000,000	(60,000,000)	0
Fed. Income Taxes Payable	35,000,000	39,000,000	(4,000,000)	0
Dividends Payable	15,000,000	15,000,000	0	
Lease Payable	0	7,000,000	(7,000,000)	0
Def. Fed. Inc. Tax	42,000,000	30,000,000	12,000,000	1
Common Stock	39,000,000	39,000,000	0	
Total Revenue (Sales)			2,079,000,000	1
Cost of Sales			1,530,000,000	0
Depre., Depletion & Amort.			7,000,000	0
Selling & Admin. Expenses			412,000,000	0
Dividends & Misc. Income			4,000,000	1
Increase in Equity			5,000,000	1
Interest Paid			9,000,000	0
Federal Income Taxes			58,000,000	0
Common Dividends			37,000,000	0
Actual Change in Cash & Short-Term Securities		$7,000,000	7,000,000	0
Net Change of Cash & Short-Term Securities per analysis		(3,000,000)		
Unexplained Difference in Retained Earnings		(2,000,000)		
Other Inarticulation of Data		$(2,000,000)		

data. A worksheet rather than an equation is used to help locate errors and discrepancies.

Next, a funds flow statement is constructed based on the sources and uses identified on the worksheet (see Table 7–10). The logic of the statement is similar to that generally used by accountants for sources and uses statements. However, we classify the funds provided and used by six primary categories, that is, funds provided by matter–energy outflows, funds used by matter–energy inflows, funds provided by time-lagged money–information marker outflows, funds used by time-lagged money–information marker inflows, funds provided by accounting adjustments, and funds used by accounting adjustments. Additionally, the increase or decrease in cash is stated separately as are sales and other matter–energy process-generated income. The cash is stated separately so that it may be used to identify gross inflows (GI) in the CPA described above. All matter–energy process generated income (revenue from operations generally) is removed to keep from duplicating information captured by CPA in MEI and Mo.

Obviously, this estimation procedure suffers from the netting of outflows against inflows and vice versa in the permanent accounts. This limitation on the data precludes directly comparing analyses across organizations. However, comparing global patterns of MEI and money–information marker flows should demonstrate that a similar feedback exists between various organizations in society. Differences can be discovered as society provides public information about both inflows and outflows on balance sheet accounts and requires such accounts as Selling and Administrative Expenses to be disaggregated to costs of materials, personnel, energy, and communications. In the meantime, however, information about additions to Plant and Equipment and other such accounts is often provided publically or may be reasonably estimated from combinations of disclosures in different accounts.

Numerous classification decisions must be made to construct the funds flow statement of Table 7–10. For example, when a company uses funds to hire labor and buy electricity, it is importing forms of matter–energy. The monetary value of such elements is recorded in the Cost of Sales account. Therefore, Cost of Sales is classified as Funds Used by Matter–Energy Inflows on Table 7–10. In addition to the $1.53 billion of such matter–energy elements as labor and energy recorded in Cost of Sales, J. C. Penney Company brought into the firm $26 million of similar items. These items are reported in the Inventory account in accordance with Accounting Research Bulletin No. 43 (AICPA, 1953). We know this because Inventory increased by $26 million during 1965. Consequently, the increase in Inventory also is recognized on Table 7–10 as Funds Used by Matter–Energy Inflows. If Inventory had decreased, Cost of Sales would have included monetary values of matter–energy elements that were actually imported during a previous period. In that case, we would deduct the decrease in Inventory from the Funds Used by Matter–Energy Inflows section.

Another example of related classification decisions concerns Funds Used by

Table 7–10
Statement of Funds Flow, J. C. Penney Company, 1965

Funds Provided by Matter-Energy Outflows:	None	
Funds Used by Matter-Energy Inflows:		
Increase in Land	$ 8,000,000	
Increase in Furniture & Fixtures	13,000,000	
Increase in Improv. to Leased Prop.	4,000,000	
Cost of Sales	1,530,000,000	
Change in Inventory, Inc. (Dec.)	26,000,000	
Selling and Administrative Expense	412,000,000	
TOTAL FUNDS USED BY MEI		$(1,993,000,000)
Funds Provided by Time-Lagged Money-		
Information Marker Outflows:		
Dividends and Misc. Income	$ 4,000,000	
Increase in Equity	5,000,000	
Increase in Accounts Payable	95,000,000	
Decrease in Accounts Receivable	120,000,000	
TOTAL FUNDS PROVIDED BY TL-MIMO		224,000,000
Funds Used by Time-Lagged Money-		
Information Marker Inflows:		
Interest Expense	$ 9,000,000	
Federal Income Taxes	58,000,000	
Increase in Def. Fed. Income Tax	(12,000,000)	
Common Dividends	37,000,000	
Decrease in Notes Payable	79,000,000	
Decrease in Accrued Taxes	10,000,000	
Decrease in Other Accrued Items	60,000,000	
Decrease in Fed. Income Tax Payable	4,000,000	
Decrease in Lease Payable	7,000,000	
Increase in Govt. Securities	53,000,000	
Increase in Prepaid Tax, Rent, Etc.	2,000,000	
TOTAL FUNDS USED BY TL-MIMI		(307,000,000)
Net Currency Money-Information		
Marker Inflows:		
Net Increase in Cash		(7,000,000)
Funds Provided by Matter-Energy		
Generated Income:		
Sales		2,079,000,000
Funds Provided and Used by Off-		
setting Accounting Adjustments:		
Increase in Total Accum. Deprec.		7,000,000
Depreciation Expense		(7,000,000)
Unexplained Uses		$(4,000,000)
Explained by Inarticulation of		
1964 Ending Balance and 1965		
Beginning Balance in R/E		2,000,000
Unexplained Inarticulation of Data		$(2,000,000)

Time-Lagged Money–Information Marker Inflows for federal income taxes. Typically, funds are used to retrieve time-lagged money–information markers termed Federal Income Taxes Payable. The record of all such markers originating during a particular accounting period is generally maintained in the account Federal Income Taxes. This account showed $58 million for 1965; therefore, we classify this as Funds Used by Time-Lagged Money–Information Marker Inflows on Table 7–10. Some Federal Income Taxes Payable are generally outstanding at the end of each accounting period, however. Any change in the amount of these outstanding payables must be taken into consideration because funds are used or provided to bring about the change. In 1965, funds were used to decrease by $4 million the amount in the Federal Income Taxes Payable account. Therefore, this amount must also be added to the Funds Used by Time-Lagged Money–Information Marker Inflows on Table 7–10.

Accounting for the time-lagged money–information markers involved with federal income taxes is further complicated by APB Opinion No. 11 (AICPA, 1967) and FASB Statement No. 95 (1987). Under GAAP, generally the account Federal Income Taxes is adjusted to reflect the product of the prevailing tax rate(s) and net income before such items as discontinued operations, extraordinary items, and the cumulative effects of changes in accounting principles. The effects of this adjustment and adjustments based on other inarticulations between taxable income and GAAP income are reflected in the account Federal Deferred Income Taxes. Federal income taxes, although often based on matter–energy flows such as investments in machinery, are strictly money–information marker flows. That is to say, the currency money–information markers extracted from the firm constitute the economic effect of these taxes. These markers are not available to entice matter–energy inflows. Therefore, we adjust the Federal Income Taxes account to reflect the deferrals or accruals in the Deferred Federal Income Tax account. This is done on Table 7–10 by deducting the 1965 increase of $12 million in Deferred Federal Income Taxes from the Funds Used by Time-Lagged Money Information Marker Inflows section. Intuitively, currency money–information markers were *not* given up to the extent that the account Deferred Federal Income Taxes was increased instead of increasing Federal Income Taxes Payable.

The information from Table 7–10 required for CPA is summarized in Table 7–11. However, Table 7–11 is more than a summary of pertinent information about funds flows as accountants typically view them. It also rearranges the relationships of the information to reflect the circuitous relationship between matter–energy flows and money–information marker flows between organizations. That is to say, it recognizes the inverse relationship between the left-side and right-side terms of identity (7–1).

In Table 7–11, matter–energy inflows are assigned positive values, and similar outflows are ignored, as discussed above. The sum of these matter–energy inflows is *MEI*. Net currency money–information marker inflows (*Mo*) are summed with *MEI* to calculate gross inflows (*GI*). Next, time-lagged money–information

Table 7-11
Concrete Process Analysis, J. C. Penney Company, 1965

MATTER-ENERGY INFLOWS (MEI):	$1,993,000,000
ADD:	
NET CURRENCY MONEY-INFORMATION MARKER	
INFLOWS:	
Net increase (decrease) in cash (Mo)	<u>7,000,000</u>
GROSS INFLOWS (GI)	$2,000,000,000
ADD:	
TIME-LAGGED MONEY-INFORMATION MARKER	
NET INFLOWS:	
Funds used by time-lagged money-	
information marker inflows $307,000,000	
Subtract:	
Funds provided by time-lagged	
money-information marker outflows <u>224,000,000</u>	
NET TIME-LAGGED MIMI	<u>83,000,000</u>
GROSS MATTER-ENERGY SYSTEM GENERANT (GSG)	<u>$2,083,000,000</u>

$$GSG/GI = 1.042$$
$$GI/MEI = 1.004$$
$$GSG/MEI = 1.045$$

marker net inflows are added to the *GI* to arrive at gross matter–energy system generant (*GSG*). This operation has the same result as subtracting net outflows. This relationship holds because to the extent that time-lagged money–information marker net outflows generated net currency money–information inflows, matter–energy process-generated income did not.

Caveat: In equation (7–2), the time-lagged money–information marker net is actually in terms of outflows, whereas the matter–energy net is in terms of inflows. Consequently, in this section of the CPA statement, funds provided by time-lagged money—information marker outflows would be assigned a positive value while the opposite treatment would be given similar inflows. In the example being used in Table 7–11, when the inflows exceed the outflows, a negative amount would be subtracted from *GI*, thus increasing the amount of *GI* to arrive at *GSG*. Intuitively, this makes sense because the firm must have forgone currency money–information markers or matter–energy to bring about inflows of time-lagged money–information markers. Consequently, the *GSG* must have been larger than the *GI*. The same end can be achieved, however, by reversing the signs of inflows and outflows of time-lagged money–information markers and adding the net to *GI*. This is what we do in Table 7–11.

Generally, this logic treats monetary assets differently than does common accounting logic (Swanson and Miller, 1988). For example, the common logic treats inflows of the time-lagged money–information marker accounts receivable (increases) as assets. Net assets are used by various societal deciders to estimate a firm's strength. What actually happens when accounts receivable are increased is that management forgoes the use of currency money–information markers. Considering the wide acceptance of the time-value-of-money model, it is unlikely that many economic actors would view as a positive development the need to forgo the use of money today in favor of its later use. With reference to matter–energy processes, increases in accounts receivable are extractions of currency money–information markers that might have been used to increase those processes, but were not. Balance sheets, statements of residuals, would reflect more accurately the processes of the organizations whose structures they represent if increases in monetary assets were netted against liabilities and owners' equity.

In the CPA discussed below, the system of ratios calculated on the Concrete Process Analysis statement in Table 7–11 is connected to relative changes over time of absolute amounts of matter–energy inflows, MEI, and used to map the influences of management actions on the growth and decay of J. C. Penney Company and W. T. Grant, Inc. J. C. Penney Company continues to be one of the largest retailers of its type. W. T. Grant, Inc., filed for bankruptcy in 1975 when it was just below J. C. Penney in size, after many years of successful business endeavor.

Figure 7–1 plots for W. T. Grant the absolute amounts of MEI and the ratio *GSG/MEI*. By using these two sets of information in tandem, the results of management actions and system feedback can be mapped at this level of aggregation.

For example, Figure 7–1 shows that in 1956 the ratio *GSG/MEI* decreased. The following year the growth rate of *MEI* decreased and the ratio *GSG/MEI* increased. In the periods 1958 and 1959, a similar pattern occurred. In 1961 a decrease in the growth rate occurred, but it was not sufficient to turn around the decreasing ratio. The *GSG/MEI* continued to decrease through 1963 while the growth rate of MEI increased dramatically. This cumulating imbalance was finally reversed in 1964 not simply by an adjustment of the growth rate, but by an absolute reduction of *MEI*. In every case, decreases in the ratio *GSG/MEI* were reversed by an appropriate degree of reduction in the growth rate of *MEI*.

Generally, when *GSG/MEI* decreased, a decrease in the growth rate of *MEI* occurred within two periods. Table 7–12 describes the adjustment process. Mostly, such adjustments occurred in the same or the following period. As the slide in *GSG/MEI* began in 1971 and grew progressively worse through 1973, however, inadequate adjustment in the growth rate of MEI was made. In fact, after an initial reduction in 1971 failed to turn the *GSG/MEI* around, large increases occurred in the growth rate of MEI in 1972 and 1973. This inadequate adjustment triggered a pathological positive feedback which culminated in bankruptcy.

Figure 7–1
MEI and GSG/MEI for W. T. Grant, 1955–1974

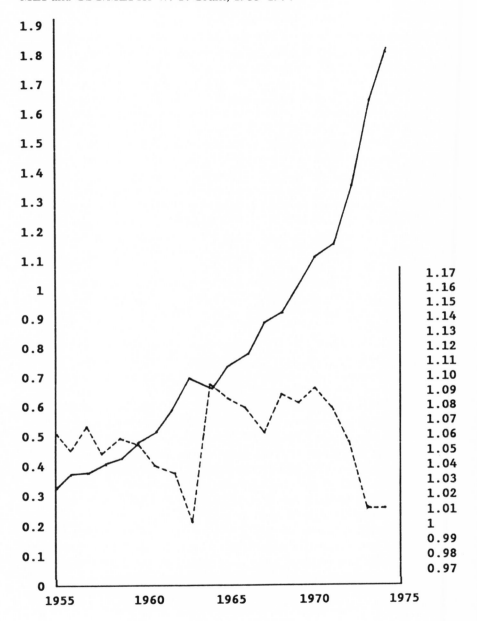

— MEI in billions of dollars on left-side scale

--- GSG/MEI using decimal scale on right side

Table 7–12
Analysis of W. T. Grant Company

Year	GSG/MEI	Increase/Decrease		Growth Rate of MEI
1955	1.061	Decrease	Decrease	6.67%
1956	1.051	Decrease	Increase	11.31%
1957	1.065	Increase	Decrease	7.77%
1958	1.049	Decrease	Increase	8.16%
1959	1.058	Increase	Decrease	5.31%
1960	1.053	Decrease	Increase	11.70%
1961	1.039	Decrease	Decrease	7.88%
1962	1.034	Decrease	Increase	14.03%
1963	1.006	Decrease	Increase	21.06%
1964	1.093	Increase	Decrease	-4.75%
1965	1.085	Decrease	Increase	10.79%
1966	1.075	Decrease	Decrease	8.10%
1967	1.062	Decrease	Increase	12.66%
1968	1.088	Increase	Decrease	3.56%
1969	1.082	Decrease	Increase	12.67%
1970	1.091	Increase	Decrease	9.49%
1971	1.079	Decrease	Decrease	6.51%
1972	1.054	Decrease	Increase	11.61%
1973	1.010	Decrease	Increase	24.27%
1974	1.013	Increase	Decrease	11.39%

For this organization, the mapping of matter–energy flows reflects a fluctuous steady-state pattern like that asserted by LST. It also suggests that when portions of the specific exchange value generated by the organization provided to creditors, owners, and socialization processes declined, a downward adjustment of the growth rate of matter–energy inflows generally occurred to rebalance the system.

This map is drawn from a highly aggregated level of accounting information. Detailed maps could be provided from disaggregated information, like that suggested in our seven proposed changes in accounting procedures, that would make it possible for readers to identify specific organization elements that contribute to imbalances requiring corrective action.

The ratio GSG/MEI goes to the very heart of an organization's endurance over time. It does this by connecting the analysis directly to matter–energy flows. GSG/MEI provides an estimate of the relative amount of a system's generated increases or decreases that contribute to matter–energy growth or decay. Changes in this relationship influence changes in the rate of growth or decay in the absolute value of MEI.

Consequently, changes in GSG/MEI may be used to forecast directional changes in the rate of growth or decay of the absolute value of MEI. This is the case because the ratio measures a signal at an earlier point in a cross-level (between organization and society) feedback loop. The development of a path-

Table 7–13
Analysis of J. C. Penney Company

Year	GSG/MEI	Increase/Decrease		Growth Rate of MEI
1962	1.093	Increase	Increase	6.19%
1963	1.059	Decrease	Increase	10.84%
1964	1.042	Decrease	Decrease	8.60%
1965	1.045	Increase	Increase	12.99%
1966	1.008	Decrease	Decrease	12.15%
1967	1.005	Decrease	Increase	13.67%
1968	1.049	Increase	Decrease	3.24%
1969	1.020	Decrease	Increase	24.87%
1970	1.030	Increase	Decrease	11.26%
1971	1.019	Decrease	Increase	12.44%
1972	1.017	Decrease	Increase	14.89%
1973	1.038	Increase	Decrease	13.07%
1974	1.045	Increase	Decrease	12.58%
1975	1.053	Increase	Increase	18.99%
1976	1.053	No change	Decrease	1.68%
1977	1.040	Decrease	Increase	10.12%
1978	1.003	Decrease	Increase	16.34%
1979	.985	Decrease	Increase	17.28%
1980	1.071	Increase	Decrease	-3.87%

ological positive feedback is not evident in the growth pattern of *MEI* itself. This is the case because society triggers bankruptcy by connecting bankruptcy law to money–information marker flows rather than to matter–energy flows. The health of the growth pattern (positive or negative) of *MEI* must be judged in the context of an organization's relationship to its suprasystem. It is likely that if that relationship falls into a pathological positive feedback that decreases in MEI fail to turn around, the organization will disintegrate.

Table 7–13 provides values calculated from actual data for *GSG/MEI* and the growth/decay rate of *MEI* for J.C. Penney Company. A similar pattern of management actions can be observed in it. For example, the 1965 *GSG/MEI* is 1.045 and increased over the previous year. That same year *MEI* increased by 12.99 percent. In 1966 the *GSG/MEI* decreased significantly and management reduced slightly the rate of growth of *MEI* (inputs of materials, personnel, energy, etc.). In 1967, however, the *GSG/MEI* remained low. During this period management again increased the rate of growth of *MEI*. Therefore, in the following year (1968), management decreased the growth rate of *MEI* greatly, and the *GSG/MEI* increased to a viable level. Also, a three-year imbalance of cumulative decreasing *GSG/MEI* and increasing growth rate of *MEI* was reversed in 1980 by an absolute reduction of *MEI*.

Obviously, we cannot draw conclusions about specific management actions on such examples. The illustration of the analysis methodology should clarify

Figure 7–2
Net Income for W. T. Grant, 1955–1974

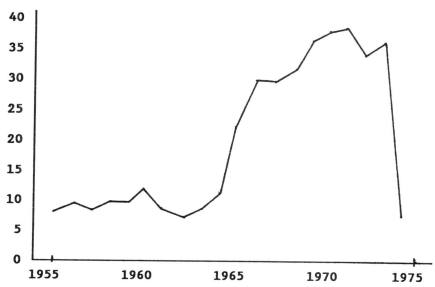

what we mean by CPA, however. While precise cosmic estimates on companies within and across industry may provide standards to evaluate and forecast management actions to some degree, we believe the larger contribution of CPA lies in analyzing disaggregated information within mature organizations over varying periods.

Living systems theory provides extensive documentation of twenty critical subsystems of organizations—processes that must be carried out for an organization to endure (Miller, 1978.) These subsystems maintain steady-state relationships (vary within relatively narrow ranges) among themselves. All of these are concrete processes and are traced by accounting information systems in some fashion (Swanson and Miller, 1986). CPA at that level of specificity may provide a basis to fully integrate on-line management and accounting information systems. How such analyses may be performed is discussed in Chapter 8.

Public Disclosure of Concrete Process Information

Within the boundaries set by GAAP, managers are given wide latitude in selecting values composing the net income amount that is disclosed in a particular period. Figure 7–2 shows that the net income of W. T. Grant was pushed to the largest absolute amount in the history of the company and generally maintained there during the period it was sliding into bankruptcy. Largay and Stickney (1980) have shown that other key accounting variables likewise did not present evidence that the company was on a slide into bankruptcy—only that many internal problems existed.

Typically, the combined effect of accounting adjustments is to remove from the net income amount much of its raw accounting measurement information. Information based on analyzing the concrete flows, both matter–energy flows and money–information marker flows, may be publicly disclosed. Such disclosure would provide a relatively unbiased, with reference to the basic accounting measurement method, referent for users to judge the effects of the various interpretive decision model assumptions now incorporated in accounting reports. Additionally, it could provide information about the concrete flows of organizations to be used in scientific investigations that are designed to aid society-level policy decisions.

The disclosure could be made initially in a footnote. Although thorough study must dictate an actual composition, the following example specifies the sort of detail that possibly should be disclosed.

Footnote 1. The concrete processes of XYZ Corporation for the period January 1, 1988, to December 31, 1988, aggregated from raw accounting measurements taken at the boundary of the entity, are as follows:

Materials inflows	000	
Materials outflows		000
Personnel inflows	000	
Personnel outflows		000
Energy inflows	000	
Energy outflows		000
Communications inflows	<u>000</u>	
Communications outflows		000
Total Matter–Energy inflows	000	
Total Matter–Energy outflows		<u>000</u>
Currency Money Information Markers (inflows-outflows)	<u>00</u>	
Gross Inflows	000	
Less:		
Credit documents (outflows-inflows)	000	
Owner documents (outflows-inflows)	000	
Socialization documents (outflows-inflows)	<u>000</u>	<u>000</u>
Gross system generated increment or decrement		<u>000</u>

Concrete processes information is based on measurements and aggregations of individual exchanges of the entity with other entities, and it describes specific exchange value in terms of dollars. No GAAP adjustments are made. The information is provided so that informed users of the accounting statements may judge the effects of various GAAP adjustments on the raw accounting measurements.

Table 7–14
ABC Company Process Report for Accounting Period Ended 19XX

MEASUREMENTS MADE ON CONCRETE PROCESSES:

Matter-Energy Inflows (MEI)	\$XXX	
Net Currency Money-Information Marker Inflows (Mo)	X	
Gross Inflows (GI)	\$XXXXX	
Net Time-Lagged Money-Information Marker Inflows	XX	
Gross Matter-Energy System Generant (GSG)		\$XXXXX

INTERPRETATIONS BASED ON GAAP

To estimate the MEI of past and current periods that contributed to revenues generated during the current period	XXX
To estimate current market values of certain residual variables that are stated in terms of specific exchange values	XX
To estimate certain observation errors and legal obligations that exist but are not yet quantified in terms of money-information markers	XX
To estimate revenues generated during the current period	(XXXXX)
GAAP Net (Income) Loss	\$ (XX)

If the public disclosure of concrete process information proves to be as valuable as we believe it may be, disclosure should be made in the body of financial statements themselves. Table 7–14 suggests a possible format that would include such disclosure.

This format explicitly distinguishes among accounting variables that may be predictive (as discussed in Chapter 2) and thus may be used forthrightly for planning and control and those variables that are prospective (anticipate the future). The section "Measurements Made on Concrete Processes" may be analyzed for patterns that persist over time. Such patterns form a basis for predicting how certain changes affect an organization's processes. The Gross Matter–Energy System Generant (GSG) is a summary variable of this class of variables. On the other hand, the section "Interpretations Based on GAAP" incorporates prospective variables that may be useful for forecasting an organization's future.

This second section is classified into three subsections, each summarizing a set of typical accounting adjustments as follows:

1. To estimate the *MEI* of past and current periods that contributed to revenues generated during the current period. Inflows of some types of *MEI* are not always exhausted during a particular accounting period. Those residuals may be used in future periods to entice additional *MEI* and, consequently, have some forecasting usefulness.

2. To estimate current market values of certain residual variables. All *MEI* is measured in terms of specific exchange value. Some types of *MEI* have value in use, and others have value in exchange. Some forecasting utility may be obtained by restating certain *MEI* residuals that have value only in exchange, in terms of estimated current exchange values.

3. To estimate certain observation errors and legal obligations that exist but are not yet quantified in terms of money–information markers. Observation errors may be made when accounts receivable are extended. Because the law requires their conversion to currency according to an implied contract (under penalty), most accounts receivable are converted. Sometimes, however, an account is extended to a person or firm who does not pay. This error in judgment may be estimated, and such estimates may provide useful forecasting information. Firms that sell products are constrained by law to warrant that their products do what they are intended to do. Because of manufacturing errors, some few products may not perform as intended. The firm is required to replace or repair any defective products. Engineers have been able to estimate within relatively narrow ranges the number of products in a large population that are defective. Consequently, this information may have forecasting utility.

Statisticians have found that residual variables often contain important information. Residual statements based on the section, "Measurements Made on Concrete Processes" of Table 7–14 can be constructed by aggregating the series of process reports beginning with an organization's inception period and progressing without omissions through each intervening period to the current one. This aggregation provides a statement of organizational structure at the instant that marks the end of the current period. The section interpretations based on GAAP give rise to additional residual variables that are believed generally to provide certain prospective information.

Summary

In Chapter 7 we discuss how LST would change accounting recording and reporting procedures. Two illustrations of the application of concrete process analyses, CPAs, are provided. One begins with measurements made on concrete process elements and restates such values in terms of GAAP. The other one reverses the action and proceeds from GAAP-adjusted variables to estimates of measurements of concrete processes. In Chapter 8 we discuss how living systems process analysis, LSPA, may be used to allocate internally concrete process measurements to the critical subsystems of organizations and other societal systems.

References

American Institute of Certified Public Accountants (AICPA). *Accounting Research Bulletin No. 43*, New York: AICPA, 1953.

_____. Accounting Principles Board, *Opinion No. 11*, AICPA, 1967.

Financial Accounting Standards Board (FASB). *Statement of Cash Flows* (FASB Statement No. 95). FASB, 1987.

Largay, J. A. III, and C. P. Stickney. "Cash Flows, Ratio Analyses and the W. T. Grant Company Bankruptcy." *Financial Analysis Journal* (July–August, 1980), pp. 51–54.

Miller, James Grier. *Living Systems*. New York: McGraw-Hill, 1978.

Swanson, G. A., and J. G. Miller. "Accounting Information Systems in the Framework of Living Systems Theory and Research." *Systems Research* (1986), 4, pp. 253–65.

_____. "Distinguishing between Measurements and Interpretations in Public Accounting Reports." *Behavioral Science* 33 (1988), pp. 1–24.

8
CONCRETE PROCESS ANALYSIS (CPA) AND LIVING SYSTEMS PROCESS ANALYSIS (LSPA)

Introduction

Systems science research is concerned with processes and structures of complex heterogeneous systems. Such systems may be composed of entirely nonliving elements, of entirely living elements, or of mixed living and nonliving elements. LST-defined living systems above the organism level typically are composed of mixed living and nonliving elements. Those living systems include man-machine systems.

Generally, natural ecological systems as distinguished from human systems, while composed of mixed living and nonliving elements, are not consciously constructed and controlled by a human decider subsystem. These systems are, in fact, competitive environments, markets, held in a fluctuant steady-state over time by both opposing and parallel forces of the competition of their components for survival. The composite of relationships that the components establish is the stuff that in some cases gives rise to higher-level living systems but in other cases simply dissipates. If all twenty critical processes are carried out at or for the higher level of organization, a higher-level living system emerges.

As humans contemplate colonizing space, they must learn to construct ecosystems based on specific survival characteristics. Such a purpose introduces a conscious human decider subsystem into those ecosystems. Consequently, such ecosystems are higher-level human living systems within the LST definition of the term.

A similar ecosystem, that is, an ecosystem consciously constructed by humans, exists on the earth; but it has not been generally recognized as such. This ecosystem is what is commonly termed the market economy. It is interesting that long before "eco-logy" came into emphasis, "eco-nomy" was being studied extensively. Yet modern ecologists who discover ecological dysfunctions brought about by human actions often seek political rather than economic solutions. It seems that a logical connection exists between the questions that concern how to correct natural ecosystem dysfunctions caused by human system intrusions and those concerned with the major human-constructed ecosystem, the economy.

Because both space habitation and Earth's economic activity involve ecosystems consciously constructed by humans, we have chosen to illustrate living systems process analysis (LSPA) by using a proposal for research to be conducted under the sponsorship of the National Aeronautics and Space Administration (NASA) (Miller et al., 1988). We first survey briefly certain other applications of LSPA, followed by a summarized description of the NASA proposal. Afterward, we discuss how the accounting measurement theory that we have developed in prior chapters and have incorporated in CPA can be integrated with LSPA.

Applications of LSPA

Although all living systems are concrete systems and therefore subject to the laws of thermodynamics, they are able apparently to defy the Second Law of Thermodynamics. In its most general form, this law of nature indicates that the most probable state of concrete systems, toward which all such systems that are isolated tend, is an equilibrium of randomly distributed molecules. Living systems are able to maintain a nonrandom and therefore improbable state because they are open systems that exchange inputs and outputs of matter and energy with their environments. Nicolis and Prigogine (1977) term this phenomenon *self-organization*.

Systems scientists use models (mainly numerical ones) to discover and display isomorphisms (formal identities) among systems of different types and levels. Models that are capable of handling the nonlinear interactions among large numbers of variables characteristic of living systems have been developed. Prigogine (1947) originated nonlinear thermodynamics, the thermodynamics of irreversible processes, to provide models for systems of this sort. Such models use various relatively new theories, for example, hierarchy theory, catastrophe theory, set theory, fuzzy set theory, and bifurcation theory. Additionally, numerous other mathematical approaches have been used to analyze data on living systems, for example, information theory, game theory, cluster analysis, factor analysis, decision theory, queuing theory, and statistical decision theory. What is being learned from this analytical science may be used within the framework of LST to test empirically various derived specific purpose theories.

Living Systems (Miller, 1978) provides 173 testable cross-level (e.g., between group and organization) hypotheses. Some of these apply to all eight hierarchical levels of living systems, and others apply to two or more levels. Several have been tested empirically. Additionally, many LST studies have been done at one hierarchical level of living systems. It is very important that measurements or indicators be developed for structures and processes of systems at all levels and that normal values and ranges of critical variables be determined. This has been achieved for thousands of physiological variables that concern human beings. Normal values and ranges of many variables of interest to psychologists are also known, particularly in areas like sensation, perception, learning, and child behavior; and many ranges have not yet been established. Such information on higher-level systems could be obtained but efforts to do so are rarely made. We believe that CPA and LSPA provide methods for establishing normal values and ranges for many important variables at these levels of life.

Multilevel Research

The first multilevel experimental test of a hypothesis derived from LST was research on information input overload (Miller, 1960, 1978). The following hypothesis was tested at the levels of cell, organ, organism, group, and organization:

As the information input to a single channel of a living system—measured in bits per second—increases, the information output—measured similarly—increases almost identically at first but gradually falls behind as it approaches a certain output rate, the channel capacity, which cannot be exceeded in the channel. The output then levels off at that rate, and finally, as the information input rate continues to go up, the output decreases gradually toward zero as breakdown or the confusional state occurs under overload. (Miller, 1978, p. 122)

Specialists in the relevant fields conducted the experiments at each level. Measurements of information input and output rates were made for (1) the cell on single fibers from the sciatic nerves of frogs, (2) the organ on optic tracts of white rats (retina or optic nerves to optic cortex), (3) the organism on human subjects working alone, (4) the group on human subjects in triads, and (5) the organization on human subjects arranged in laboratory ''organizations'' composed of nine subjects.

For example, at the organization level, one form of experimental organization consisted of two groups of three people who simultaneously received information inputs. Each of these groups consisted of two members serving as input transducers and a third member who served as output transducer. Each input transducer member received a different sequence of visual inputs. These members sent electronic signals to the third member of the group who output them to a display before one member of a three-person group in another room. Each of those members forwarded the signals received to a final person in a second room, who acted as decider and output transducer for the organization level. This person compared the signals, made a decision about them for the total organization, and output the decision to a recording device.

The results of the experiments confirmed the hypothesis of a formal identity in this aspect of information processing at those five hierarchical levels of living

Figure 8–1
Theoretical Curve on Logarithmic Coordinates Based on Average Perfor-
mance Data of Five Levels of Living Systems under Various Rates of Pulse–
Interval Coded Information Input

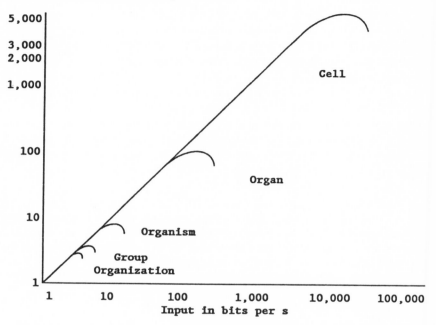

Source: James G. Miller, **Living Systems**, McGraw-Hill, 1978.

systems. Data from all five levels yielded information input-output curves alike
in form. Each curve rose sharply at first, leveled off, and then, as the channel
capacity of the systems was exceeded, fell toward zero. Average transmission
rates at which transmissions were processed were lower at each higher level (see
Figure 8–1).

Organization-Level Research

LSPA provides a method for analyzing the structures and processes of organizations in order to discover malfunctions that reduce effectiveness in achieving
their purposes. This method has been used to study several different kinds of
organizations. Some examples follow:

1. Hospitals (Merker and Lusher, 1987)
2. The components, variables, and possible pathologies of the subsystems of the inpatient
   psychiatric unit of a university hospital (Chase, Wright, and Ragade, 1981)

3. Several public schools in a community (Banathy and Bell, 1985)

4. A public transportation system (Bryant and Merker, 1987)

5. U.S. Army battalions (Ruscoe et al., 1985)

6. An IBM study of organizations generally (unpublished)

The last two examples are briefly described below.

Measurements of effectiveness may be made with reference to financial variables, such as profit indicators or costs per unit of goods or services output. They may also relate to less global indicators, such as mortality rates of hospital patients, rates of attendance at performances or meetings, or numbers of people applying for admission to a university. The factors that contribute to effectiveness within an organization can be revealed by monitoring flows of matter–energy and information through components or subsystems of the organization rather than using only inflow-outflow measurements at the boundary of the organization itself.

Different types of organizations are specialized for different subsystem processes of the society to which they contribute. A particular system may be very different from other types in the subsystems that are emphasized and in the types of living and machine components that carry out its processes. Organizations of the same type may also differ in many aspects of structure and process. Consequently, it is necessary to observe how an individual organization being investigated is structured and what living and nonliving components are involved in each process.

The first large-scale application of LSPA was a three-year study of forty-one U.S. Army battalions (cited above). The objective of this study was to use LSPA to explain how battalions function and to relate the quality and quantity of flows of material and information to battalion effectiveness.

Three types of data were collected: (1) findings of the army's traditional evaluation methods, which combine performance indicators, command indicators, and perceptions of personnel; (2) process perception data, which include opinions of unit personnel on how well each matter–energy and information process is being performed in terms of several process variables, the time spent on each by members of the unit and the unit as a whole, and the importance of each process; and (3) process objective data, which include such things as the percentage of the unit's vehicles that are operational at a particular time.

The data were collected by using standardized questionnaires, personal interviews with key management personnel, records and reports available within each unit, surveys provided by brigade-level managers, and check sheets completed by surveyors. More than 5,000 officers, noncommissioned officers, and other enlisted personnel from battalions in both the continental United States and Europe participated in the study.

Two sets of effectiveness criteria were employed: (1) the traditional army criteria and (2) a new set based on living systems theory. The living systems criteria led to conclusions similar to those based on traditional measurements about distinctions among battalions. However, the LST-based data revealed much more about the dynamics of the military units studied.

Among other discoveries, the study clearly revealed a relationship between information processing and effectiveness. The better a unit's information sub-system processes, the more effective it was. Where unit personnel possessed greater appreciation of and skill in information processing, a unit scored discriminately high on effectiveness indicators. Consequently, the information variables of meaning, lag, volume, cost, and distortion were repeatedly shown to be good indicators of unit effectiveness.

In addition to its findings, this study is significant because it developed field research procedures for applying LST empirically. We refer to such procedures developed in the army study and elsewhere as LSPA.

In unpublished studies within IBM Corporation, James Grier Miller and others are designing a comprehensive study similar in scope to that conducted for the U.S. Army. However, this study concerns all types of organization-level systems and uses several technological improvements. Civilian corporations and military battalions are different in many ways, but they have many similarities, including carrying out the same life processes. Consequently, many of the procedures developed in the army study are transferable. The IBM study differs from the army study in the following ways:

1. To be consistent with studies of organizational behavior over the last quarter of a century (Forrester, 1961), five rather than three concrete flows are measured. Instead of tracing flows in terms of the general classifications matter, energy, and information, this study monitors the following classifications of flows: materials (MATFLOW), energy (ENFLOW), communications (COMFLOW), money and money equivalents (MONFLOW), and personnel (PERSFLOW). Basically, these are the same matter–energy and information flows used in all other living systems research. Because such distinctions are clearly observable in organizations, information is divided into two classifications (communications and money) and an indivisible bundle of matter–energy (personnel) is recognized.

2. Only subjective information was collected in the army study. All objective data were taken from existing records. The IBM study uses badges with infrared sensors and transmitters that send signals to a central computer to actually track movements of the five classes of throughputs within organizations. The resultant data are used to confirm and interpret the subjective data collected by the procedures developed in the army study.

3. The army study used human interviewers to collect data. In the IBM study, subjects gave their responses to computers in standardized interviews.

4. Computerized expert systems were used to analyze the data. Two types of analyses were performed: (a) analyses on the interactions of components within an organization (ALIGH) and (b) analyses on interactions between an organization and the local, national, or supranational market in which it competes (IMPACT).

5. Three separate criteria of internal organizational effectiveness were used. They are: (a) independent opinions of several judges (chief executive officers) on the best strategy in different situations, (b) effectiveness criteria derived from the army study, and (c) effectiveness and productivity data from the extensive literature on organizations.

The above descriptions of the latter two examples of organization—level LST studies provide general insights into what we mean by LSPA. In the following section, we supply a larger description of a study proposed to be conducted under the auspices of NASA.

A Proposed NASA Study Using LSPA

Following preliminary studies at the California Space Institute, principal investigator James Grier Miller and a team of specialists in various sciences and technologies have proposed a NASA study applying LST to human space habitation. A synopsis of the proposal is presented in the following paragraphs.

The proposal is for a long-term systems research on space habitation. Its initial phase involves a twenty-four–month preliminary systems analysis of the flows and interactions of materials, energy, information, personnel, and money in an eight-person space station. A second phase (thirty-six months) contemplates the production of an artificial intelligence expert system to analyze and identify possible improvements in how living and mechanical components function in a space station prototype.

This study would have significant implications for other space habitations that may be established in the future on the moon, on Mars, or elsewhere. All the work is carried out within the conceptual framework of LST, an integrative biosocial theoretical and applied approach to living systems and technology that has been developed and tested over more than thirty years.

The study concentrates on the total mixed living-nonliving system composed of the space station and its components on the spacecraft. Quantitative readings are taken on component variables, and such readings are compared to normal values for each variable of each component to determine whether they are within normal ranges. A continuous record of their fluctuations is kept. In addition, if any variables exceed normal ranges in any direction that could indicate the presence of a problem or dysfunction, a knowledge-base-driven expert system in the network determines the best actions to correct it. If there is time for a human decision on the matter, the situation is reported to the officer of the watch together with a recommendation for action. If the time is inadequate, the computer system takes the action immediately.

The proposal integrates such a hardware-software system with components of the space station currently under consideration by NASA. In the initial two-year phase, the procedures developed in the study would be tested on whatever mock-up or simulation of the space station is indicated by NASA to be appropriate.

A dynamically programmable logic module, or DPLM (see Rumelhart,

Figure 8–2
Adaptive LST Expert System (ALEXSYS)

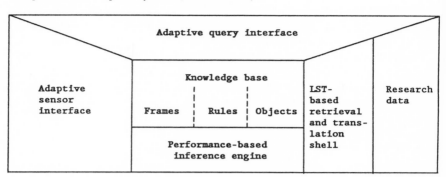

McClelland, and the PDP Research Group, 1986), network of special combinatorial architecture continuously receives signals from all living and nonliving inhabitants. A prototypical interface to planned technological information-processing computer systems is developed that employs sensors throughout the spacecraft itself, as well as sensors of human behavior. These sensors send signals on-line in real time to on-board parallel processing DPLMs. These signals report on the current states of variables of numerous flows of materials, energy, communications, personnel, and money and money equivalents in a very large number of living and nonliving space station components. When the space station is deployed, all such information will be stored for on-board analysis and also telemetered in real time to Earth.

The first phase of the research project is comprised of a rather complex progression of activities that culminate in what the researchers term an adaptive LST expert system (ALEXSYS). Figure 8–2 is a symbolic representation of the relationship of the activities and their products. To construct an ALEXSYS for a space station, the following activities are proposed:

1. Compile an extensive collection of research data and findings relevant to extraterrestrial habitation and human performance.

2. Construct an LST-based retrieval and translation shell. This software will make it easier for scientists to search systematically through human performance research data and to format those findings as required to create, expand, and maintain a working knowledge base.

3. Develop a performance-based inference engine. This artificial intelligence implementation will feature both forward and backward chaining and will take into account research findings about environmental constraints on human performance, sometimes termed the performance envelope.

4. Develop a query sensor interface to the knowledge base. This interface will (a) allow researchers to test and update the knowledge base, (b) provide human performance

and system management experts a means to input expert rules and scenarios into the knowledge base, and (c) give astronauts a tool for living systems status reporting and knowledge-base query.

5. Develop an adaptive sensor interface that can, in conjunction with a network of DPLM processors, monitor, evaluate, record, report, and, if necessary, improve space system performance and correct dysfunctions in real time.

6. Conduct a space personnel development study for systems analysis and management of the increasing number of spacefarers that are likely to go into space in the future. Beginning with the space station, there will probably be an ever-growing need for a space personnel deployment system (SPDS). The SPDS will be concerned with a personnel relocation cycle, including selection, recruitment, training, orientation, transportation to and incorporation into a space community, and finally re-entry to Earth and reaccommodation to it. The findings of this segment of the research are incorporated into the data set of item 1 above.

A set of symbols has been designed to represent the levels, subsystems, and major flows in living systems (see Figure 8–3). They are intended for use in simulations and various forms of diagrams. They can also be used in graphics and flow charts. These symbols are compatible with the standard symbols of electrical engineering and computer science.

Figures 8–4 and 8–5 illustrate major flows and the subsystems they concern. All of these flows are monitored in the manner described above. For a small system such as the space station to survive in an alien environment, the importance of such monitoring procedures is obvious.

The Integration of LSPA and CPA

Life processes similar to those described in the NASA study are performed by every living system on Earth, including organizations (e.g., corporations, government agencies, and not-for-profit entities). The space station seems to be a highly complex project when, in fact, it is quite simple compared to the life processes performed by a typical multinational corporation or the United States Government.

Because these higher-level systems process information more slowly, however, the ranges within which critical variables fluctuate are likely much greater. These greater ranges coupled with the relatively large quantities of scarce economic goods provided by past new frontiers and new discoveries of raw resources often have allowed managers to neglect monitoring many basic life processes. Furthermore, societal deciders in the past could rely quite extensively on ignorance to differentiate levels of organization—within the organization level between echelons of management and within supranational systems between levels of living systems. By this statement we mean that individuals operating at one living system level did not have the means to discover how those operating at a higher level functioned.

Figure 8–3
Living Systems Symbols

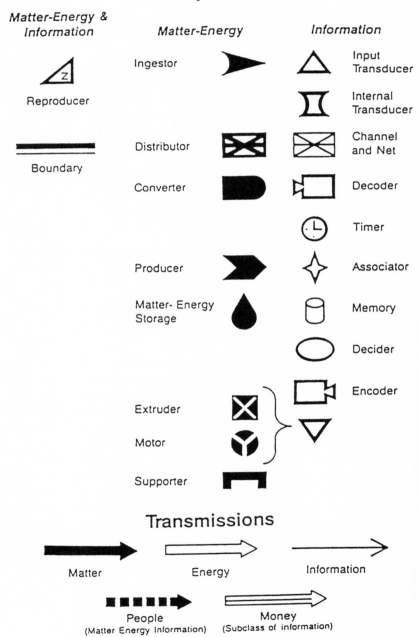

156

Figure 8–4
Matter Flows in the Space Station

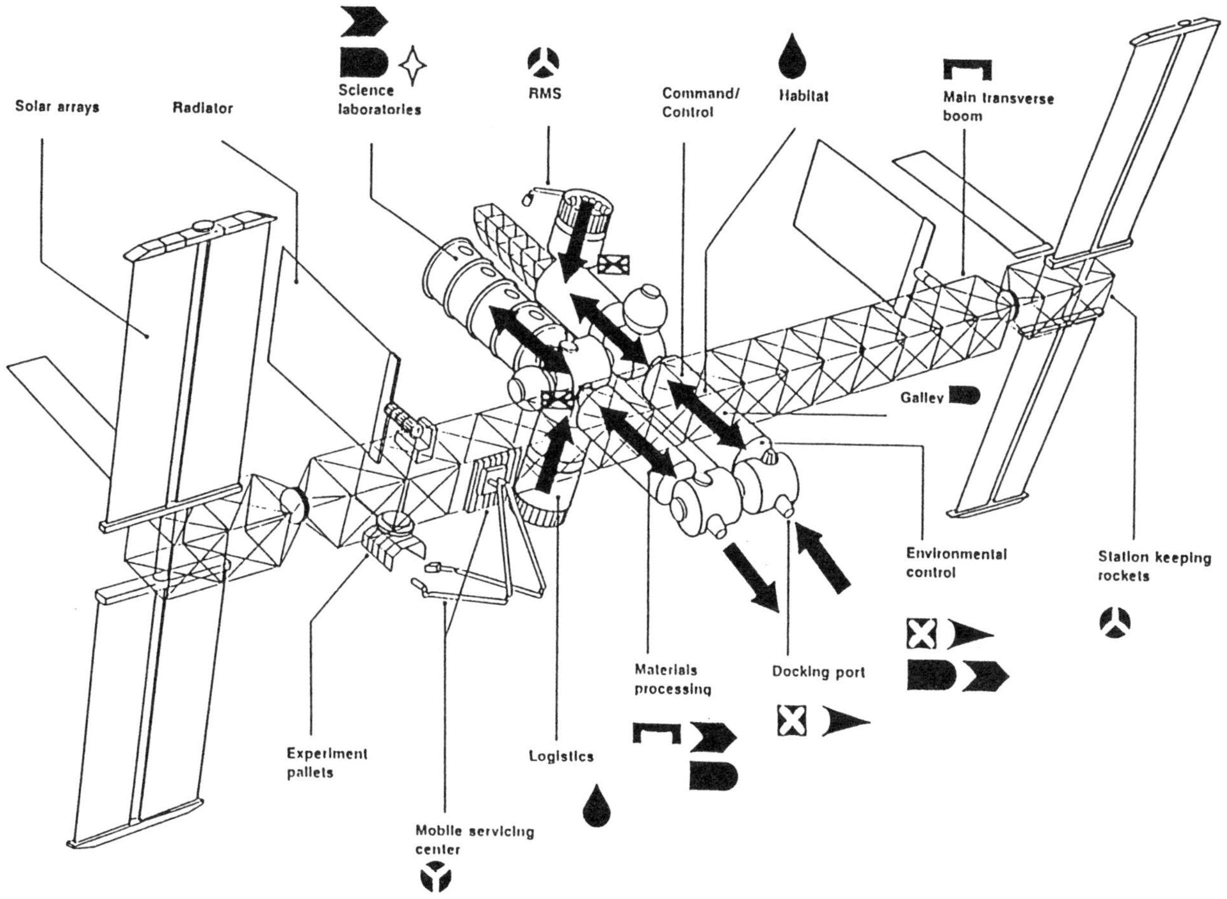

Figure 8–5
Energy Flows in the Space Station

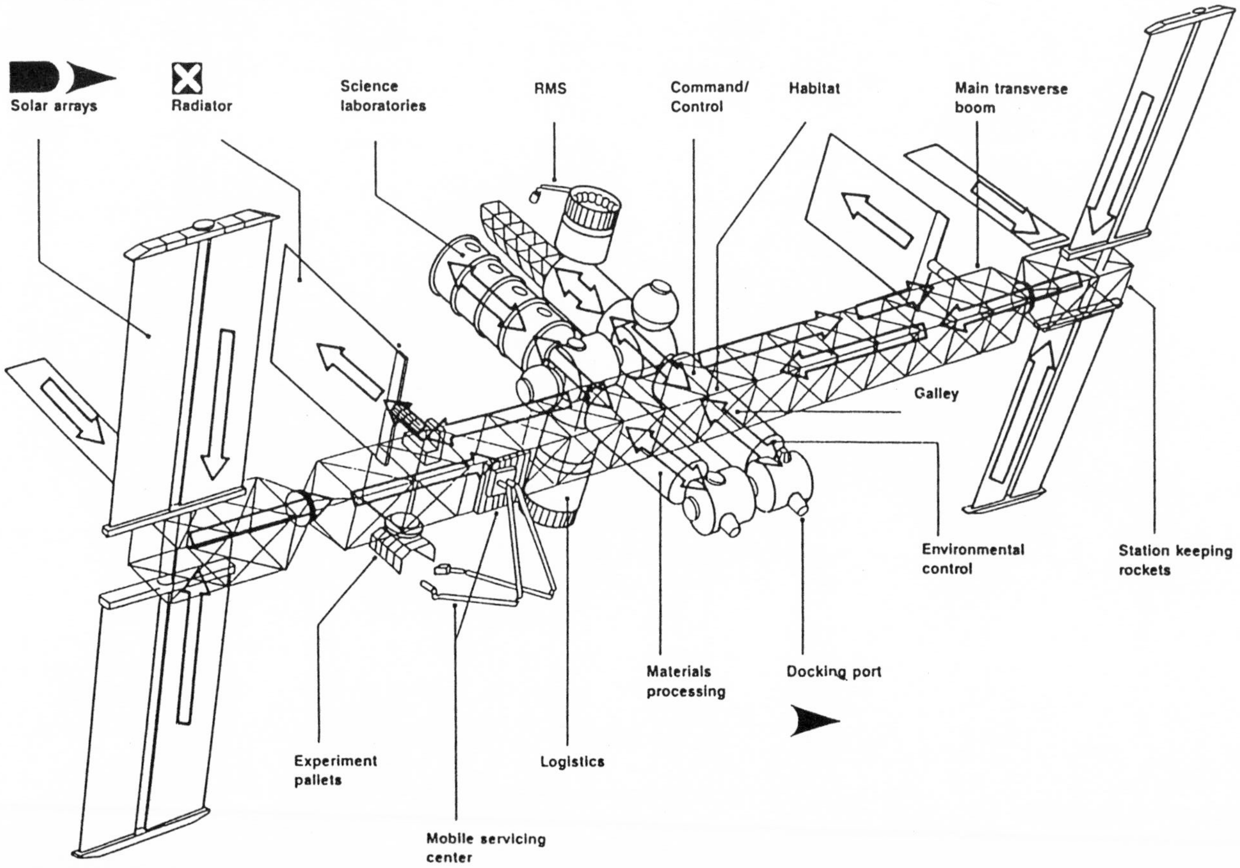

With the advent of the information era, it is likely that to preserve the multiple-level organizations that make modern civilization possible, societies will have to consciously and rationally provide information disconnects between levels of living systems. Indeed within corporations and governmental structures, such disconnects should be considered.

For example, artificial intelligence software can now construct stand-alone self-organizing data files. The data of such files are raw inputs. No aggregation or other data reduction procedures are applied to them. They are interpreted only by the decisions to collect them. The heralded purpose of such files is to make available to all levels of organization deciders as much information as possible. Such ultimate decentralization of information is supposed to capture the ultimate ingenuity of an organization and thus enhance its competitive prowess. What is overlooked in such a theory is the glaring reality that all observable successful organizations are hierarchically structured and that such structures are information structures controlled by decider subsystems. Such subsystems collect filtered information and control the organization by further filtering that information through decision processes. To provide all data to all levels of management may ultimately force an organization to be governed by political consensus of internal specialties. If this internal situation were to occur, it is likely that the global considerations (relationships between a company and its markets) would be neglected. Such neglect might lead to the termination of a company in bankruptcy.

Because Earth's economy (an ecosystem consciously constructed by humans) is highly complex, critical life processes are not always obvious to an observer. This ecosystem controls the distribution of goods and services—a vital function. Consequently, conscientious scientific efforts should be made to discover empirically how obscured life processes work.

This ecosystem is constructed by humans using elements of natural ecosystems. It is an accepted tenet of science that humans are constrained by the laws (relationships that exist among elements) that govern those natural ecosystems, and thus we attempt to discover such laws by empirical investigation. Because the economy is constructed by humans, there may exist a general presumption that we understand the relationships of this ecosystem. The presumption often is demonstrated to be false but, nevertheless, it persists.

Notwithstanding its construction by humans, the modern economy likely is not understood well. This is the case because it is possibly the first human step toward an artificial intelligence system (a system in which intelligence cannot be traced to specific biological systems) and, as such, is capable of self-programming. Furthermore, many relatively independent individuals contribute to its construction over long periods.

Consequently, empirical investigations of the relationships that exist among its elements should be undertaken. LSPA and CPA provide means for monitoring the relationships among its elements. Using the measurements and assessments of these procedures, normal values and ranges of many variables of interest to diverse social actors may be demonstrated. Such normal values and ranges can be used to discover problems and dysfunctions in the subsystems of organizations and between an organization and its suprasystem. In the following discussion we explain how CPA and LSPA can be integrated to provide a comprehensively integrated information processing methodology that may be useful for both real time management and biosocial research purposes.

In the prior chapters, we developed a theory of accounting measurement that identifies clearly and specifically the object (attribute) of measurement that is measured by the monetary scale. This attribute is specific exchange value and it is measured at the boundary of an organization in an exchange process.

Our confidence in such a value depends largely upon the relative independence of the parties to an exchange. Generally, as independence increases, our confidence in the values generated also increases. Because of this characteristic, confidence in such values generated within a particular organization is difficult to have. Consequently, our greatest confidence is in values generated in ''arm's-length transactions in the marketplace,'' that is, in exchanges at the organization boundary and not at boundaries of its subsystems or components.

The monitoring of internal flows is an important management need. If this were not the case, cost accounting and other internal allocation procedures never would have arisen. Currently, internal allocation procedures contribute to both management planning and control.

A weakness of the current procedures is that they are arbitrary with reference to the cosmic accounting measurement scale. That is to say, allocations are made on the basis of logics other than the logic of the accounting measurement methodology. They are interpretive by the nature of such logics.

Although internal allocation variables are often based on concepts other than those of GAAP, the internal mixing of measurements and interpretations may obscure measurements of critical concrete processes within an organization in much the same way as GAAP-adjusted variables do outside.

To improve systems for monitoring internal processes, we need to actually take measurements on such processes. Recent technological advances in information processing make it possible to do so in many situations. For example, transmitting badges may be attached to inventory items to monitor their movements through production processes or component boundaries can be fitted with computer sensors to record the movement as items pass over a boundary.

However, efficiencies are obtained within organizations by combining various living systems processes, often in unique fashion; and such combinations cannot always be measured efficiently by direct space-time observations. For example, time spent in a particular location may not distinguish between the information-processing functions and the matter–energy processing functions of a particular person.

Furthermore, the persistence of cost allocation procedures for performing estimates on concrete processes amidst the rapid advancement of sensor technology may indicate a need for cosmic accounting information in decisions affecting and effected by an organization's internal subsystems. In other words, measurements of intrinsic physical attributes are often needed for such functions as those provided by the producer and the converter subsystems. Such measurements, however, are not sufficient to measure the overall cost or contribution of a component to the coherent processes of an organization as a whole. This latter type measurement must be cosmic, that is, a measurement made on diverse physical objects on a single attribute.

As discussed in prior chapters, the measurements made on the spatiotemporal accounting scale are cosmic measurements on the attribute specific exchange value. Costs based on such measurements, and not adjusted to GAAP specifications, are themselves cosmic measurements. No doubt this characteristic explains the persistence of cost allocation procedures.

Again, to improve the system for monitoring internal processes, we actually need to measure such processes. Consequently, to monitor processes in terms of a cosmic measurement, we would like to take actual cosmic measurements on these processes similar to those measurements taken at the boundary of an organization.

A fundamental characteristic of all living systems prevents such measurement, however. Every critical subsystem except the decider subsystem of a living system may be dispersed upwardly, laterally, or downwardly to other systems. Without a decider subsystem of its own, a living system at any of the eight hierarchical levels cannot exist. The decider subsystem controls the system. Consequently, independent exchanges between the subsystems of a system can occur only to the degree allowed by the decider. Therefore, our confidence in values generated by exchanges within an organization is severely limited by the bias of the decider subsystem.

Because of this difference in a fundamental characteristic between the internal and the environmental conditions of concern to organization managers, we must forgo our desire for a direct cosmic measurement of internal processes analogous to that of the money–information marker measurement of society-level processes. Although the ideal direct cosmic measurements are not available, we still have the cosmic measurements taken at the boundary of an organization. Because we cannot measure the matter–energy these values represent as it frays-out through (is divided among) an organization's components to achieve specialization of functions, we must allocate them. Now we have argued ourselves out of measurement and back to allocation. Nevertheless, our desire to improve the system for monitoring internal processes persists.

We believe that the internal allocation of costs may be improved by using LSPA. Such allocations would provide information about the critical life processes of organizations on the basis of a cosmic measurement and an allocation logic that is relatively unbiased by a particular decider subsystem (management). The danger of researcher bias that is ever present in scientific investigations is not absent from management investigations. When costs are allocated on the bases of management-selected logics, an ever-present tendency exists to select those that serve management purposes. To the extent that this tendency prevails, the purpose of measurement is defeated. Costs can be allocated in ways to self-fulfill the prophecies of management rather than to provide high-fidelity feedback based on the concrete processes being managed.

Such allocation is based on LSPA studies of a firm or set of firms. As discussed in the examples of research presented in this chapter, these studies use both subjective and objective data to determine the quantities of certain flows (e.g., material and personnel) dedicated to each of the twenty critical life processes (Table 4–1). Ratios for allocating related costs can be derived from those quantities.

The allocation of CPA-based costs within organizations according to LSPA would provide a means of monitoring the internal processes of organizations that are analogous to a set of processes that society can monitor on its various organizations. This multilevel commonality is important. How information about integrated hierarchical systems is broken down may either obstruct or enhance understanding those systems.

When top management changes occur, organizational charts are often changed and actual physical relocations of departments and people performing various functions are sometimes imposed. One way of getting on the business publication best seller list is to contribute to what someone has termed the Framework of the Month Club. Putting together a list of important aspects of business processes and supporting their importance with testimonies from various successful firms can provide temporary business guru status.

We believe that, although conceptual frameworks should evolve, they should not be so transient. They should be much more fundamental, concerning life processes that all types of organizations must perform or have performed, for them to survive.   When they concern hierarchically constructed systems, frameworks should be able to distinguish both commonalities and differentials across levels.

LST organizes processes and structures in a way that is applicable at all levels of living systems. It is a framework that has evolved over a long history from the physical sciences to the biological sciences and more recently to the social sciences. Information broken down according to LST-defined subsystems can produce analyses of fundamental processes common to all types of organizations and comparable across both organizations and hierarchical levels. Such an information break-down can be performed on accounting data using LSPA to allocate CPA costs.

Certain ranges exist at all hierarchical levels in which the ratios among the concrete inflows and outflows of important subsystems fluctuate. If any of these relationships are pushed beyond their steady-state ranges, internal stresses occur that provide either negative feedback to stabilize the system as a whole or positive feedback to destabilize it towards growth or decay.

Whether LSPA-allocated, CPA-based costs should be used for pricing decisions awaits further research. Neither should this allocation procedure simply replace standard costing procedures and those that impose budgetary controls in the accounts themselves. Nevertheless, the concept of unbiased measurement (with reference to the measurement methodology) has important implications for how those systems should be used.

Expert Systems Technology May Be Used to Integrate LSPA with CPA

The recent rapid advancement of expert systems technology provides new tools for integrating LSPA with CPA. Although traditional data processing systems may be used, this new technology provides interactive knowledge retrieval capabilities, easily updated data bases, and flexible system architecture. These features make a system user-friendly and thus increase its usefulness to organizations.

In the last five years, thousands of systems based on artificial intelligence (AI) concepts have been developed. Most major universities offer courses in this technology. Expert systems comprise a type of AI systems, and these systems are beginning to be important to accounting and its concerns. For example, a Coopers and Lybrand study (1988) found that 43 percent of major financial services institutions are using, developing, or actively researching expert systems applications. That this technology has significantly penetrated the domain of accounting concerns was shown by the more than 100 participants at the First International Symposium on Expert Systems in Business, Finance, and Accounting conducted by the Expert Systems Program for the University of Southern California School of Accounting.

Expert systems technology may be applied to at least three types of problems: (1) those involving prescriptive or proscriptive rules, (2) problems of planning complex and time-extended activities, and (3) ill-structured and fuzzily delimited problems. The Audit Research Group of Peat, Marwick, Main found expert systems technology especially helpful for the last type of problems. Such problems are common in auditing. Similar problems are encountered to allocate CPA-generated costs on the basis of LSPA.

A system architecture termed *blackboard* is being used by several expert systems developers. This architecture involves a shared data structure that can be accessed and modified by several separate knowledge bases. Models are built using meta rules to determine when to use subordinate rules. Coopers and Lybrand Knowledge Engineering Group, London, designed an expert system for international taxation using this architecture (Gleeson and West, 1988; Brown, 1988). Their system includes a corporate model (a hierarchy of companies) and an international model (a set of modules containing information about tax laws of each country). A similar system could be built to integrate information based on LSPA cost allocations with judgments of experts, measurements of concrete processes, and the various decision models used to interpret those measurements.

Many applications of expert systems are being made by adding this technology to existing data processing systems. This procedure provides a relatively inexpensive means for implementing it broadly and suggests that expert systems technology may become an important part of the now proliferating integrated systems software. We believe that this technology will enhance many accounting and financial analyses now performed by corporations and governments. One enhancement should be the implementation of CPA and LSPA.

A specific description of how artificial intelligence/expert systems technology may be used to integrate LSPA and CPA is provided here. The description is based on Jacques J. Vidal's research at the Distributed Machine Intelligence Laboratory UCLA Computer Science Department and Brain Research Institute.

The technology of the proposed adaptive LST expert system (ALEXSYS) introduced above may be used to integrate LSPA and CPA. This technology provides an alternative to the now popular analog neural nets in the field of neural networks. In that field the problem of responsibility assignment in functional space slowed progress for several years. However, the development of Rumelhart's Reverse Error Propagation Algorithm (Rumelhart, McClelland, and the PDP Research Group, 1986) and other recently developed algorithms have revitalized the field.

Parallel research on distributed programming algorithms for programmable logic networks has provided a foundation for developing a general combinatorial architecture (Martinez, 1986; Verstraete, 1986; Verstraete and Vidal, 1987a; Vidal, 1984, 1983). This architecture is based on a radical concept that brings together many fundamental issues and views computing systems as compromises of parallel and sequential architectures. The idea is to use a massively parallel "connectionist" approach patterned on the reflex scheme as a general form of calculation using digital logic components. Many control problems are most easily stated or may be restated in terms of propositional logic. Deduction can then be implemented by a network compiled in Boolean logic to represent chains of propositions.

Such networks provide completely parallel digital implementation of logic arrays. These arrays constitute a uniquely manageable form of knowledge representation. Vidal and others (Adler and Vidal, 1986; Verstraete and Vidal, 1987a, 1987b) developed the Residue Propagation Algorithm to ameliorate the responsibility problem in the space of logic functions. Despite Boolean space lacking the smoothness of the restricted functional sets of analog sigmoid functions used in reverse propagation, complete general heuristics becoming deterministic when specific restrictions are imposed have been developed.

Using this architecture, the function of a network is modified incrementally in response to logic rules (instances) being passed to the network one by one. Each instance makes the network evaluate its behavior. It then adds the new logic rule to the previously assumed set of rules and deletes earlier rules when they cause contradiction, also removing unused nodes. This is a local mechanism involving only communications between adjacent neighbor nodes.

ALEXSYS incorporates dynamically programmable logic modules, or

DPLMs. Vidal (1983) has generalized the programmable propositional logic algorithm concept with elements that are individually and reversibly programmable. Networks of these DPLMs form a distinctively novel class of massively parallel processors. Their dynamic programmability allows them to adapt to external problem changes and potentially to internally self-organize.

This new technology may be used in organizations to implement a system for internally allocating specific exchange value costs based on LST. Such a system would integrate LSPA and CPA, providing estimates of the cosmic impact of the twenty vital functions identified by LST. In the process, many additional analytic variables could be measured or estimated as well, for example, employee morale and resources devoted to communications.

Studies of stress adaptation have indicated that the processes of living systems can occur only within certain sets of limitations. The organizational set of limits is composed of a large number of interacting physical, biological, and social variables beyond which stresses cannot force the system without risking its termination.

Research data on these variables can be collected into a knowledge base and classified in terms of LST levels and subsystems. An ALEXSYS system can search this knowledge base to determine which variables are in danger of exceeding the established norms and recommend adaptations to correct the imbalance. ALEXSYS is a learning system. Consequently, it can use operational information analyzed in the context of prior information to update the knowledge base. Incorporating in this system specific exchange monetary information generally and CPA specifically provides the ability to view an organization as a coherent whole from the societal level. Furthermore, it provides data for estimating the cosmic contribution of various organization components.

Summary

In this chapter, we discuss the application of LST to organizations through concrete process analysis (CPA) and living systems process analysis (LSPA). CPA is an application of the theory of accounting measurement of concrete process that we develop in Chapters 5 and 6. LSPA is a set of research procedures developed in the social sciences and applied to organizations based on the LST conceptual framework.

We suggest that CPA should be used to analyze the performance of organizations at some global level and illustrate one way to construct such analyses in Chapter 7. In Chapter 8, we suggest that measurements made on concrete processes may be allocated, based on LSPA, internally to various critical concrete processes of organizations. Such allocation provides a means for monitoring those vital processes in terms of cosmic measurements.

References

Adler, Gabriela, and Jacques J. Vidal. "Top-Down Functional Decomposition in Digital Perceptrons," UCLA-CSD–870014 (1986).

Banathy, B. S., and S. R. Bell. "The Application of Living Systems Process Analysis in Education." *ISI Monograph* (1985), pp. 85–87.

Brown, C. E. "Tax Expert Systems in Industry and Accounting." *Expert Systems Review for Business and Accounting* 1 (June, 1988), pp. 9–16.

Bryant, D., and S. L. Merker. "A Living Systems Process Analysis of a Public Transit System." *Behavioral Science* 32 (1987), pp. 293–303.

Chase, S., J. H. Wright, and R. Ragade. "The Inpatient Psychiatric Unit as a System." *Behavioral Science* 26 (1981), pp. 197–205.

Coopers and Lybrand. *Expert Systems in the Financial Services Industry Survey Report.* New York: Coopers and Lybrand, 1988.

Forrester, J. W. *Industrial Dynamics.* Cambridge, MA: M.I.T. Press, 1961.

Gleeson, J. F., and M. L. West. "CLINTE: Coopers & Lybrand International Tax Expert System." In *Research and Development in Expert Systems IV*, ed. D.S. Moralee. New York, NY: Cambridge University Press, 1988, pp. 18–31.

Martinez, T. "Adaptive Self-Organizing Logic Networks," Ph.D. dissertation, University of California, Los Angeles, 1986.

Merker, S. L., and C. Lusher. "A Living Systems Process Analysis of an Urban Hospital." *Behavioral Science* 32 (1987), pp. 304–14.

Miller, J. G. "Information Input Overload and Psychopathology." *American Journal of Psychiatry* 116 (1960), pp. 695–704.

_____. *Living Systems.* New York: McGraw-Hill, 1978.

_____, principal investigator, et al. "Living Systems Applications to Human Space Habitation." Submitted to NASA, Information Science and Human Factors, Code RC, Office of Aeronautics & Space Administration, through the University of California, San Diego, with the endorsement of the California Space Institute, 1988.

Nicolis, G., and I. Prigogine. *Self-Organization in Non Equilibrium Systems: From Dissipative Structures to Order through Fluctuations.* New York: John Wiley, 1977.

Prigogine, I. *Edute Thermodynamique des Processus Irreversibles.* Liege: Desoer, 1947.

Rumelhart, D. E., J. L. McClelland, and the PDP Research Group. *Parallel Distributed Processing: Explorations in the Microstructure of Cognition.* Volumes 1 and 2. Cambridge, MA: M.I.T. Press, 1986.

Ruscoe, G. C., et al. "The Application of Living Systems Theory to 41 U.S. Army Battalions." *Behavioral Science* 30 (1985), pp. 7–50.

Verstraete, R. A. "Assignment of Functional Responsibility in Perceptions," Ph.D. dissertation, University of California, Los Angeles, 1986.

Verstraete, R. A., and J. J. Vidal. "Decomposition of Boolean Functions on a Network of Polyfunctional Nodes." UCLA, CSO–87008 (1987a).

_____. "Assigning Parallel Distributed Logic Networks by Residue Propagation." Submitted for publication (1987b).

Vidal, Jacques J. "Silicon Brains: Whither Neuromimetic Computer Architectures." *Proceedings of the IEEE International Conference on Computer Design—VLSI in Computers* (1983), pp. 17–20.

_____. "Knowledge Representation with Reconfigurable Logic." *Proceedings, Workshop on Applications of Supercomputers* (December, 1984).

9

LST GENERAL RESEARCH HYPOTHESES AND ACCOUNTING INFORMATION SYSTEMS

Introduction

In Chapters 1 through 8, we have developed from the conceptual framework termed living systems theory a theory of accounting measurement, illustrated the application of that theory using concrete process analysis, and illustrated living systems process analysis, suggesting that this latter analysis may be used to internally allocate CPA-derived values among organization subsystem processes. We believe that those analyses provide an additional useful set of information for decisions of management and other social actors and, consequently, should be performed and the results publicly reported. To do so would clearly distinguish between accounting measurements and interpretations of those measurements that are commonly introduced into public accounting reports. Those prior chapters concerned the application of LST to the practice of what may be termed accountancy.

In this chapter, we leave the question of accounting practice and focus attention on scientific research that involves accounting information systems. Here a clear distinction should be made between the fundamental social process that we term *accounting*, the development of which may be traced from prehistory, and modern *professional accountancy*. In the past there has been a rather involved debate on whether accounting/accountancy is art or science. This debate typically confused accounting and accountancy. Many concluded that accounting is not a science and is possibly better described as an art.

This situation is similar to that of the medical profession. While few practitioners would deny that many aspects of medicine involve the experiential judgments of art, over this generation medicine has become increasingly an applied science. Only a few years ago, doctors commonly measured about 25 biological variables on the centimeter, gram, second scales when examining a patient. Today, as many as 171 variables are measured for an annual checkup. At the same time doctors continue to exercise informed judgments and to respect the feelings of patients. However, a clear distinction is made between those measurements and the diagnosis (judgments) of an individual doctor and of the medical profession itself. The rules of measurement theory and science apply clearly to those measurements. A clear understanding of what the numbers mean enhances the professional judgment of doctors. A similar distinction is blurred in modern accounting procedures.

By distinguishing between accounting (based on measuring concrete processes) and accountancy (based on consensus interpretations of the resulting measurements), we may rigorously apply scientific methodology to accounting and use accounting measurements in scientific investigations. On the other hand, as such investigations reveal new knowledge about higher-level living systems, the art of accountancy may be enhanced by that knowledge.

One way modern societies generally and fundamentally control their components is to provide and withhold money–information markers in a feedback relationship. As a part of the process of allocating goods and services in society, organizations receive societal feedback through money–information marker flows (described in Chapter 7). Therefore, the quantities of inputs and outputs of money–information markers to and from organizations reflect this feedback relationship.

Generally, the basic purpose of organizations is survival because, in terms of economic hazards and advantages, they form sheltered environments for individual persons and groups. Survival and growth are related. As a consequence, organizations seek growth. Such growth is encouraged or discouraged by, respectively, positive or negative feedback from society. Such feedback is generally processed through both currency and time-lagged money–information marker flows.

Accounting information systems map the concrete flows of organizations, communities, societies, and supranational systems. Dual-entry procedures record both the money–information marker flows and the goods and services flows. As a result, accounting figures contain information about the feedback processes of these multiple levels of human systems.

Because the levels of human systems are hierarchically related and are maintained by feedback across levels as well as within levels, research on accounting information systems involves cross-level questions. Living systems theory (Miller, 1955, 1965a, 1978) is a conceptual framework that characterizes such human systems as concern the accounting discipline in a hierarchical relationship that takes into account such feedback processes. Any general hypothesis for research involving accounting information systems should take into explicit consideration the cross-level characteristics of the accounting environment. Consequently, LST may provide a conceptual framework for research involving accounting information systems.

Conceptual frameworks that guide research should help investigators generate hypotheses because hypothesis testing is a time-proven method of scientific analysis. This chapter develops a set of general hypotheses for research involving accounting information systems. It does so first by distinguishing between conceptual frameworks for research and those for practice. A subsequent discussion details important considerations of empirical research generally and hypothesis testing specifically. The term *general hypothesis* is defined, an LST general hypothesis for research involving accounting information systems is developed, and differentiation of general hypotheses into specific research hypotheses is discussed and demonstrated. Finally, we discuss in some detail how the LST general hypothesis that is developed in this study may contribute to the continuing advancement of empirical research in the modern accounting profession.

Distinguishing between Conceptual Frameworks for Research and Those for Practice

Conceptual frameworks obviously are products of human minds, whether individual or corporate. As a consequence, they are purposeful. Different useful purposes exist for constructing conceptual frameworks. These different purposes are functions of the goals of the concrete human systems that produce them. A useful conceptual framework is generally the result of a recursive process that begins with the internal purpose of survival, progresses to an array of external goals based on this purpose, and then frays out the internal purpose of survival (develops a preferential hierarchy of values) based on achievement of external goals (Miller, 1978, pp. 39–41).

The accounting literature is fraught with research that concerns conceptual frameworks (Anthony, 1983; Chambers, 1966; FASB, 1978; Ijiri, 1981; Mattessich, 1964; Sherman, 1984; Sterling, 1979). Virtually all of the discussion has centered around developing a consensus on what general ideas should govern the development of GAAP and of individual practitioner decisions in the absence of specific GAAP pronouncements. Such discussion is expected and necessary because a basic purpose of the accounting profession is to provide generally understood accounting information based on agreed-upon disclosure in an evolving market society. Accountants are becoming more aware that such frameworks, while not changing from moment to moment, should evolve over time in response to the changing environment of which the accounting profession is an important component.

Research on accounting information systems is a different proposition. The modern connotation of the term research is scientific research. Science and accounting are different professions. Each tenaciously pursues and protects its purposes, goals, and methodology.

While these professions are different, they are similar in several respects. Possibly the most important similarity is that distinguishing all professions from individual persons, libraries, business corporations, governments, educational institutions, and the like. Both infiltrate those other kinds of systems with pre-scriptions and proscriptions that have been proven useful for the survival and advancement of higher-level human systems such as societies. The fundamental elements on which both professions collect data do not belong to the profes-sions—they belong to those other kinds of systems.

As a result of this ability to penetrate other systems, both science and ac-counting penetrate each other. The question of how accounting penetrates science is not discussed in this study. We are concerned, however, with the question of how science may be applied beneficially to investigations that involve accounting information systems.

Conceptual frameworks that instruct research involving accounting informa-tion systems are the products of science. Those that instruct the practice of accountancy are constructed by the accounting profession. Obviously, contri-butions made by scientific investigations will be incorporated over time into the unique configurations of the accounting profession's conceptual frameworks. However, by clearly distinguishing between conceptual frameworks based on the different purposes of science and accountancy, debilitating conflicts resulting from paradoxes created by arbitrarily mixing two different sets of logic may be avoided.

This chapter discusses a particular conceptual framework (LST) based on science for research involving accounting information systems. These discussions apply only indirectly to such conceptual systems as the FASB's conceptual framework project (discussed in Chapter 10), which is based on accounting profession consensus and is a useful mechanism of a market-based society.

A distinction that is as important as that between scientific and accountancy professional conceptual frameworks is the distinction between different degrees of abstractions. That is to say, it is important to designate whether a framework focuses on basic or applied aspects of scientific investigation. Applied science areas such as engineering and medicine are founded on certain basic sciences. Consequently, conceptual frameworks that instruct applied disciplines like ac-counting should concern both basic and applied considerations. Applied frame-works should be built on basic ones. Likewise, specific hypotheses that concern applications should be differentiations of general hypotheses that represent im-portant characteristics of a basic conceptual framework. If they are not, generally the results of testing them may be ambiguous and fail to contribute to an orderly development of a discipline of knowledge.

Scientific Methodology, Experimentation, and Hypothesis Testing

Scientific methodology need not be limited to experiments that test hypotheses. Because this methodology is tried and proven, however, it offers a reasonable primary methodology for research involving accounting information systems.

Generally, a *hypothesis* is an assertion that is stated in a way that it can be confirmed or disconfirmed by empirical evidence using understood methodology and methods. Such assertions are made on the basis of sets of theory and a priori knowledge. When a hypothesis is not formulated on the basis of well-developed theory, the results of a valid test are ambiguous. This is so because in the absence of the theoretical framework relating the predicted results to what is already understood, we have no basis for minimizing coincidence as a viable alternative explanation of the results. For this reason, one of the measures of the maturity of a scientific discipline is the detail and rigor it has achieved in its theoretic frameworks.

Experimentation is basically the ingenious construction of physical (matter–energy) boundaries, impermeable to elements to be excluded from observation, in such a manner that an experimenter can vary by a measured amount an element of interest and measure the covariance of a theorized (hypothesized) related element. As the complexity of systems increases from nonliving ones through a hierarchy of living ones, the actual rearrangement of physical boundaries becomes more and more difficult. For example, it is quite possible to separate plutonium from other elements or an amoeba from other amoebas without affecting their intensive quantities (internal characteristics often termed qualities). It is difficult, however, to separate an organ from an organism without affecting its function intrinsically and extrinsically and even more difficult to isolate the individual human organism from organizations. The increasing difficulty of experimentation at higher levels of living systems is related directly to the emergent characteristics of the system boundaries.

LST defines boundary as the subsystem at the perimeter of a system that holds its components together, protects them from environmental stresses, and excludes or permits entry to various sorts of matter–energy and information (Miller, 1978, p. 3). According to LST, boundaries serve three basic functions:

1. They form barriers to the free flow of matter–energy and information in and out of the system.
2. They selectively filter matter–energy and information flows.
3. They maintain a steady-state differential between the interior of the system and its environment.

Such boundaries often do not exist for nonliving systems; are continuous, while also having many gaps, in living systems from cell to the organism levels; and, at higher levels, include common information boundaries in space-time, that is, limits of the channels over which they communicate. Obviously, for living systems, such boundaries can be discovered empirically. Observers, however, must sort out many boundaries of higher-level living systems, for example, groups, organizations, and communities; and apparently many boundaries of nonliving systems must be set by an observer (for example, physicists may set boundaries by constructing certain lab facilities).

Given these emergent characteristics, it is not surprising that investigators of social systems have developed methods of quasi experimentation. In the general case, these methods neither attempt to change the natural boundaries of the systems they investigate nor vary an element of interest. Instead, they measure an observed change in an element of interest and the covariance of a hypothesized related element. Having forgone the power to manipulate an element of interest, the strength of such experimentation rests with the discovery of natural (existing) boundaries and their characteristics and the ability to make measurements at such boundaries.

At these higher levels, system boundaries are information-intensive; that is, they consist of the boundaries of channels and nets, and portions of these subsystems as well as parts of other information processing subsystems (e.g., decoders and transducers) are often dispersed to other organizations, groups, and individual organisms. As a consequence, after discovering the physical boundary, the information flow itself must be filtered to determine the information belonging to a system of concern to a researcher. In the absence of a well-defined theory based on previous empirical evidence of the connection between a variable of interest and a hypothesized related variable, it is difficult, if not impossible, to eliminate chance correlation as a viable alternative explanation of the results of quasi experimentation.

Notwithstanding this well-understood limitation, quasi experimentation by the social sciences generally has paid scant attention to discovering the concrete boundaries of living systems and to studying the interrelationships of such systems and their elements. Empirical quasi experiments by accounting researchers often follow a pattern similar to that of the social sciences.

Miller (1965b; 1978; 1986, p. 73) formulates this research problem in terms of abstracted versus concrete systems: "The units of abstracted systems are relationships abstracted or selected by an observer. These relationships are observed to inhere and interact in selected concrete, usually living, systems. The units of concrete systems, on the other hand, are other concrete systems (components, parts, or members). The relationships of concrete systems are spatial, temporal, causal, or results of information transmissions." He believes that largely because of the great influence of Talcott Parsons (Parsons and Smelser, 1946; Parsons, 1979, 1980) on the theory of sociology and other social sciences between the late 1940s and the 1960s, the dominant systems theory of these disciplines is stated in terms of abstracted systems. Because the theoretic statements that characterize it are difficult to test by any form of data collection, abstracted systems theory has produced no large body of measured quantitative research to support it. Alternatively, experience has shown that it is less difficult to conduct quantitative research based on hypothesis testing that investigates propositions concerning measurements of variables of concrete systems.

A General Hypothesis Defined

A definition of what we mean by a general hypothesis is necessary because the term *hypothesis* is commonly used to designate a variety of related but not identical concepts. A general hypothesis is an assertion

—that encapsulates an essential aspect of a general theoretic framework,

—that may be empirically confirmed or denied,

—by differentiating it into specific research hypotheses consistent with detailed elements of the general theoretic framework, and

—testing those specific hypotheses by scientific experimentation or quasi-experimentation.

A general hypothesis should:

1. Be of a medium degree of abstractness, neither vague, obvious, trivial, incapable of confirmation, nor so specific that it is not widely relevant.

2. Be stated in terms equally applicable to the different hierarchical levels of living systems involved.

3. Be capable of being represented ultimately by a mathematical statement of a formal identity across levels, in which different variables show regular changes across levels of living systems, across types of living systems at a particular level, and across individual systems at a particular level.

4. Be stated so that the observations (measurements) made at each level and within levels can be precisely compared. Thus, analogous measurements must be made on the same dimensions of the same space or on related dimensions with understood transformations among them.

LST can provide this kind of general hypothesis for research involving accounting information systems. From such a hypothesis, we may expect several general (cross-level) formal identities to be formulated. Some researchers call such formal identities *general theories* because from them various specific mathematical research hypotheses can be derived. Consequently, we use the term conceptual framework to designate the broader verbal theory such instrumental general theories describe.

LST General Hypotheses for Research Involving Accounting Information Systems

Miller (1978, chap. 4) approaches the question of hypothesis generation by constructing a taxonomy of hypotheses based on similar hypotheses taken from various scientific disciplines. The adapted hypotheses are related by a matrix of nineteen critical processes, subsystems characteristic of all living systems, each occurring at seven biological and social levels in an evolutionary hierarchy. He believes that this ensemble of hypotheses may apply to more than one level of living systems and specifically states more than 150 such hypotheses.

Notwithstanding the major emphasis his theory places on hypothesis generation and testing, Miller does not state a general hypothesis (as it is defined in this chapter) that is uniquely characteristic of LST. However, he does assert that the unique contribution of LST is his arrangement of the research findings of others into a particular mosaic that is based on the thesis he terms *shred-out* or *fray-*

out. This thesis actually generalizes the theory of biological evolution to include man-made systems above the organism level. The generalization is more mechanistic, or methodical, than organismic, although he unfortunately used the organismic metaphor to describe it at a time when this metaphor was falling into disuse. Actually, the thesis asserts that all living systems are highly dynamic and complex, and it is therefore necessary to examine their components as they interact with each other and the system environment. To do this, it is necessary to rely on the previous research of multiple disciplines and tried-and-accepted methods of instrumental, or formal, reasoning.

For such a thesis to be more than pedagogically useful, that is, useful for the expansion of knowledge resulting from understanding as well as its explanation (propagation among individuals), the thesis must provide the basis to postulate a unique linkage among important elements of the systems the conceptual framework concerns. In the case of LST, those systems are concrete living ones.

Four basic concepts from which a unique linkage of concrete elements can be hypothesized are: (1) concrete systems, (2) the fluctuous steady-state principle, (3) the principle of fray-out, and (4) hierarchy theory. The particular connections LST makes among these concepts provides the conceptual framework for asserting the following general hypotheses, and they are discussed following the statement of the hypotheses.

The Hypotheses

1. *A General Hypothesis for Research on Organizations.*
   Nonpathogenic organizations maximize growth of aggregate matter–energy inflows over indefinite periods of time within a set of dynamic constraint imposed by communities, societies, and supranational systems. Likewise, within a particular organization, various combinations of components maximize growth of matter–energy inflows within a set of dynamic constraints imposed by the organization.

2. *A General Hypothesis for Using Accounting Information for Research on Organizations.*
   Nonpathogenic organizations maximize the specific monetary exchange value of aggregate matter–energy inflows (specifically, materials, personnel, energy, communications, and currency money–information markers) over indefinite periods within a set of dynamic constraints imposed by communities, societies, and supranational systems that are communicated to the organization by the specific monetary exchange value of time-lagged money–information markers (specifically, owner documents, credit documents, and socialization documents).

3. *A General Hypothesis for Research on Accounting Information Systems.*
   Nonpathogenic accounting information subsystems maximize growth of aggregate matter–energy concrete inflows over indefinite periods within a set of dynamic system constraints by transducing information (in both monetary and physical measurement units) about concrete flows within organizations, communities, societies, and supran-

ational systems, which information is used by a particular system to maximize growth of aggregate matter–energy inflows within a set of dynamic constraints imposed by higher-level systems.

4. *A General Hypothesis for Using Accounting Information for Research on Accounting Information Systems.*

Nonpathogenic accounting information subsystems maximize the specific monetary exchange value of matter–energy inflows (specifically, materials, personnel, energy, and communications) over indefinite periods within a set of dynamic system constraints by transducing information (in both monetary and physical measurement units) about concrete flows within organizations, communities, societies, and supranational systems, which information is used by a particular system to maximize the specific monetary exchange value of aggregate matter–energy inflows (specified above) within a set of dynamic constraints imposed by higher-level systems by the specific monetary exchange value of time-lagged money–information markers (specifically, owner documents, credit documents, and socialization documents).

The Conceptual Framework Used to Generate the Hypotheses

As stated above, the linkage of concrete elements embodied in these four hypotheses is based on the particular connection LST makes among four concepts, that is, concrete systems, fluctuous steady state, fray-out, and hierarchy theory. In this section, each idea is discussed in turn, followed by a description of how LST connects these concepts.

Concrete Systems

Concrete systems are accumulations of matter and energy in specific regions of physical space-time. Living systems are a subclass of the class of concrete systems. As such, to endure over time in Earth's environment, they are subject to the natural laws that govern concrete systems, for example, the laws of thermodynamics.

By constructing a framework based on concrete systems, research is connected to behavior (physical actions) that may be observed. This connection clearly distinguishes between questions of a metaphysical nature and those that may be empirically investigated using measurement theory.

Similarly, this connection distinguishes between roles and individual actors within systems. One reaction to the surge of methodologies based on analysis in modern science is revived emphasis on synthesis (Swanson, 1987a, pp. 4–5). Perhaps more than any other discipline, advocates of general systems theory (GST) and other systems thinkers have influenced science to take a more integrated or systemic view of research questions. This is particularly true in efforts to make investigations by the social sciences more rigorous.

These sciences now generally recognize that living systems, like organizations, develop their own cultures in which roles emerge and endure over time, being filled by different individual actors. Unfortunately, there is a tendency to attempt to investigate directly these emergents of higher-level systems. The actions of individual actors can be observed and measured. Distinguishing what actions belong to what roles is difficult.

Because such roles are conceptual emergents of higher-level living systems, they are the results of the complex interactions of the concrete components of living systems. That is to say, the interactions of concrete components of living systems create roles, not the reverse. Consequently, it is reasonable to investigate such roles by determining how these concrete-component progenitors of roles interact.

A modern formulation of the *Gestalt* (Kohler, 1921) may be used to illustrate this point. Foerster (1962) points out that in systems, components or subsystems coalesce so that interacting elements follow a superadditive composition rule, that is, a measure of the sum of a system's units is larger than the sum of that measure of its units; $0(x+y) > 0x+0y$. For example, if 0 is the square, then $(x+y)^2 > x^2+y^2$, because $x^2+y^2+2xy > x^2+y^2$ by the interaction term $2xy$. The interaction term is dependent on the particular relationships among the other terms, that is, it arises from the peculiar interrelationships of the elements of a particular system. Roles may be represented by interaction terms. The interaction terms that represent most roles are highly complex, however, and their compositions are unknown.

Many different elements interact in complex relationships in living systems such as organizations to produce roles. Because we cannot know a priori the composition of an interaction term representing an emergent role, it makes sense to investigate the composition of such terms by identifying and observing the physical elements that produce them (i.e., the x^2 and y^2 terms).

Fluctuous Steady State

The steady-state principle has long been investigated by scientists. In LST, it rests on the idea that the state of each unit of a system is constrained by, conditioned by, or dependent on the state of other units.

The steady-state principle as used in this study is described by Miller (1978, p. 34):

When opposing variables in a system are in balance, that system is in equilibrium with regard to them. The equilibrium may be static and unchanging or it may be maintained in the midst of dynamic change. Since living systems are open systems, with continually altering fluxes of matter–energy and information, many of their equilibria are dynamic and are often referred to as *flux equilibria* or *steady states*. These may be *unstable*, in which a slight disturbance elicits progressive change from the equilibrium state—like a ball standing on an inverted bowl; or *stable*, in which a slight disturbance is counteracted so as to restore the previous state—like a ball in a cup; or *neutral*, in which a slight disturbance makes a change but without cumulative effects of any sort—like a ball on a flat surface with friction.

All living systems tend to maintain steady states (or homeostasis) of many variables, keeping an orderly balance among subsystems which process matter–energy or information. Not only are subsystems usually kept in equilibrium, but systems also ordinarily maintain steady states with their environments and suprasystems, which have outputs to the systems and inputs from them. This prevents variations in the environment from destroying systems. The variables of living systems are constantly fluctuating, however. A moderate change in one variable may produce greater or lesser alterations in other related ones.

There is a *range of stability* for each of numerous variables in all living systems. It is that range within which the rate of correction of deviations is minimal or zero, and beyond which corrections occur.

This statement is generally consistent with the LeChatelier principle (1888), which was adapted for open systems by Prigogine (1955, p. 82).

Various authors have maintained that some principle like that of LeChatelier operates at all levels of living systems to maintain important variables in steady state. For example, Pareto (1935, p. 1435) observed it in social systems. Weiss (1959, p. 8) described the principle in organisms. Cannon (1939) termed the concept *homeostasis* and suggested its cross-level generalization to include the organism and industrial, domestic, and social organizations. Schumpeter (1939), Leontief (1953, 1966), and many others have applied it to economic systems. Ashby (1954) has applied it to living systems in general, including the brain; Kaplan (1957, pp. 6–8) has applied it to political systems. And Kempf (1958) points out that every level of organization (atomic, molecular, crystalline, enzymatic, protoplasmic, cellular, organismic, and social, among others) has components interacting in space and time, maintaining internal and external equilibria amidst stresses capable of disturbing them. If they did not, they would cease to exist.

The Fray-Out Principle

The fray-out principle is the central proposition that justifies unifying ideas from various disciplines in a hierarchy. This principle asserts that because of their common cosmological origin, an evolutionary process exists whereby less complex living systems give rise to more complex expressions of life by specialization of functions. For example, heart and blood cells specialize in circulating nutrients to other types of cells, and nerve cells specialize in transmitting information to form organs. At the organization level, some individual organisms specialize to produce communications systems while others produce commodities usefully identifiable by their physical forms. Miller (1978) terms this process *shred-out*, but in later writing he terms it *fray-out* because this term better describes the process.

While it results in emergents at higher levels, social evolution is not independent of biological evolution. Taking into consideration the wealth of information collected on the detail of the evolution of various subsystems, it is reasonable to base a hierarchical theory of levels of life on an evolutionary principle. As a result of fray-out, commonalities across levels of life may be expected. LST identifies twenty subsystems (processes) that are common to eight hierarchical levels of life (see Chapter 4). It may be asserted that cross-level formal identities, of definitive quality similar to single-level identities developed by various disciplines, can be formulated and empirically confirmed (Miller, 1986). The accounting discipline is directly and obviously concerned with at least three hierarchical levels of living systems: organizations, societies, and supranational systems. Consequently, such cross-level formal identities may be developed by accounting research.

Hierarchy Theory

At first glance, the principle of fray-out seems to explain fully the function of hierarchy theory in LST. Hierarchy theory plays a much more important role, however. The fray-out concept gives rise to a simple hierarchy that describes quite adequately what happens. In that it describes process, it is dynamic to some extent, but not fully so. In LST, hierarchy theory is the antithesis of the fray-out principle. Whereas fray-out explains the existence of commonalities across levels of living systems, hierarchy theory explains the differences, the emergents at higher levels. In tandem, these two concepts form a Hegelian dialectic that describes not only what processes exist but also how they work— a fully dynamic theory.

When discussing hierarchy theory in the context of LST, two problems emerge: (1) in a sense, modern hierarchy theory is broader than LST, and (2) LST is a verbal theory only now beginning to be quantified, whereas hierarchy theory is fundamentally a quantitative theory only now beginning to be given understood verbally expressed applications. Given these problems, when we assert that hierarchy theory is a vital component of LST, we refer to the idea that it expresses so well, that of differentiating levels of organization based on measurements made on a spatiotemporal scale, for example, in terms of rate criteria and spatial criteria.

Many hierarchy theorists distinguish clearly between epistemological and ontological theories and make no ontological claims for hierarchy theory (O'Neill et al., 1986; Allen and Starr, 1982). Rather, it is perceived as a highly useful tool that may be used to decompose complex systems into explanatory elements— a tool of mechanistic or methodical thought. In this sense, hierarchy theory is broader than LST because, depending on the orientation of a particular question, hierarchy theory may be used to differentiate levels of organization in addition to those that correspond to physical boundaries. As a result, it is not limited necessarily to differentiating levels of organization based on entities with such boundaries. Hierarchy theory can be used to identify important relationships of elements that are physically components of different levels or of different entities at the same level of organization. Consequently, it might provide some important methods for quantitatively operationalizing LST. On the flip side of the coin, LST might provide important physical details about processes of higher-level human systems (e.g., organizations and societies) that surely affect the bio as well as the eco levels of virtually all earthbound living systems.

Notwithstanding the operational difficulties of merging two more or less independently developed bodies of literature, the fundamental idea on which hierarchy theory is built—that levels of organization may be orderly differentiated—constitutes a vital aspect of LST. It is the antithesis of the fray-out thesis. Together, these concepts provide the dynamic for a progressive synthesis of opposing elements into organizations that endure over time. This configuration of coupled opposing concepts provides the basis for the unique arrangement of the elements of the LST conceptual framework into a general hypothesis.

The Linkage of the Four Basic Concepts

In this section, we discuss the linkage of the concepts of concrete systems, fluctuous steady state, fray-out, and hierarchy theory first as they are integrated to produce the general hypothesis for research on organizations (1). Then we discuss the three stated adaptations of this hypothesis, (2), (3), and (4).

The concept of concrete systems focuses the hypothesis on physical and thus observable and measurable entities and elements. The designation of the particular levels of entities (organizations with individual organisms and groups designated components, communities, societies, and supranational systems) are based on commonalities asserted by the fray-out concept and differentials asserted by hierarchy theory.

The fundamental assertion of the hypothesis, that organizations and components *maximize growth of concrete processes,* is deduced from the central thesis of LST, fray-out, as might be expected. The roots of the explanation, however, reach into the concept of fluctuous steady state. Fray-out extends the principle of survival in a competitive environment from biological evolution theory to the study of higher-level human systems. The concept of fluctuous steady state generalizes the Second Law of Thermodynamics from relatively closed systems to open systems. In a general sense, this law asserts that all physical systems are moving toward a state of disorganization—that is, away from survival. The concept of fluctuous steady state explains how living systems overcome this action to perpetuate their existence over some indefinite period. They do this by processing inputs of various forms of matter and energy higher in organization than their outputs, using the difference for repair and growth. Thus, growth and survival are connected; and in the uncertain world of a competitive environment, such systems display a propensity toward growth as a means of survival.

The concept of maintaining a range of stability among important physical variables of organizations provides a set of measurable but dynamic constraints that makes it possible to treat the survival of such systems as an optimization within constraints problem. Pathology may then be identified by suboptimal performance, and depending on the detail of the observation grid, may be traced to specific faulty components.

When such components are identified, what we are learning in specific scientific disciplines may be applied to solve the problem. For example, if the problem is traced to a factory production line, variance analysis may be used to determine whether it is a pricing or efficiency problem. If it is determined that the problem is efficiency, various methods developed by the social and management sciences may be used to discover the specific causes which, when sufficiently delineated, may be corrected.

The selection of fray-out as the central thesis of LST, and thus the thesis term of a thesis → antithesis → synthesis directional conceptual system which itself evolves with new discoveries, effectively sets the normal vector of living systems towards growth. It is important to realize that LST asserts more than that opposing variables are coupled in organizations. It asserts that the coupling normally occurs in such a manner that the fundamental purpose of the organization is survival; and, in the context of the fluctuous steady state, survival translates directly to growth.

The importance of this idea to constructing a cosmos of methodical thought capable of guiding pragmatic research on concrete social systems can hardly be overstated. The concept makes it possible to construct a system that achieves a next higher degree of closure, a fully dynamic closure, than those circuitous systems of mechanistic thought that have contributed so prodigiously to improving modern life, for example, double-entry bookkeeping in accounting and the conservation of energy in physics. Those systems make it possible to mechanistically, or methodically, examine any element within the system in terms of all other elements in the system. However, they are static systems to the degree that the system itself offers no cosmic justification for arranging and ordering its elements, that is, no dynamic. They are simply accounting devices.

Closure in those accounting systems is achieved by assuming that net increases or decreases in the total system constitute another element of the system and arranging this assumed cosmic element in such a way that the total inputs and outputs of the systems are equal. Such a condition of equality is suggested by the circuitous nature of the dynamic of the physical systems those thought systems model. This degree of closure assures a complete accounting but also makes it easy to arbitrarily and eclectically decouple the system in many different arrangements.

A logical next higher degree of closure is one that captures arrangement and order by identifying the normal direction of the assumed cosmic element that is used to close the circuitous mechanistic thought system. The element that closes those first-degree-of-closure systems is a residual that is assumed to continue to be part of the system. Therefore, we need not expect that the closure component of a next-higher-degree-of-closure system be more than an assumption. We might expect, however, that such an assumption would follow from the circuitous nature of the physical systems the thought system purports to model.

While a first-degree-of-closure accounting system provides a highly flexible model for examining the interrelationships of system variables, it obscures the cosmic increases and decreases of the system. In fact, depending on how numbers are assigned to various terms, the assumed term of the thought system may or may not be a measurement of the cosmic increases or decreases of the physical system being mapped. Furthermore, simply accounting for relationships provides no basis to assert causation. It tells us nothing about how the relationships came to be and, consequently, how to maintain or change them.

Obviously, the circuitous systems we are trying to map do exhibit cosmic increases and decreases. Consequently, we need an assumption that allows us to bring such increases and decreases into the mechanistic thought system and that furthermore allows us to assert causation. A simple means of satisfying this need is to directionalize the assumed term of the first-degree-of-closure system. LST provides the rationale for assuming that the normal vector of the cosmic increase/decrease term points toward increase. Consequently, the general hypothesis incorporates the directionalization provided by the fray-out thesis by asserting maximization of growth. Unconstrained maximization, of course, is a fully open-ended system. The antithesis, hierarchy theory, provides the constraints that, in tandem with maximization of growth, close the system.

A brief statement should be made about a subtle and important relationship that this discussion draws between mechanistic and teleological thought systems. Generally, teleologists view mechanistic thought systems as a set totally different from, or a subset of, teleological ones. This discussion asserts that it makes sense to retain a proven-useful mechanistic thought system but include in the dynamic of this system a teleological view of the concrete system it maps and studies.

O'Neill et al. (1986, pp. 94–96), discussing hierarchy theory based on the rate criterion, point out that, at particular levels of organization, holons (individuals) operate on the same spatiotemporal scale and thus can interact. Such interaction is termed *symmetric relations*. On the other hand, asymmetric relationships, which they call "constraints," occur between hierarchical levels. This term is used because these higher levels are relatively unresponsive to the many changes at lower levels but constitute "immovable" barriers to certain behavior of lower levels. For example, the importance of ecological constraint can be illustrated by contrasting population growth of organisms in a laboratory and their natural environment. When the constraints of the environment (e.g., food, space, predators) are removed, the population increases at some maximum potential rate. Thus hierarchy theory provides the rationale for successive hierarchical constraints that may be used to close a more fully dynamic mechanistic thought system and to provide a general hypothesis.

In sum, the unique linkage that LST postulates among important elements of concrete systems is that lower-level living systems maximize concrete process inputs up to a certain potential characterized by internal steady-state relationships among its components and constrained by higher-level system relationships. This hypothesis is substantially different from the common perception that firms maximize profit. In accounting terms, our hypothesis means that nonpathogenic firms generally maximize expenses and nonmonetary assets. This fundamental maximization is achieved in the circuitous economic process by maximizing liabilities, capital stock, and sales as well. Interest, dividends, and monetary assets are managed generally in a manner to maximize noninterest expenses and nonmonetary assets. Within an organization, various components compete to maximize their own portion of the expenses, thus receiving salaries, services, and so on, for their own uses.

Hypotheses (2) and (4) adapt the general LST hypothesis for research on organizations to the specific use of accounting information based on Chapters 1 through 8. Hypothesis adaptation (3) is based on our assertion that, when viewed from the organization level, accounting information systems are components of the internal transducer LST-defined subsystems.

Differentiating General Hypotheses into Specific Research Hypotheses

General hypotheses form an important link between the ever-growing and diversifying collection of scientific knowledge and rigorous, but more limited, general mathematical theories. Such theories are reductions of this knowledge and are achieved within methodical thought systems that employ various schemes of instrumental reasoning. In terms of LST, general hypotheses are verbal conceptual systems that assert the specific abstracted systems (limited sets of relationships) that, in turn, are studied by constructing and manipulation quantitative conceptual systems.

General hypotheses may be differentiated into specific research hypotheses that may be empirically confirmed or disconfirmed by employing understood measurements and statistical techniques. Ideally, such general hypotheses should be differentiated first into unique instrumental reasoning or general mathematical theories and then into the specific research hypotheses of particular methodologies. The question of how general is general is ever present, however. Furthermore, because of their uniqueness, such general theories depend greatly on the ingenuity of researchers, not already developed methodologies; and thus their emergence cannot be predicted or regularly anticipated.

Therefore, it is important to realize that researchers can differentiate general hypotheses directly to specific research hypotheses of particular already-developed methodologies and often do so. This "leap-frog" procedure actually contributes to the construction of general instrumental reasoning or mathematical theories by providing an array of specific relationships that may not be apparent in the statement of the general hypothesis itself. *Caveat*: In no way does this statement imply that we are suggesting differentiation by loose analogy, which may overlook important elements of an isomorphism, whether verbal or numeric.

Important differentiations should attempt to hypothesize well-defined relationships between components within an organization and between such components and the organization's environmental components based on a general hypothesis. For example, concerning an organization, let

MEI be aggregate matter–energy inflows measured by the money–information marker transmissions of exchanges

Mo be the net change in the residual of currency money–information markers that remain in the circuitous system unconverted to *MEI*

MEI + *Mo* be termed *GI* (gross inputs)

Cr be creditor documents

O be owner documents

S be socialization documents

GI − (*Cr* + *0* + *S*) = *GSG* (gross system-generated increase or decrease)

Then,

$$GSG/GI \cdot GI/MEI = GSG/MEI.$$

(These relationships are fully developed in Chapters 7 and 8. A method for sorting accounting report information into these classifications is also given there.)

According to the general hypothesis, we may expect the organization to maximize *MEI* within constraints imposed by *Cr*, *O*, and *S*. That is to say, the organization will increase *MEI* unless signaled by the aggregate of *Cr*, *O*, and *S* flows to change. Creditors, owners, and socialization institutions provide positive feedback signals when organizations are providing an acceptable level of currency money–information marker outputs to these markets. When the output falls to an unacceptable level, negative feedback signals are sent, and the organization decreases *MEI*. Consequently, given the circuitous mechanistic thought system defined above and the dynamic of the general hypothesis, we may hypothesize the following:

Ho: For organizations and in terms of direction of change (increases or decreases), no important and orderly relationships exist between changes in the ratio *GSG/MEI* and time-lagged changes in the absolute amount of *MEI* measured over time for certain connected periods of the same length.

Ha: For organizations and in terms of direction of change (increases or decreases), an important and orderly relationship connects change in the ratio *GSG/MEI* and time-lagged changes in the absolute amount of *MEI* measured over time for certain connected periods of the same length.

However, we expect that feedback processes are generally efficient in profit organizations. Consequently, we expect directional changes in rates of change in *GSG/MEI* and *MEI* to constitute feedback signals. Therefore, we hypothesize:

Ho: For organizations and in terms of change (increases or decreases), no important orderly relationship connects changes in the *rate of change* in the ratio *GSG/MEI* and the *rate of time-lagged changes* in the absolute amount of *MEI* measured over time for certain connected periods of the same length.

Ha: For organizations and in terms of directional change (increases or decreases), an important and orderly relationship connects changes in the rate of change in the ratio *GSG/MEI* and the time-lagged changes in the rate of change in the absolute amount of *MEI* measured over time for certain connected periods of the same length.

Even this latter hypothesis is relatively general. Two elements are loosely defined: (1) the length of the period over which the flows are accumulated and (2) length of the time lag between changes in rate of change in the ratio *GSG/MEI* and the rate of change in the absolute amount of *MEI*. However, this illustrates the nature of the process of discovery through hypothesis testing. As individual studies hypothesize specific values for these elements, those values for which the null hypothesis cannot be rejected are eliminated one by one, and we move closer to discovering how organizations function. Furthermore, we expect that different types of organizations and, indeed, different organizations themselves will exhibit different certain but dynamic values for these variables. Therefore, individual studies also may hypothesize these values for individual organizations and types of organizations. A variety of specific mathematical and statistical methods and procedures may be justified and used in such individual studies.

This particular example of what we mean by differentiating a general hypothesis into specific research hypotheses is only one among many that may be differentiated to study various levels of living systems and their subsystems. LST provides a 5 × 20 matrix that directly concerns accounting information systems. It specifically identifies and connects levels of living systems (group, organization, community, society, and supranational systems) and their subsystems (identified on Table 4–1, Chapter 4). These systems and subsystems combine in unique configurations in a competitive environment to survive indefinitely. Modern accounting is actively attempting to solve problems at each of the five levels. The twenty subsystems are discussed extensively in the literature (Miller, 1978; Swanson and Miller, 1986). The LST general hypothesis may be differentiated into specific hypotheses designed to investigate 100 different but specifically connected concrete system components that involve accounting information systems.

One Possible Accounting Research and LST Connection

The term *empirical research* certainly conveys to different groups of investigators different notions. Nevertheless, all are associated with the idea of rigorous observation. To further explain the term and to show how it fits into one aspect of current accounting research, we discuss our concept of empirical research in the context of the positive accounting theory that Watts and Zimmerman (1986) review. These researchers consider this set of theory an empirical science because it postulates what they believe are empirically confirable hypotheses. The discussion presumes their interpretation of the development of this body of research.

The phrase *positive accounting theory* as used by Watts and Zimmerman designates a set of theories and methodologies underlying economics-based empirical research on accounting information systems. Generally, these studies are based on theories and methodologies adopted from the disciplines of economics and finance. This line of research began in earnest with Ball and Brown (1968), progressed through tests based on numerous variations of the efficient market hypothesis (EMH) and the capital asset pricing model (CAPM) to a theory of accounting practice based on two theories adopted directly from economics, that is, the theory of the firm and the theory of regulation.

This group of investigators espouses a "scientific" view of theory; that is, the object of theory is to explain and predict. By prediction they mean that "the theory predicts unobserved accounting phenomena . . . not necessarily future phenomena" (Watts and Zimmerman, 1986, p. 1). Such theory can provide hypotheses about attributes of firms, and those predictions may be tested with historical data. This general view is not significantly different from that of LST.

The manner of applying the general view to produce specific hypotheses and tests, however, differs in the following important aspects: (1) the method of constructing and applying theory, (2) the use of measurements versus surrogates, (3) the degree of differentiation between the accounting information system and the decision processes of economic actors, and, perhaps most importantly, (4) the focus of investigation.

(1) We have described how LST is applied; that is, a general hypothesis is developed from a conceptual framework of a scientific discipline, and, in turn, differentiation of specific research hypotheses is guided by the dynamic of the general hypothesis and the detail of the conceptual framework. Positive accounting theorists have adopted hypotheses based on relatively limited conceptual frameworks from the economics and finance disciplines. As particular theories proved inadequately broad, additional theories were adopted; and eventually an integrative theory of accounting practice was formed. It is expected that some adopted theories and methods will be disregarded and that others will be more firmly integrated as the theory evolves.

These two methods of constructing and applying theory are obviously different. LST integrates not only economics and finance but also the biological, social, behavioral, and systems sciences. Can we expect that as positive accounting theory progresses, it will incorporate theories from these other disciplines? Given the organized special interest groups in the accounting profession, and if the underlying thrust of positive accounting theory is empirical investigation involving accounting information systems (we believe it is), the answer is possibly yes. Therefore, might it be possible to expedite the development of empirical research in those collateral areas by merging the LST integration with the positive accounting theory momentum, quantitative methods, and knowledge of data bases?

Watts and Zimmerman (1986, p. 357) list the major limitations of positive accounting theory as:

1. Developing proxy variables that actually represent contracting and political costs.

2. Specifying the cross-sectional models.

3. Collinearity among the contracting variables.

Contracting and political costs are costs associated with roles. As discussed above, theoretic statements about roles are difficult to test by any form of data collection. All three limitations are the result of attempting to test theories about roles directly.

Theories that make statements about measurable attributes are less difficult to test. Over many centuries the accounting information system has evolved to process information about observable physical systems. The elements (measurable attributes) of these systems provide ready variables for models based on concrete system measurements. The information the accounting system processes about elements of other systems and subsystems are the variables that combine in unique patterns to create the principal-agent and regulator-regulated roles. Consequently, we believe that the general scientific view of theory may be applied more directly by observing these measurable progenitors of those roles and inferring from such observations certain characteristics and limits on those roles.

(2) The use of surrogates (proxy variables) is immediately connected to attempting to observe roles directly. Their use is symptomatic of a problem that underlies modern accounting thought and, indeed, much of the thought of the social disciplines. A clear distinction between measurements of concrete processes and their interpretations is not always made. In fact, in too many cases, modern measurement theory is perceived to allow any form of quantified surrogation. This application of such a liberal theory for assigning numbers to observations can easily quantify interpretations right along with measurements. In this situation, it is possible to quantify nonempirical elements, mix them with empirical ones, and give the whole exercise an air of empiricism.

We believe that accounting researchers have not yet pushed back the frontiers of accounting knowledge based on measurable elements of concrete processes. This is a fundamental exercise of empirical research and should be attempted.

Observing the day-to-day information-processing activities of the accounting information system, it is difficult to understand why such fundamental research is not a major focus of current accounting research. The answer may lie in the neglect of double-entry bookkeeping by many modern researchers. Mattessich (1984, pp. 407–408) explains this neglect:

The neglect which this model has suffered in the hands of the younger generation of academic accountants may be explained by two factors. The first is a natural reaction to what they regard as a symbol of the past, representing mere description without any analytical challenge. The second, not unrelated to the first, lies in a misunderstanding of the nature of the double-classification model. They regard it as an occasionally convenient but purely coincidental classification device, thereby overlooking the empirical and general "physical" foundation underlying this conception.

As discussed in Chapters 5 and 6, we believe that modern measurement theory provides the basis to rigorously identify the measurement characteristics of this double-entry (double-classification) model and to develop methodologies and mathematical models that exploit its characteristics for rigorous empirical research. Such measurements can be used to infer characteristics of complex roles from empirical data, providing an alternative to selecting proxy variables (surrogates).

(3) The degree of differentiation between accounting information systems and the decision processes of individual economic actors is related directly to clearly distinguishing measurements of concrete systems and their interpretations. Nobody denies that accounting (the measurement focus) and management (the interpretation focus) are related, but distinctly different, functions.

Possibly, economics and finance are disciplines that primarily study problems from the perspective of the decider subsystem (management). Thus, we would expect that they are rich in quantified conceptual systems (decision models) that attempt to study, in a comprehensible frame, large accumulations of elements in extended space and time.

Finance is possibly a field of study that attempts to provide empirical confirmation or disconfirmation of various purely conceptual economic models. Because it is more an extension of economics (a decider subsystem orientation) than accounting (a transducer subsystem orientation), whose empirical numbers it uses, a bias toward confirmation of the model might exist. Such a bias might be expected because information is also processed to and from the decider subsystem by transducer components other than the accounting information system, providing the decider with information additional to that provided by accounting. Up to a point, more information is generally perceived to be better. Consequently, data that is perceived to be empirical (such as accounting data) may be put into a model in an arrangement that the researcher believes captures some of that additional information as well. The model thus may mix measurement data and interpretive data (the specific arrangement of data and its assigned meaning). Certainly, such an approach is not unreasonable when viewed from the functional position of the decider subsystem. However, it does fall short of the degree of empiricism obtainable from accounting measurements.

Viewing the process from the functional position of the internal transducer emphasizes information quality. In terms of the accounting information system, this emphasizes concrete system feedback and thus the empirical observations contained in accounting data. Those observations become the basic building blocks of quantitative models, that is, differentiations and syntheses of the accounting data into unique configurations that concern management questions. We believe that LST, as we have discussed it, can help establish an accounting orientation for empirical research involving accounting information system measurements of the concrete elements of organizations.

(4) Because the theories that were adopted early on were themselves narrowly focused, a relatively narrow focus may be expected of positive accounting theory. Clearly, the positive accounting theory focus of investigation is expanding. While many of the studies are focused on aspects of one type of organization (e.g., the New York Stock Exchange), applications of the theory to auditing are much broader.

Positive accounting theory depends fundamentally on a firm's (organization's) value, and this value is some combination of the market value of the firm's ownership and debt securities. Such values are determined by another organization such as the New York Stock Exchange. Thus the focus of positive accounting theory is on the particular information exchange between a particular firm and one or two other firms. Although positive accounting theory studies involve many other variables, all are ultimately evaluated by how they contribute to or obstruct increases in firm value. The problem we see is that such firm value is managed within the constraints of the stock exchange organization and constitutes only one aspect of the overall growth-maximizing function of the firm. In fact, over some indefinite period, this value actually may be managed purposefully downward.

On this point, LST comes close to asserting a hypothesis opposite to that of positive accounting theory. Rather than an opposing hypothesis, however, we believe that the LST general hypothesis may be viewed as broadening the focus of positive accounting theory. By substituting ''the optimization of the specific exchange monetary value of aggregate concrete inflows of the firm'' for ''the optimization of firm value,'' positive accounting theory could be expanded for use in empirical research on all sorts of organizations, profit-oriented and otherwise, and connected directly to measurable concrete flows. This statement does not suggest that specific investigations that attempt to identify the relationship of profit-oriented and regulated firms to different specific market organizations should be discontinued. Rather, it suggests an additional specific type of investigation.

Such a broadening of focus is both lateral and vertical—lateral in that it includes more of the accounting domain at the theoretic level of positive accounting theory and vertical in that it extends the research from its present theoretic level toward the practical level. Discussing agency theory, Mattessich (1984, p. 406) considers this latter type of extension important.

One of the most crucial tasks, however, has hardly begun, that of relating this impressive ''economic theory'' for management accountants to the daily purpose-oriented details of academic management accounting theory proper (which consists in the formation and testing of specific purpose-oriented hypotheses about realization, valuation, allocation, classification, and so forth). To our mind, a prerequisite for the emergence of an instrumentally useful management accounting theory is the connecting of the latter object-area to the meta-areas of the agency theory.

We are not suggesting that Mattessich is necessarily arguing our case. By building formal models of contractural relationships, the positive accounting theory researchers may be closer to the extension Mattessich envisions than is the research we advocate. Nevertheless, he doubtlessly argues for extension in the direction of theories that are useful for empirical investigations of concrete systems.

In modern times, a distinction is sometimes made between sciences that concern statements that are in principle irrefutable by experience (i.e., purely analytical) and those that concern statements that are refutable by experience. Mattessich (1978, pp. 7–10; 1984, p. 400) makes this distinction concerning applied social sciences such as accounting.

Watts and Zimmerman definitely view positive accounting theory as empirical science and yet acknowledge that the statements it concerns are not directly refutable by experience—proxy variables must be developed. Such variables are part of the extension from purely analytical science to "the daily purpose-oriented details of academic management accounting theory proper" advocated by Mattessich.

Mattessich accepts a clear distinction between analytical sciences and empirical ones. Nevertheless, this polarization might be a great benefit to accounting if analytical and empirical researchers collaborate in fruitful teamwork similar to that between theoretical and experimental physicists, if analytic and empirical accounting research is integrated into a coherent overall framework of accounting theory, and if theoretic achievements are practice-oriented and find ultimate application. We believe that one way, among several, to bring together analytical research and empirical research is to adapt the methodology of positive accounting theory to statements made directly about the concrete processes of organization that we are describing.

Summary

Can LST provide general hypotheses for research involving accounting information systems? We believe it can.

LST is a scientific conceptual framework based on a mosaic of general principles and ideas that have developed within numerous scientific disciplines and that are related to accounting thought in one way or another. Among its many concepts, four are particularly significant in developing a general hypothesis for research involving accounting information systems: (1) concrete systems, (2) fluctuous steady state, (3) fray-out, and (4) hierarchy theory. Based on these concepts, LST postulates a unique linkage among important elements of the concrete processes of organizations. From this linkage, a general hypothesis is formulated and three adaptations are developed.

Because scientific research is perceived differently by different groups, what we mean by this term is explained by distinguishing between conceptual frameworks for research and those for practice; overviewing the general process of scientific methodology, experimentation, and hypothesis testing; and examining the connection between selected current accounting research and that which we advocate in this study. These discussions clearly define a type of research that may contribute to the advancement of empirical research involving accounting information systems.

References

Allen, T. F. H., and T. B. Starr, *Hierarchy: Perspectives for Ecological Complexity*. Chicago: University of Chicago Press, 1982.

Anthony, R. N. *Tell It Like It Was*. New York: Richard D. Irwin, 1983.

Ashby, W. R. *Design for a Brain*. New York: John Wiley, 1954.

Ball, R. J., and P. Brown. "An Empirical Evaluation of Accounting Income Numbers." *Journal of Accounting Research* 6 (Autumn, 1968), pp. 159–178.

Cannon, W. B. *Wisdom of the Body*. New York: Norton, 1939.

Chambers, R. J. *Accounting, Evaluation and Economic Behavior*. Englewood Cliffs, NJ: Prentice-Hall, 1966.

Financial Accounting Standards Board (FASB). *Objectives of Financial Reporting Business Enterprises*. FASB, Stamford, CT: (SFAC 1), 1978.

Foerster, H. von. "Communication Amongst Automata." *American Journal of Psychiatry* (1962), pp. 118, 866–67.

Georgescu-Roegen, N. *Energy and Economic Myths*. New York: Pergammon Press, 1976.

Ijiri, Y. *Historical Cost Accounting and Its Rationality: Research Monograph No. 1*. Vancouver, B.C.: The Canadian Certified General Accountant's Research Foundation, 1981.

Kaplan, M. A. *System and Process in International Politics*. New York: John Wiley, 1957.

Kempf, E. J. "Basic Biodynamics." *Annual of the New York Academy of Science* (1958), pp. 894–95.

Kohler, W. *Die physischen Gestalten in Ruhe und in stationaren Zustand*. Braunschveig, Vieweg, 1921.

LeChatelier, H. "Recherches Experimentales of Theoriques sur les Equilibres Chimiques." *Annales des Mines*, Huitième Sevie, Memories, 12, Dunod (1888), p. 200.

Leontief, W. *Input-Output Economics*. New York: Oxford Unversity Press, 1966.

Leontief, W., H. B. Chenery, D. G. Clark, J. S. Duesenberry, A. R. Ferguson, A. P. Grosse, R. M. Grosse, M. Holzmann, W. Isard, and H. Kistin. *Studies in the Structure of the American Economy*. New York: Oxford University Press, 1953.

Mattessich, R. *Accounting and Analytical Methods*. Homewood, IL; New York: Richard D. Irwin, 1964.

_____. *Instrumental Reasoning and Systems Methodology*. New York: D. Reidel, 1978.

_____. *Modern Accounting Research: History, Survey, and Guide*. Vancouver, B.C.: CGA Research Foundation, 1984.

Miller, J. G., "Toward a General Theory for the Behavioral Sciences." *American Psychologist* 10 (1955), pp. 513–31.

_____. "Living Systems: Structure and Process." *Behavioral Science* 10 (1965a), pp. 337–79.

_____. "Living Systems: Cross-Level Hypotheses." *Behavioral Science* 10 (1965b), pp. 380–411.

_____. *Living Systems*. New York: McGraw, 1978.

_____. "Can Systems Theory Generate Testable Hypotheses? From Talcott Parsons to Living Systems Theory." *Systems Research* Vol. 3, No. 2 (1986), pp. 73–84.

O'Neill, R. V., DeAngelis, D. L., Waide, J. B., and Allen, T. F. H. *A Hierarchical Concept of Ecosystems*. Princeton, NJ: Princeton University Press, 1986.

Pareto, V. *The Mind and Society*. New York: Harcourt, Brace, 1935.

Parsons, T. "Concrete Systems and "Abstracted' Systems." *Contemporary Sociology* 8 (1979), pp. 696–705.

_____. "Concrete Systems and 'Abstracted' Systems." *Behavioral Science* 25 (1980), pp. 46–55.

Parsons, T., and N. J. Smelser. *Economy and Society*. New York: Free Press, 1946.

Prigogine, I. *Introduction to Thermodynamics of Irreversible Processes*. New York: Charles C. Thomas, 1955.

Schumpeter, J. A. *Business Cycles*. New York: McGraw-Hill, 1939.

Sherman, H. D., ed. *Conceptual Frameworks for Financial Accounting*. Boston: The President and Fellows of Harvard College, 1984.

Sterling, R. R. *Toward a Science of Accounting*. New York: Scholars Book Co., 1979.

Swanson, G. A. "An Inquiry into the Utility of a Parallel System for Providing Insights into the Development of an Accounting Conceptual System." *Advances in Accounting* 4 (1987a), pp. 3–12.

Watts, R. L., and Zimmerman, J. L. *Positive Accounting Theory*. Englewood Cliffs, NJ: Prentice-Hall, 1986.

Weiss, P. "Animal Behavior as Systems Reaction." *General Systems* 4 (1959), p. 8.

10
ACCOUNTING MEASUREMENT OF CONCRETE PROCESSES APPLIED TO SOCIETIES

Introduction

Although they apply generally to all higher-level living systems, previous chapters emphasize the organization level. This emphasis occurs because the focus of modern accounting is on organizations. From the perspective of a firm, managerial accounting is termed *internal accounting* and financial accounting is viewed as *accounting for external reporting*.

Because organizations are relatively independent components of societies, their accounting information systems are not components of society-level accounting information systems. Rather, their reports provide relatively independent data, which in turn are gathered by information processing subsystems of societies for societal uses.

To recognize that GAAP-regulated accounting itself is not societal accounting is important. GAAP accounting is a product of organizational deciders who cause the information to be encoded and output-transduced according to a particular set of rules and regulations. On the other hand, societal accounting is a product of the internal transducer subsystem of a society. Such subsystems are always components of society-level living systems—and not necessarily exponents of a subsystem of any particular lower-level system or set of systems.

Accounting is recognized widely to include the actions of recording and reporting for planning and control. At the societal level, these actions occur first in the money–information marker flows. The movements of goods and services are both recorded and reported in this information medium by the exchange process itself. Control is exercised by societal forces limiting the money supply and planning is accomplished by individuals on the basis of their residual and estimated potential money–information marker flows.

Consequently, in a modern market society (one organized around relatively independent economic flows), the most basic societal accounting is done primarily by the money–information marker flows themselves. To a degree, those flows are influenced by every individual human decider in the society. Goods and services that pass among people are recorded in the money–information marker flows by how those people choose to spend their money. Of course, this fundamentally simple process is complicated by allowing credit in the economic system and by the characteristics of the banking and other financial institutions of a society.

Governments and other corporate societal deciders derive reports from the raw information contained in the monetary flows by causing observers to be placed at certain spatiotemporal locations to record measurements of both the attribute specific exchange value and physical attributes such as volume of coal in tons or of milk in gallons. Statistics such as those based on national accounts attempt to estimate overall social economic activity. Such statistics are used in various society-level policy decisions.

In this chapter, we propose to extend the theory of accounting measurement of concrete processes that we describe in prior chapters to the society level of living systems. In practice, such an extension should be relatively easy, because the work of Leontief (1966) on input-output economics provides a widely understood system for analyzing information about concrete processes from that perspective.

Leontief's recognition of a need for an empirical science of economics pioneered a major movement toward empirical analyses of economies. He states, "The engine of economic theory has reached, in the last twenty years, a high degree of internal perfection and has been turning over with much sound and fury. If the advance of economics as an empirical science is still rather slow and uncertain, the lack of sustained contact between the wheels of theory and the hard facts of reality is mainly to blame" (Leontief, 1953, p. 4). We believe that concrete process analysis, CPA, may be used to expand the empirical orientation of this movement.

Consequently, we propose that a new branch of input-output economics be developed based on measurements of both goods and services and money–information marker flows. Such measurements would provide more precise empirical evidence in much greater volume than the current system provides. To explain our proposal in some detail, we first discuss how input-output modeling of societies differs from that of organizations. How Leontief's basic input-output tabulation of information and specification of important relationships may be adapted for use with accounting measurements of concrete processes is discussed and illustrated. We discuss the importance of cross-level information disconnects generally, the Financial Accounting Standards Board in the context of information disconnects, and, finally, some additional comparisons of FASB's conceptual framework with our proposals.

How Concrete Process Analyses Differ for Societies and Organizations

Without doubt, concrete processes examined at each of the two levels of living systems termed *society* and *organization* are the same basic processes. Any difference in analyses made at the two levels is a matter of perspective. That is to say, the spatiotemporal location of observers and observation devices differs significantly in the two types of analyses.

At the organization level, observations are made from within an organization as various forms of matter, energy, and money–information markers cross an organization boundary. Both the input and output of every transaction are formally observed and quantitatively equated. Generally, this observation process equates money–information markers measured on a monetary scale to various forms of matter and energy, thus restating the matter–energy in terms of monetary units.

On the other hand, at the society level input-output analysis is concerned generally with observing and equating the inputs of a particular organization or set of organizations with the outputs of another organization or set of organizations. To do so, it accepts information outputs (reports) from organizations as its primary data. This use of the methodic thought system underlying the input-output model is different from its use at the organization level.

As we discuss in detail in previous chapters, both positive and negative growth occurs over time in the concrete systems being mapped at the organization level by the input-output model. If the construct logic of the model itself is not violated, the residual used to close the input-output conceptual system is a cosmic measurement of that growth. Thus, growth that occurs over time is measured in terms of a spatiotemporal scale consisting of a monetary ratio scale and discrete but connected periods. From within organizations, this growth is determined with relative ease because a direct comparison is made between the inputs and outputs of a particular system that survives by maintaining a dynamic equilibrium, purposefully biased toward growth, among such inputs and outputs.

These same inputs and outputs may be viewed from the perspective of society. That is to say, they may be viewed from a vantage point that is external to particular organization-level systems. From this vantage point a recognized important question has been that of identifying the patterns of goods and services transferred within an economy among its components. An input-output model based on a closed methodical conceptual system may be used to analyze such movements.

Within such a conceptual system, the inputs equal the outputs. This is not the case because a residual is used to close the system as in the organization-level double-entry model. Rather, in the society-level model inputs equal outputs because they constitute two expressions of the same measurement on particular flows. That is to say, a particular input to one organization or sector of an

Figure 10–1
Different Uses of Input-Output Modeling by Organizations and Societies

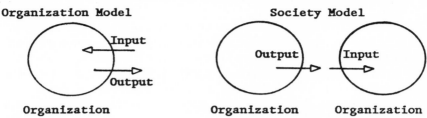

economy of a matter–energy form, such as 2 million tons of coal, came from somewhere. Where it came from is the output.

This observation is significantly different from an organization-level observation that equates money–information markers to other forms of matter–energy as they are exchanged in a transaction. No growth, positive or negative, occurs in a particular transaction between organizations. Growth occurs within organizations by making two or more transactions. Of course, a person may view a transaction as if part of a value received is profit. To do so, however, he or she must have knowledge of a previous transaction that assigned specific exchange value to the object given in the later transaction. Growth is calculated at the organization level by comparing total inputs of a particular organization to the total outputs in a period. In the society-level input-output model, the inputs of one or more organizations are simply acknowledged to be the outputs of others.

So at the organization level, accountants use double-entry bookkeeping to record the two distinct actions of a transaction, inputs and outputs. This conceptual system involves the entire concrete economic system, both money–information markers and goods and services. Currently, at the society level a single-entry model is used to construct double records of the same element that obviously are equal, barring recording errors. If $a = c$ and $b = c$, then $a = b$. Figure 10–1 illustrates the difference between the two observation and modeling methods.

Double-entry at the organization level records the inputs and outputs of a particular exchange, generally involving both goods or services and money. Single-entry at the societal level generally analyzes the outputs of an organization or sector as the inputs of others, making two records of each particular flow of goods and services by recording each amount twice or by recording one set of amounts and calculating the other set. In the organization model, the total input-output equality for a period is forced by adding the difference between inputs and outputs to the smaller of the two. The society model provides total equality of inputs and outputs because in some sense anything is equal to itself.

The Extension of Double-Entry Bookkeeping to the Societal Level

The changes we suggest in accounting information-gathering and reporting procedures (Chapter 7) would make it possible to extend double-entry bookkeeping to society-level accounting. Such an extension should be made on the basis of concrete process analysis, CPA, and not on the basis of GAAP. The changes we suggest in Chapter 7 may be made incrementally, involving at a particular increment only minor methodological adjustments. Implementing three-dimensional double-entry bookkeeping (monetary units, time, physical units) and requiring public reporting of concrete processes aggregated to a certain degree would provide data for using double-entry bookkeeping at the societal level.

Such a system would measure at a certain level of aggregation the specific exchange value of all transactions among components (e.g., organizations and people) of society. That measurement would increase significantly the information available for intrasociety and intersector analysis. It would allow investigators to examine such feedback processes as we describe in Chapter 7 among sectors or industries. It would allow reasonable transformation equations to be constructed to restate summary specific exchange values measured in monetary units of transactions between sectors into summary units of physical attributes for particular periods. Fundamentally, it would base the national accounts on measurements of a population rather than on extrapolations of measurements of samples or on opinions of surveyees. Fisher (1987) discusses some of the shortcomings of data collected by those latter methods. Basically, current census structures do not provide for collecting data on all variations of the production of a particular good.

At first glance, our proposal might appear to involve an overwhelmingly large data collection system. It does not. Already, most industrial societies collect, on the scale we are proposing, two different and separate sets of data, that is, data based on GAAP and data based on tax law.

Initially, the extension of double-entry bookkeeping to societies should be made by using the classifications of aggregated flows that we describe in prior chapters (materials; people; energy; communications; currency money– information markers, or MIM; credit MIM; owner MIM; and socialization MIM). Such flows should be measured as they flow in and out of the twenty critical processes (subsystems) of societies (see Table 4–1). The industrial classifications currently used are based on no fundamental conceptual system that can explain why they are arranged as they are. Increasingly, conglomerate corporate organization diminishes the usefulness of information arranged by the current industrial scheme. In such an environment, identifying who or what provides critical processes is difficult but increasingly important as societies grow more complex.

In the following pages, we discuss how the current societal accounting system based on Leontief's studies may be adapted to incorporate our proposals. An important aspect of expanding the societal accounting system is the construction of upward information flow disconnects. If a free-market type of society is to be retained under expanded information flows, provisions must be made to consciously block some information flows. We include a discussion of this aspect with descriptions of the current basic input-output economics model and the societal double-entry bookkeeping that we propose.

Input-Output Economics

Future accounting historians may view the works of Wassily Leontief and his colleagues as progenitors of society-level accounting. Their seminal work on input-output economics provides a frame that may be used to analyze the economic processes of societies. This work underlies a system of national accounts now used by many nations to study their economies. What is possibly the most familiar of all economic statistics, the gross national product, is generated by this system of accounts.

According to Leontief, "The input-output method is an adaptation of the neoclassical theory of general equilibrium to the empirical study of the quantitative interdependence between interrelated economic activities" (1966, p. 134). The conceptual systems that underlie the accounting input-output model, Leontief's input-output model, and LST have important similarities. Leontief's model concerns flows of inputs and outputs of various forms of matter, energy, and information through a set of sectors (industries) in an economy. Both LST and the accounting input-output model are concerned with those same forms of matter, energy, and information. Both Leontief's and the accounting models are based on closed methodic thought systems. Both the accounting and the input-output economics models allow perceptions to be manipulated only as quantities.

Accountants for organizations provide information in a highly disaggregated form by using many more accounts than would be necessary to provide information on the five general forms of matter–energy and the twenty critical processes of living systems discussed in prior chapters. Similarly, the national accounts mapped 370 separate industries in 1963 (National Economics Division of the Office of Business Economics, 1969, p. 16). As we demonstrate in prior chapters, many of the organization accounts can be shown to provide information about LST-defined elements of concrete systems. Likewise, many of the industries mapped can be identified as components of LST-defined societal subsystems.

In the model used for national accounts, it is possible to trace the flow of any particular good or service from its original producer through each of the industries that use it to its final destination in households, governments, or exports. Alternatively, the inputs to a particular producer from other producers and from labor that are required to produce a particular good or service are easily calculated. Consequently, regularly updated computerized input-output models are maintained by governments to provide detailed information about the interrelationships among their societies' industries. Those models are also used to study the effects of anticipated or hypothetical changes in demand for or availability of a good or service.

The Importance of Cross-Level Information Disconnects

Leontief provides a method for tracking concrete observable economic flows by using a system of input-output balancing equations. His system allows certain statistical disconnects between the actual measurements taken on concrete processes that are classified and aggregated by accounting systems at the organization level and the estimates processed by the society-level accounts. These disconnects (e.g., sampling) apparently are not the results of conscious efforts to construct disconnects because of some perceived need to do so. Rather, they exist in the system as a result of the difficulties of collecting empirical data.

Likely, a societal accounting system that does not incorporate information disconnects between the society level and the organization level can become overly connected. Hierarchy theorists provide models for observing disconnects in eco systems of various sorts.

If such disconnects do not exist, the constraints provided by higher hierarchical levels do not exist. Without such constraints the lower-level elements simply grow unrestrained by higher-level patterning. The type of disconnect that prevents such dissipation of higher-level systems is one that blocks the flows of certain information downward to lower-level systems. The type of disconnect that statistical sampling may provide is one that blocks the flow of certain information upward from lower-level systems, for example, organizations, to higher-level systems such as society. Although the study of this type of disconnect is not emphasized by hierarchy theorists, it is nevertheless very important to the study of human social structure.

Leontief's work may very well be a major contribution to the ability of the West to build a social structure that incorporates societal strength while maintaining "independent" organizations as its components. Paradoxically, had historical developments in accountancy not denied him the degree of empiricism that he possibly was attempting to capture, these critical disconnects might never have been incorporated into his system. If the national accounts had been based on full measurement, the independence of organizations would have been difficult to maintain. As it turned out, alternative channels to those of the system of national accounts had to be opened for information flow before politicians could exercise more control over organizations, for example, those provided by civil rights and occupational safety legislation in the United States. In the absence of disconnects for certain upward information flows, it is likely that society itself eventually becomes an organization-level living system. That is to say, all of the diversified decider subsystems of individual organizations become nested in the decider subsystem of the system that collects and thus controls the information.

In view of this situation, if a proposal is made to base societal accounting on direct measurements, and we make such a proposal, it must contain conscious provisions for disconnects of certain upward information flows. If such disconnects are not constructed, the modern free-market system likely may degenerate into a vast bureaucracy.

One way to construct appropriate upward information disconnects is *not* to require public reporting of quantities disaggregated beyond a certain degree and of classifications detailed beyond some agreed-upon level. For example, perhaps aggregates for less than one year or one quarter should not be reported publicly and labor should not be subclassified into more categories than hourly wages and salaries. Other perhaps ingenious methods for disconnecting certain upward information flows may be conceived.

Perhaps history is now providing a societal laboratory to identify useful information disconnects. The Eastern bloc of nations is attempting to use market forces in a limited manner. Because such limited expressions may be expected to be less complex than the expression of an entire market-based society, the disconnects that create limited expressions may be varied and the covariance of the market expressions studied. On the other hand, when upward-flow information *connections* are created within mature market societies, it is difficult to measure their effects. The ingenious construction of upward-flow information disconnects in societies with limited market expressions may provide an economic rather than a psychological means of attaining a high level of social welfare.

The dawning of the information age has thrust upon the human race the necessity of purposefully limiting information flows, both upward and downward. The West must discover and preserve those important *disconnects* that have provided the degree of individual freedom achieved and the important *connections* that have provided the unification to produce its historically unparalleled wealth. The East may provide the setting for learning what disconnects and what connections are important.

How a Societal Double-Entry System Compares to Input-Output Economics

Obviously, the salient difference in input-output economics and societal concrete process analysis is the manner in which the two systems collect economic data. The data collection methods that provide data for input-output economic analyses use various forms of statistical inference. Societal double-entry uses only aggregation within the constraints of the accounting measurement scale discussed in Chapter 5. Consequently, the quantities used in the input-output models of Leontief likely differ from those used for societal double-entry accounting.

Table 10–1

A Matrix of Quantitative Input-Output Relationships Stated in Monetary Units (Millions)

| | | Purchaser | | | Total |
Producer	Iron	Food	Building	Households	Output
Iron	10	20	30	20	80
Food	-	80	-	100	180
Building	10	20	30	110	170
Households	15	30	50	20	115
TOTAL INPUT	35	150	110	250	545

Societal double-entry bookkeeping consists of derived measurements taken on physical processes by organizations and reported publicly. Such reports are made at regular intervals on the time continuum. This system is not at all competitive with input-output analysis itself, only with its current methods of data collection. In fact, the regular flow of information provided by a double-entry system may be used to validate the conclusions of various input-output analyses and to update vital coefficients (ratios relating unit inputs to unit outputs). This latter use would help ameliorate an acknowledged difficulty with the current system (Wienrib, 1987).

In input-output economic analysis, information about inputs and outputs of various sectors of an economy is tabulated on a matrix of producing (output) and purchasing (input) industries. As discussed previously, the inputs-outputs are two statements of single entries. Consequently, the matrix formats inputs and outputs on a single set of industries as illustrated in Table 10–1.

Obviously, this short discussion omits many important details of the basic input-output model and, of course, its many analytic variations, for example, Auger's (1985). Our purpose is to show in the simplest form possible the fundamental changes our proposal entails. Because they are fundamental and involve data characteristics rather than model structure, these changes may be incorporated in most of the available analytic variations of input-output models.

Tables 10–1, 10–2A, 10–2B and 10–3 are recognizably fictitious. They demonstrate important tabular format and relationships, however. On Table 10–1 the total output of the iron industry is 80 as listed in the last column. That industry's total input from other industries is 35, the total of Column 1. Of course, the input-output must be stated on a common denominator such as dollars for the table to be columnar additive.

Three dimensional double-entry accounting would provide two matrices on the same set of sectors, one matrix in terms of monetary units measured as

Table 10–2A
A Table of Quantitative Input-Output Relationships Stated in Terms of Physical Attribute Measurements (In Millions)

Producer	Iron	Food	Purchaser Building	Households	Total Output	Meas. Unit
Iron	5	9	18	11	43	Tons
Food	-	150	-	190	340	Lbs.
Building	.0001	.00015	.00025	.0014	.0019	Units
Households	1.5	3.2	4.5	2.0	11.2	Man Hrs.

Table 10–2B
A Table of Quantitative Input-Output Relationships Stated in Terms of Monetary Units of Specific Exchange Value (In Millions)

Producer	Iron	Food	Purchaser Building	Households	Total Output
Iron	11	20	32	18	81
Food	-	90	-	95	185
Building	10	22	28	105	165
Households	16	34	48	20	118
TOTAL INPUT	37	166	108	238	549

described in Chapters 5 and 6 and the other in terms of the dominant measurements of physical attributes.

This societal double-entry differs from currently used organization-level double-entry. Organization-level double entry records the specific exchange monetary value as in Table 10–2B. In that system, however, information about the intrinsic physical characteristics of the goods and services of a transaction is categorical. Relying on three-dimensional double-entry recording and reporting procedures, the societal double-entry described in Table 10–2A uses ratio scale information, such as tons, to upgrade physical attribute measurements from a categorical scale to a ratio scale.

In addition to providing increased precision by measuring physical flows (both matter–energy and money–information markers) instead of inferring them based on probability theory, this expanded system provides vital price information

Table 10–3
A Table of Quantitative Input-Output Relationships Stated in Terms of Average Specific Exchange Prices per Period

Producer	Iron	Food	Buildings	Households	Total Output	Meas. Unit
			Purchaser			
Iron	2.20	2.22	1.78	1.64	1.88	$/Ton
Food	-	.60	-	.50	.54	$/lb.
Building	100,000	146,667	112,000	75,000	62,105	$/Unit
Household	10.67	10.63	10.67	10.00	10.54	$/Man Hr.

about how well various sectors are faring in the competitive environment. By dividing the amounts of Table 10–2B by the related amounts of Table 10–2A, a cross-dimensional table of average prices for sector-to-sector exchanges can be derived, as shown in Table 10–3. Numerous policy decisions of both sector deciders and global deciders hang on such information.

Generally, this expansion increases the types of analyses possible by providing money–information marker flow measurements of the transactions between sectors rather than estimating the average price of such transactions and using it to restate physical units into monetary units or simply measuring the monetary units and statistically adjusting those for general price changes. It effectively expands the empirical data base used by most, if not all, current variations of models and simulations based on input-output economics. It provides information directly about both the matter–energy flows and the money–information marker flows. The monetary information incorporates the actual cosmic measurements of the economy on the attribute specific exchange value, providing information for the many decisions based on such measurements.

Concrete Process Measurement and Statements of Financial Accounting Concepts (SFAC)

Throughout prior chapters, we have discussed in depth the differences between the concrete process measurements we propose and the adjusted amounts commonly reported by accountants (based on what is often termed generally accepted accounting principles, GAAP). Statements of Financial Accounting Concepts (SFAC) are part of the eclectic approach to accounting theory which underlies GAAP. Consequently, to some degree, this entire book distinguishes between reported amounts based on concrete process measurements only and those based on the SFAC. However, some theoretic implications of the SFAC currently are not reflected broadly in GAAP. Such implications and the purpose served by the SFAC are discussed below.

In recent years, the Financial Accounting Standards Board has issued five SFAC, which together commonly are called the FASB conceptual framework project. These statements concern the same concrete process measurements that we discuss throughout this book. However, they generally assume the existing eclectic approach to accounting theory while attempting to systematize to some degree future developments in official pronouncements. This means that they fundamentally accept current GAAP while attempting to provide a consistent basis for determining how different theories should be applied in the overall application of theory to accounting practice.

As we stated in Chapter 9, this framework clearly is based on a different purpose than that of those constructed for research on accounting information systems and, indeed, organizations. The conceptual framework for research on accounting information systems and their suprasystems suggested in that chapter is, on the whole, in no important way a substitute for or parallel with the FASB conceptual framework project.

An important connection between the two frameworks, however, is that both concern measurements on concrete system processes. To the extent that this connection exists, FASB theorists should take into consideration theory of the accounting measurement of concrete processes. How, if at all, this theory fits with the several theories of the eclectic approach within the purposes of the accounting profession should be the concern of those theorists.

The FASB conceptual framework project is a useful component of a society-level accounting information system. It is part of an important upward information flow disconnect between the organization and society levels of living systems. This disconnect is important because it allows organization-level systems in market-based societies to do certain things outside of the control of a central society-level decider subsystem—that is, it diversifies the society-level decider subsystem.

In the United States this disconnect has developed as a result of a fundamental societal decision that securities laws should be based on disclosure of information rather than on government control of organizations whose stock is publicly traded. The U.S. Congress has delegated authority to set accounting procedures for those organizations to the Securities and Exchange Commission (SEC), which in turn generally has deferred in these matters to the accounting profession. As a result of this societal strategy, decisions about what information must be disclosed are at least twice removed from the Congress itself.

This is a political process—a sort of market environment where some kind of vote constitutes the medium of exchange and the standard of value. This process decides what procedures govern on the basis of compurgation. As such processes mature, living systems emerge to perpetuate their important aspects. The SEC is now a full-blown organization-level system with very few of the twenty critical processes upwardly, laterally, or downwardly dispersed. The FASB, if not there, is rapidly evolving the same maturity.

Such mature systems emerge as internal specialization of functions occurs.

FASB was created (i.e., its template [charter] stipulated that its purpose is) to issue authoritative statements concerning accounting and reporting procedures. Now, in terms of LST, it is evolving critical subsystems. Initially, FASB was very actively amassing information through studies, exposure drafts, and the like. Because its template provides for information processing at the society level, the FASB organization may be expected to emphasize information-processing subsystems.

Information storage is a memory function. The memory subsystem is one of two primary learning functions. It cannot become sophisticated without a corresponding advancement of the associator subsystem function. The FASB conceptual framework project is part of the development of an associator subsystem.

Recall that all functional LST-defined subsystems are composed of concrete structures and processes. This means that people, machines, and so on carry out those processes. The recent expansion of the FASB input transducer subsystem by constructing the Emerging Issues Task Force illustrates this phenomenon.

Because many attempts to provide a conceptual framework for the accountancy profession have failed, many accountants, both practitioners and theorists, predict the failure of the FASB project. We anticipate that it will succeed. Our judgment is based in no important way on the meanings contained in the SFAC. We believe that some of those are misguided. Our judgement is based on an LST analysis.

As long as the rule-setting body was a component of the American Institute of Certified Public Accountants (AICPA), little propensity existed to specialize internally to provide the twenty critical LST subsystem processes. Once this body is made freestanding under the charter of FASB, those processes come under the control of the FASB decider subsystem. Under the FASB charter, the association of information is well defined by the purpose of the organization and is much narrower in scope than the association of information by the AICPA. That is to say, the dominant purpose is to associate information to analyze and propose procedures for accounting and reporting emerging processes, both concrete and conceptual. The AICPA is concerned with many other purposes as well.

As a consequence of the function it serves in a concrete system, we anticipate that the conceptual framework project will endure. As with all concrete system components, it will also evolve—now emphasizing one pattern of meaning and then another but always connecting the evolving different meanings in a formal pattern of association.

Fundamentally, the FASB conceptual framework would be improved significantly by distinguishing clearly between measurements and interpretations as we have described in previous chapters. The FASB framework has actually taken three important steps in this direction, that is, (1) the concept of earnings, (2) the concept of comprehensive income, and (3) the concept of cash flow. These are discussed briefly below.

(1) *The concept of earnings.* SFAC 5 defines earnings as a measure of entity

performance during a period. As defined, this derived amount excludes certain accounting adjustments from previous periods such as the cumulative effect of changes in accounting principles. This definition is put forward without rejecting GAAP income. Consequently, it provides the basis for an additional disclosure of information. We have suggested that such additional disclosures be made. Our suggested additional disclosure, however, would begin with eliminating all accounting adjustments and progress on the basis of cohesive theory toward "earnings" disclosure.

(2) *The concept of comprehensive income.* SFAC 5 defines comprehensive income as all recognized changes in equity other than those arising from investments by and distributions to owners. The idea of comprehensive income, a total systemic increase, is a movement in the correct direction, but this definition provides a basis to continue using the proprietary model. For more than fifty years, this model has not mapped adequately the dynamics of modern organizations whose stock is publicly traded. What the entity model suggests, a systems approach, is needed.

We suggest a systems-based accounting model that explicitly recognizes that owners and creditors, while they possess time-lagged money–information markers of different particular legal characteristics, are only two of several important types of human components that compete within organizations. The decider subsystem must balance the demands of all components, and the particular influence of any one type varies from organization to organization and over time within organizations. Furthermore, we distinguish between measurements of specific exchange value and various estimates of other types of value such as replacement cost, market value, net realizeable value, and present value of future cash flows. SFAC 5 does not make this distinction and thus encourages accountants to continue to mingle measurements with interpretive data.

(3) *The concept of cash flows.* We have already illustrated in Chapter 7 that concrete process analysis, CPA, and the cash flow statement advocated by the FASB are different analyses. The powerful idea that underlies the cash-flow statement is that all of the amounts that the statement generates can be traced directly (in the accounts) to money–information markers, a concrete process. CPA can be made from the vantage of money–information markers as well as from the view of matter–energy flows as we have done. Possibly at some level of application the money view is more easily used. A money–oriented CPA would move a long way in the direction of the analyses we advocate. The cash-flow statement is a big step in that direction.

However, the arrangement of the information on the cash-flow statement continues to be strongly influenced by certain decision models. Consequently, it mingles (indiscriminately with reference to the accounting measurement methodology) money–information marker account balances with balances of the accounts that record the underlying economic activity (goods and services movement). Such arrangements obscure the fundamental measurements. The statement could be improved by first disclosing the actual inflows and outflows of important classes of money–information markers and then adjusting disclosures based on various decision models that have proven to be useful.

Summary

In this chapter, we advocate extending accounting measurement of concrete processes based on the double-entry model to the function of accounting for societal policy decisions. Constructing information disconnects between levels of living systems is an important aspect of this extension. The SEC, the FASB, and GAAP form important existing disconnects.

Extending concrete process measurement to societal accounting would connect both organizational and societal decision processes to a common measurement methodology. Furthermore, it would provide an expanded empirical data base for societal decisions.

References

Auger, P. "Hierarchically Organized Economics: Input-Output Analysis." *International Journal of Systems Science* Vol. 16, No. 10 (October, 1985), pp. 1,293–1,304.

Financial Accounting Standards Board (FASB). *Objectives of Financial Reporting by Business Enterprises* (SFAC 1). Stamford, CT: FASB, 1978.

—————. *Qualitative Characteristics of Accounting Information* (SFAC 2). Stamford, CT: FASB, 1980a.

—————. *Elements of Financial Statements of Business Enterprises* (SFAC 3). Stamford, CT: FASB, 1980b.

—————. *Objectives of Financial Reporting by Nonbusiness Organizations* (SFAC 4). Stamford, CT: FASB, 1980c.

—————. *Recognition and Measurement of Financial Statements of Business Enterprises* (SFAC 5). Stamford, CT: FASB, 1984.

Fisher, W. Halder. "Turning Input-Output Analysis to Technology." *Mechanical Engineering* (January, 1987), pp. 46–49.

National Economics Division of the Office of Business Economics, U.S. Department of Commerce. "Input-Output Structure of the U.S. Economy." *Survey of Current Business* (1969), p. 11.

Leontief, W. *Input-Output Economics.* New York: Oxford University Press, 1966.

Leontief, et al. *Studies in the Structure of the American Economy.* New York: Oxford University Press, 1953.

Wienrib, Janet M. "Richard Cyest: Managing to Get Into the Details." *Mechanical Engineering* (January, 1987), pp. 56–61.

11
SUMMARY AND CONCLUSIONS

An eclectic approach to accounting theory has resulted in obscuring information about the concrete processes of organizations in public accounting reports. Living systems theory may be used to arrange the many specific but disconnected theories of the eclectic approach into a coherent mosaic that forms a basis for providing public information about concrete processes.

Eclectic accounting theory underlies a system of generally accepted accounting principles that obscures information about concrete processes by not distinguishing between measurements taken on such processes and their interpretations. LST, in tandem with modern measurement theory, offers a way to distinguish between measurements of concrete processes and interpretive data based on various decision models in accounting reports.

The double-entry bookkeeping methodology, which emerged over a long period, uses small bundles of matter–energy, termed money–information markers, to track the inputs and outputs of various forms of matter–energy and information (goods and services) to and from organizations. Likely, such markers began to emerge in prehistoric times, becoming obvious with the invention of coins about 700 B.C. and continuing to evolve over time to such modern forms as electronic funds transfers. This methodology monitors and records both the inflow and outflow of transactions of concrete elements at the boundary of organizations.

Money–information markers are accounting artifacts by which specific monetary exchange value emerges as an attribute of the concrete elements that comprise social systems. This attribute exists only in the context of a higher-order system that has components connected by a money–information marker subsystem. It is a relational attribute and not intrinsic to the elements themselves. It is a true emergent of the higher-order system. Accounting measurements of various different forms of matter–energy processes are made on this common attribute, providing a view of organizations as cohesive wholes.

The money–information markers used to track goods and services are stated in monetary units that are all alike. Taken together, these units comprise a monetary scale that can be described as a ratio scale and is fully analogous to other measurement scales used by science. Because we have little confidence in point measurements taken on such economic processes, however, the accounting measurement scale incorporates the monetary scale but is not encompassed by it. The accounting measurement scale is four-dimensional, measuring attributes both in three dimensions of space and one dimension of time. It measures the societal attribute specific exchange value in a prescribed period. Point measurements of specific exchange value cannot provide information on an organization as a coherent whole. Our confidence in such cosmic measurements is based on aggregates of specific exchange values over some defined period. Consequently, accounting measurement is "periodaneous" and not instantaneous. The unique characteristics of this measurement methodology generally have not been taken into consideration by accounting theorists.

Measurement may be distinguished from other methods of assigning numbers by requiring that objects of measurement be compared to a scale. Observers select measured abstracted systems by comparing elements of a concrete system with some sort of scale or standard contained in the concrete system. They assign numbers based on the relationships established by the scale because they observe similar relationships among elements of a concrete system of interest to them. To observe those similarities, the scale—being a conceptual system—must be on information markers that can be located in spatiotemporal proximity to the object being measured.

On the other hand, observers select quantitative surrogated abstracted systems by comparing elements of a concrete system with a conceptual system composed of units that cannot be identified individually with specific information markers. The absence of a standard within a concrete system (i.e., in terms of identifiable information markers) makes it difficult to establish any assurance that a surrogated abstracted system corresponds in any important way to elements of a concrete system.

The main purpose of measurement theory is to provide a means of public observation to minimize the biases of different individual observers. When objects and processes are compared to a scale, the data are biased by the scale and not by any particular observer, barring measurement error. The demand of measurement theory that isomorphism be established between the scale and the system for assigning numbers encourages observations about primitives of near-decomposable explanatory systems. The degree to which the primitives (the structural givens of an explanation) persist over time determines the degree of predictive power of an explanation. To establish isomorphism, elements that have relationships that persist must be identified.

Accounting reports generate statements of "what was" in terms that attempt to describe physical reality (concrete systems). The reduction criterion for this explanation can be formalized as "matter–energy flows." Reduction based on this criterion achieves near-decomposability in that physical reality is widely understood to consist of arrangements of these fundamental elements. These structural givens are sufficiently persistent to serve as explanatory principles with some degree of prediction power.

We have developed a theory of accounting measurement of concrete processes to the degree of practical application to both organization- and society-level living systems. Application of this theory has the potential to expand dramatically empirical investigations (both economic and scientific) at and across those levels of living systems. To provide more complete data for such investigations, we propose these seven changes in current accounting information-gathering and reporting procedures:

1. Implement three-dimensional (monetary units, physical quantities, time) double-entry bookkeeping.

2. Record all inflows and outflows in separate accounts.

3. Distinguish accounts that record measurements of concrete flows, both matter–energy and money–information markers.

4. When possible, require that public accounting statements report certain aggregated inflows and aggregated outflows.

5. Estimate and report the aggregate measurement error on those accounts in procedure 4 that is accepted by auditors in assessing materiality.

6. Define accounting assumptions systematically and operationally in the context of LST, and analyze (and possibly disclose) their individual influences on publicly reported accounting derivatives.

7. Provide estimates generated by the accounting information system on the twenty critical LST subsystem processes.

These changes make it possible to use concrete process analysis and living systems process analysis to discover and correct dysfunctions within and between organizations. CPA can provide quantitative information, unbiased with reference to the accounting measurement methodology, about the concrete processes of a society and organizations within it. That is to say, this analysis can provide quantities that can be changed only by actual economic exchange processes and not by accounting adjustments based on various decision models and management influence.

LSPA can provide a method for internally allocating costs based on what science is learning about living systems, including organizations and societies. Since managers may select methods according to their perceived needs, current reporting suffers from a bias akin to researcher bias. As a result, reports may contain self-fulfilling prophecies instead of vital feedback on concrete processes. LSPA, being based on LST, is relatively independent of manager bias.

Living systems theory, LST, is a conceptual framework that attempts to integrate scientific findings about the evolving hierarchical structures of life: (1) cells, (2) organs, (3) organisms, (4) groups, (5) organizations, (6) communities, (7) societies, and (8) supranational systems. Systems at all of these levels differ in many obvious ways; but because of their common evolution, they have in common twenty critical life processes performed by subsystems, that is, subsystems that process both matter–energy and information, Reproducer and Boundary; subsystems that process matter–energy, Ingestor, Distributor, Converter, Producer, Matter–Energy Storage, Extruder, Motor, and Supporter; and subsystems that process information, Input Transducer, Internal Transducer, Timer, Channel and Net, Decoder, Associator, Memory, Decider, Encoder, and Output Transducer.

Information on these twenty processes is comparable across organizations and societies. Public accounting reports should disclose such information to increase their comparability. Accounting information systems are components of the internal transducer subsystems of such higher-order systems as organizations, societies, and supranational systems. The internal transducer subsystem is the sensory subsystem that receives, from subsystems or components within the system, markers bearing information about significant alterations in those subsystems or components, changing them to other matter–energy forms of a sort that can be transmitted within it. The accounting information system services the twenty critical subsystem processes by monitoring the inflows, throughflows, and outflows of various forms of matter, energy, and information. Thus, they could provide information on those processes.

We have drawn a clear distinction between conceptual frameworks that serve the practice of accountancy and those that serve the scientific investigation of accounting information systems, organizations, societies, and so on. The Financial Accounting Standards Board (FASB) is an organization that functions as an important upward information disconnect between the organization and society levels of an advanced market-based society. We believe that the FASB conceptual framework project will endure because it is a vital associator subsystem function of an enduring organization. This framework serves the accountancy profession. On the other hand, we have provided a general hypothesis based on LST (a scientific conceptual framework) for research on accounting information systems and organizations.

LST is applied to research on systems that concern accounting by developing a general hypothesis from the conceptual framework and, in turn, differentiating specific research hypotheses that are guided by the dynamic of the general hypothesis and the detail of the conceptual framework. A general hypothesis for using accounting information for research on organizations is:

Nonpathogenic organizations maximize the specific monetary exchange value of aggregate concrete inflows (specifically, materials, personnel, energy, and communications) over indefinite periods within a set of dynamic constraints imposed by communities, societies, and supranational systems that are communicated to the organization by the specific monetary exchange value of time-lagged money–information markers (specifically, owner documents, credit documents, and socialization documents).

The suggested changes in accounting procedures also make it possible to extend double-entry bookkeeping to the societal level of living systems. The work of Leontief on input-output economics makes this extension relatively easy. By requiring public reporting of concrete processes aggregated to a certain degree, the data of three-dimensional double-entry bookkeeping could be provided to all components of societies. Such an extension would increase significantly the empirical data available for society-level policy decisions.

In sum, by distinguishing clearly between measurements of concrete processes and their interpretations in accounting reports, we believe public accounting information can be made more intelligible and thus more useful. In this book, we provide one means of accomplishing this task.

INDEX

About the Authors

G.A. SWANSON is Professor of Accounting and Department of Accounting and Business Law Chairperson at Tennessee Technological University. He has published more than 50 scholarly works, including articles in *The Accounting Review*, *Systems Research*, *Behavioral Science*, *Journal of Accountancy*, *The Accounting Historians Journal*, *Advances in Accounting,* and *Journal of Education for Business*. Swanson is a Tennessee Certified Public Accountant (CPA). He is a member of the American Institute of Certified Public Accountants, the Tennessee Society of CPAs, the American Accounting Association, the Institute of Internal Auditors, among other professional organizations, and co-founder and first President of the Tennessee Society of Accounting Educators.

JAMES GRIER MILLER is Adjunct Professor of Biobehavioral Science and Psychiatry at the University of California at Los Angeles. He has been Editor of *Behavioral Science* for over 30 years. Miller has written or coauthored numerous books, including the seminal work in living systems theory entitled *Living Systems*, and published more than 100 scientific and scholarly articles. He originated the modern use of the term ''behavioral science,'' founded and directed the Mental Health Research Institute at the University of Michigan, was first head of EDUCOM (the Interuniversity Communications Council), and is founder and first President of the University of the World. Miller is past President of the University of Louisville.